P9-EEG-565

AESTHETICS, WELL-BEING AND HEALTH

Aesthetics, Well-being and Health

Essays within architecture and environmental aesthetics

Edited by
BIRGIT COLD
Professor, Architect
Faculty of Architecture, Planning and Fine Arts
Norwegian University of Science and Technology
NTNU Trondheim

Ashgate

Published by
Ashgate Publishing Limited
Gower House
Croft Road
Aldershot
Hants GU11 3HR
England

Ashgate Publishing Company
131 Main Street
Burlington, VT 05401-5600 USA

Ashgate website: http://www.ashgate.com

British Library Cataloguing in Publication Data
Aesthetics, well-being and health : essays within
    architecture and environmental aesthetics. - (Ethnoscapes)
    1. Aesthetics 2. Architecture - Environmental aspects
    3. Architecture - Human factors
    I. Cold, Birgit
    720.1

Library of Congress Control Number: 2001091659

ISBN 0 7546 1856 0

Printed and bound by Athenaeum Press, Ltd.,
Gateshead, Tyne & Wear.

Contents

Preface

Renowned professionals with scientific and practical knowledge within architecture and the social sciences were invited to write essays on the subject **aesthetics, well-being and health**. Their challenge was to write on this subject and its significance for their work. The background of the editor is from practising, teaching and researching architecture, and her knowledge and interest first of all lie in the aesthetic quality of the environment. To promote a better understanding of the significance of environmental aesthetics and beauty for our well-being it is necessary to investigate the relations between aesthetics and well-being and aesthetics and health from various perspectives. Our first step was to publish the book *Aesthetics, Well-being and Health - abstracts on theoretical and empirical research within environmental aesthetics* (1998). The main aim of this publication was to make a selection of the research literature on people's aesthetic relations with the environment more readily available for those interested in the field.

This volume is the second step, and with it we are addressing professionals, students and anyone interested in environmental aesthetics and its significance for well-being and health. Together, the essays are like a colourful meadow sprinkled with various plants, some very cultivated, some sturdy and common, others more rare, colourful and remarkable. The open form of the essay has allowed the contributors to write imaginatively, informatively or reflectively from the heart. They were free to choose how they wished to present their essays: as a letter, a "confession" of their thoughts or a description of their ideas, research and work. Many of the contributors know each other and the editor, and because of this the essays have a confident and open feel to them.

It is, however, in its place to ask why the scientific world wants to shed light on a subject through a collection of essays. Perhaps it is the intellectual pleasure of following other professionals as they reflect on their work and concepts, challenging these and other's conventional and scientific theories. It may also be the desire of professionals to dig behind rational and scientific facts in order to comprehend more implicit, indefinable, irrational, spiritual and existential thoughts and ideas and reflect upon connections between their own professional field and the surrounding world in a free and open form.

It is a great pleasure to present these essays and we would like to thank all the essayists for their enthusiastic participation in this project and willingness to share their knowledge and thoughts with us all. Thanks also to John Anthony who "washed" the language to give us a "clean English", without pretending that this volume is written entirely by persons whose mother tongue is English.

Introduction

The intention of the introduction to this volume is to balance between information and discussion on the subject *Aesthetics, Well-being and Health* and a stimulating presentation, leaving the reader eager to investigate the essays further. This introduction and the essays should not be approached in the same way as a collection of scientific articles. The nature of the volume and the subject itself do not encourage categorical statements but rather call for a dialectic approach to discussions and argumentations inspired by the views of the contributors and coloured by the editor's curiosity and enthusiasm for the subject.

The opportunity to discuss this subject, agreeing or disagreeing with other professionals' views and ideas, is fascinating because it concerns both the public and experts, and yet we seldom discuss it professionally. Nor do we reflect seriously on environmental aesthetics and beauty in the surroundings nor the impacts on well-being and health. What is perhaps even more odd is that it is not a more common subject within environmental psychology, the multidisciplinary field concentrating on the relations between people and the environment. Perhaps the reason is that this field is dominated by social scientists who are more occupied with social and environmental behaviour and how the environment interacts with people's minds than the significance of environmental, aesthetic quality and beauty related to people's well-being. Or perhaps they fear entering a subject with a discussion traditionally dominated by the belief that beauty and aesthetic quality are matters of personal taste, and therefore find it is not a subject to approach scientifically or profes-

Fig. 1. St Giorgio Maggiore, Venice (B. Cold).

sionally. We want to challenge this belief because it undermines and blurs the importance of trying to understand the roots to aesthetic preferences and well-being, not as a static phenomenon, but as an interactive relationship between persons, culture and the environment.

We want to discuss various approaches to *personal taste and cultural preferences* to discover if it is possible to define *general environmental qualities and beauty* in a wide perspective, and to see how we can connect these to well-being and health. The reader may disagree as to whether it is possible to discuss aesthetic quality and environmental beauty as intersubjective or objective matters. Doubt is always raised about any attempt to argue positively for, shall we call it, *general aesthetics*. Throughout history we find many significant examples of aesthetic theories claiming to present the right ideas and blueprints for architectural beauty. History's judgement, which in a way is also the judgement of the people, and knowledgable professionals' evaluations show that these differing theories were all "true". When we experience, analyse and judge buildings and environments which still exist as preserved examples of these theories, we may have our preferences, but we may also agree on their undeniable aesthetic and general quality (Fig. 1). The closest we may come to grasping the idea of objective aesthetics and beauty is through a combination of aesthetic knowledge, psychological understanding and artistic empathy. Here we discuss if an environmental-psychological and architectural-artistic approach might help us to gain deeper insight into more

2

general relations between environmental-aesthetic quality, beauty and the experience of well-being and health. The essays are an attempt to approach this subject in a multidisciplinary way.

Why it is important to discuss this subject
- Aesthetic quality, concern and neglect

We feel compelled to study aesthetics and the effects on well-being and health because this field has been so neglected for many years. Why have aesthetics and beauty come last in the discussion on planning the environment? Are aesthetic needs really the last human needs as proposed by Maslow in his hierarchy of needs and discussed by Roderick Lawrence in his essay? Or is aesthetics a total integrated part of all needs as many of the essays proclaim? Is it altogether relevant to operate on the level of basic needs in our well-fed, well-housed and affluent part of the world?

Today environmental aesthetics is discussed in many fora. People generally feel that authorities, planners, architects, builders and politicians on all levels have neglected environmental aesthetics and beauty, creating unpleasant, ugly, hostile, unfamiliar, unfriendly and unhealthy environments. Schools, hospitals, workplaces, traffic-areas, large housing estates and many public and semi-public spaces are generally experienced, both by architects and the public, as having aesthetically deprived exterior and interior design, and lacking maintenance and care. Why? It would appear as if we are more focused on formal teaching of subjects than learning, more on diseases than sick people's recovering, more on productivity than the well-being of employees, more on cars, comfort and speed than public life in aesthetically pleasant places, more on quantity than quality, more on rational and intellectual matters than sensuous and emotional ones. If so, this means that our minds are concentrating on formal, rational and materialistic matters, the "hardware" of tasks, productivity and science, private comfort, profit and prestige rather than on ethical and aesthetic values benefiting us all.

Juhani Pallasmaa argues in his essay that the aesthetic quality of works, objects and environments is a product of our minds and values. The discussion should then focus on how aesthetics and ethics are related to each other and how the environment should mirror our minds and values.

Environmental aesthetics concerns not only the fine arts and architecture but more or less all professions dealing with people and environments, indoors and outdoors. Debates on how the quality of environmental aesthetics is the responsibility of these professions, however, is rare, even though our day-to-day lives are influenced by the aesthetic quality of our physical and public surroundings. Paradoxically, we generally are concerned about the aesthetic quality of our private sphere. Perhaps this concern does not encompass the aesthetic quality of public environments because we are too busy and have a rational and instrumental relationship with the surroundings, or perhaps we have surrendered in the battle with the responsible bodies and individuals who we find aesthetically ignorant. Public areas and our workplaces, be they universities, schools, hospitals or other public institutions, are underestimated as aesthetically influential environments for our well-being and health. It is not easy to find a single explanation for the low level of concern and care in our rich Western societies. Nonetheless, several reasons why aesthetics in the public environment is neglected come to mind:

- *There are no societal ideals, hopes or beliefs to celebrate*
The environment is a symbol of society and mirrors its values, ideals and hopes, and if there are no such feelings there is nothing to celebrate and no inspiration for creating beautiful environments. Or rather we have not consciously worked out how to celebrate the values of a democratic society, a view advocated by Pallasmaa. It would appear as if a democratic society *prefers* the lowest common denominator, which in the end gives us neither high aesthetic quality nor beauty.

- *Backsliding of responsibility for aesthetic, environmental quality*
In a democratic society the aesthetically educated people seldom have the responsibility for the public environment or the responsibility has been given to aesthetically unscholared bureaucrats or politicians who may have the best intentions but not the necessary skills or knowledge. This may be one reason for the aesthetic neglect of public environments and institutions.

Fig. 2. Grandma's sitting room (B. Cold).

- Care of the private sphere and neglect of the public
We have become more and more selfish and concerned only with ourselves and our families, concentrating on what we can control and overcome, our home, car and clothes, and we cannot be bothered with the huge indefinably public environment. There are no main truths, no "concrete" heaven or hell anymore. Perhaps our beliefs and doubts have become so complex or diffuse that we do not find it worth fighting for or investing in beautiful public surroundings or aesthetic quality. We fail to see if it means anything as long as we can "hide" in our private sphere (Fig. 2).

- In industrial mass production aesthetics and well-being are not emphasized
Industrial mass production of goods and environments is designed for and based on a rational, cost-benefit view. The touch and care of human hands

and minds, as we know so well and love in the arts and crafts, is not present and we do not identify with or care for mass-produced entities. On the other hand, could not mass production give us just as high aesthetic quality if we investigated what makes people feel well and healthy, and if great attention and resources were invested in experimental prototypes?

- Aesthetic skills and knowledge are concentrated on speed and communication
Perhaps we have moved our aesthetic skills and interest to refinement of industrial modern, high-tech products connected with speed and communication, real or virtual transport, speed vehicles and virtual soft and hardware. It feels more lucrative and inspiring to invest resources in artefacts, which are either quickly outdated or which have an immediate attraction, luxury image or status for a person, company or state. An aesthetic improvement of the built environment, be it a neighbourhood, park, street, hospital or schoolyard, has less appeal than, for example, a speed boat, because we need these surroundings, we use them and become familiar with them irrespective of their aesthetic quality.

- A lack of aesthetically inspiring models and a poor, aesthetic background
If teachers, civil servants, managers of institutions and other persons with environmental responsibilty have little or no aesthetic education and training, and no awareness or interest in environmental aesthetics, then as there are few inspiring models for creating modern environments with aesthetic quality, it is difficult or impossible to create an awareness of the significance of an aesthetically qualitative atmosphere in learning, working or publicly accessible environments. We do not believe that modern man has less aesthetic potential than earlier generations, which created what we consider today to be much more aesthetically satisfactory environments than modern ones. The pre-industrial environments were more in tune with place and people, at least we think so today, and the buildings and surroundings were either a result of traditional crafts with well-known materials, cultivated structures and details or they were monumentally and beautifully designed by the most clever architects and artists of the age, who were given time and resources to create masterpieces for their clients. We would be hard pressed

Fig. 3. Røros Norway (World heritage).

today to find clever craftsmen and builders, extremely talented architects, and aesthetically conscious clients with great resources and time to develop "sweet" or sublime beauty. One hope lies in developing a common environmental awareness, aesthetic knowledge and artistic talents, mutually dependent on each other (Fig. 3).

- Environmental creators are poorly trained in aesthetics or have little influence on public environments
We cannot deny the possibility that architects, engineers and developers responsible for creating the aesthetic quality of the public environment are poorly educated and trained in aesthetics, with an over-emphasis on all other environmental criteria than aesthetic ones. Many of the post-war instru-

mental but aesthetically poor industrial housing estates, institutions, transport areas and office-blocks were designed by architects and civil engineers and also put into production by the latter. Noting that only ten percent or less of the built environment today is designed by architects makes us realize that having well-educated architects and designers is not enough when the majority of built environments and public spaces are in the hands of bureaucrats, clients, developers and professions devoid of any aesthetic awareness and knowledge, training or ambition to create beauty.

These reflections are implicitly based on the assumption that it is possible on a professional level to describe, discuss, teach, train and learn what *aesthetic quality* is or can be, how it influences our lives and how to understand and deal with it, not as a static phenomennon, but rather as a dynamic one having historic, cultural, common biological and individual roots, and a theoretical and practical content.

Does this discussion of aesthetic quality mean anything at all for the well-being of people? If it means anything, it might be that we are becoming aware of the long way we have to go before we understand why the environmental-aesthetic status is so low and take the necessary steps to rectify this. First of all, however, we have to agree, that we feel better and are more happy *in the long run* in aesthetically qualitative environments than in environments lacking aesthetic quality, even if these are functioning as intended.

Another vital question, which we have already touched on, is how to define and who should define aesthetic quality and beauty. We have no other answer to give than that each person defines and decides what is most aesthetically appropriate and attractive in his or her private sphere. In the public sphere, on the contrary, we have to trust those with a relevant, aesthetic education and training, in the belief and hope that they know how to define, promote and create environmental-aesthetic quality, which, in the long run may be pleasurable to both lay people and aesthetes. To ensure this, the experts educated in aesthetics need knowledge of the relationship between aesthetic quality of the environment and people's feeling of well-being. Empathy, observation, historic and cultural knowledge, user communication and knowledge of relevant research are necessary factors for the experts. Architects cannot be content with their own feelings and aesthetic preferences, nor can user groups take over responsibility for the aesthetics. In his essay, David Uzzell proposes a process-based approach to visual assessment based on a comprehensive and systematic *aide memoire* of criteria which are based on consideration of factors thought to be important in good design. This may be a good way to learn from user evaluations because it is open to new solutions and still reminds the experts as well as the clients and users of certain factors which have to be considered and agreed on at each level of the planning and design process. The difficulty may be to develop this *aide memoire* into an open, creative and yet informative format for the process and avoid an endless list of checkpoints and rules adding to all the plethora of legislation and regulations.

The teaching of environmental psychology to architect students is another positive attempt to create an attitude to human environmental needs and an understanding of one's own and people's environmental preferences. The aim of the study, as advocated by Sue-Ann Lee in her essay, is to make students understand that their own perceptions of the built environment and its problems and solutions may not be shared by others, that perceptions are contextual, that people seem to need something they define as beautiful, that it is necessary to learn from systematic studies of environments-in-use, to both feed forward and feedback to design, and that they should leave their designs open-ended to allow the users to express individual control and to enable fine tuning for well-being and comfort.

Aesthetics, Well-being and Health

Aesthetics

Throughout history aesthetic knowledge has, with varying emphasis, focused on the

- *perceivable side of the world through the senses,*
- *the nature of beauty and*
- *the theoretical and philosophical theories of aesthetic criticism in the arts.*

We link aesthetics with well-being and health in order to investigate and discuss the sensuous, psychological aspects of aesthetics and ideas of the significance and meaning of environmental beauty.

Man's first impression of the surrounding world is aesthetic, through the senses of sound, smell, touch, movement and vision (Fig. 4). This direct aesthetic perception is the gateway to the emotional and cognitive processes, when we become aware, discover, are stimulated by, recognize and assess the environment. The opposite to the descriptive sensuous-aesthetic perception, also the original meaning of the word aesthetic, is anaesthetic, when we are not capable of perceiving the surrounding world or ourselves because we are anaesthesized. The positive meaning of aesthetics in everyday speech may originate from the fact that it is necessary and pleasurable to be aware, with all senses alert, and not only to survive but enjoy life and the environment sensuously.

The theoretical meaning of the concept aesthetics can be traced back to the ancient philosophers. *Poetica* by Aristoteles (384 - 322 B. C.) is consid-

Fig. 4. My grandson Noa (B. Cold).

ered to be one of the first works on aesthetic theory in the art of poetry. He emphasized the unity of three constituents in a dramatic work: time, place and action and opposed Plato's (his teacher) view that ideas had their own existence separated from things. He argued that ideas existed in the things as their very nature, a modern view we may agree with today as well.

In the middle of the eighteenth century the German philosopher Baumgarten wrote *Aesthetica* (1750) in which he introduced aesthetics as one of the three normative disciplines: Aesthetics dealing with beauty, ethics with good and logic with truth. Beauty was looked upon as a natural imbedded or human-created high quality of objects, environments or works of art, in the spirit of Aristoteles. The opposite of aesthetic then becomes non-aesthetic, the ugly, messy or malformed. Norms of beauty and comprehensive theories for understanding and assessing aesthetic performances in the arts and architecture have been developed within the respective discip-lines and profes-sions engaged in aesthetic matters. Nations, regions, cultural and subcultural groups also develop aesthetic norms of behaviour, rituals, music, looks, things and surroundings. Such norms are long or short-lived depending on the status and policy of "the group" and on external social, economic and

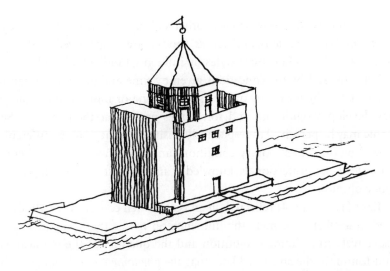

Fig. 5. Il Teatro del Mondo, Venice 1978 by Arch. Aldo Rossi (B. Cold).

political circumstances. One may say that the stronger a nation's, profession's or group's identity is attached to such norms, the longer they will last or the slower they will change. History and architectural styles show that the norms of beauty are not static. Some norms of beauty are robust, they disappear for a while and reappear in a renewed version.

We find norms of beauty in architectural theories and practices throughout history, written down in theories and built or imbedded in architectural works, models and styles. These norms become influential when they are studied, revived and used as inspiration for new performances. For example, we can take a quick look at 2500 years of history, starting with antiquity and Pythagoras' mathematical system of numbers interpreted as the microcosmos and the macrocosmos, which inspired Vitruvius, who was studied by the Renaissance's Alberti, who was studied by Palladio, who again was studied by the eighteenth-nineteenth-century classical architects, who dominated L'Ecole .des Beaux-Arts, which inspired and taught classical architecture, studied recently by the twentieth-century modern and post-modern architects Rossi and Venturi, and post-modern-eclectic architects Krier (Leon), Moore and Terry (Fig. 5).

Man and society mirror each other culturally and the four categories *spirit, intellect, emotions and senses* (body) are emphasized with varying intensity in the architectural styles by influential individuals, cultural ideals and visions, and by the conditions given by time and place. A human being or a society which over or under-estimates one or more of these categories may develop a significant and sometimes narrow, aesthetic profile. Such a profile may be perceived as respectively positive and negative in different eras, depending on contemporary conditions and needs, awareness and empathy of the aesthetic professionals, knowledge and interest of those in power, and public opinion.

Kant (1724 - 1804) reflected on an issue which concerns everybody interested in aesthetics, namely the influence on the aesthetic cognitive process respectively from human cognition and the qualities of the physical world. Kant found, in the spirit of Plato, that *the phenomenon of beauty* which can be perceived and recognized, is different from *the idea of beauty*, which in itself can not be recognized. A qualitative, aesthetic assessment therefore has to be taken without an idea of perfect beauty or perfect aesthetic quality, but rather with a disinterested awareness, a reflected and cognitive observation (listening) without any thought of utility, purpose, worthiness or meaning, or the degree in which the phenomenon is comfortable or not.

This state of disinterested awareness, however, may be an illusion, at least when we deal with environmental assessments. A pure sensuous-aesthetic perception, whether being of a field of flowers, a housing block or a village silhouette in a mountainous landscape, or situated in an atmosphere of awareness, calls immediately upon our emotions. It is virtually impossible to talk exclusively about *pure sensuous perception* because our knowledge about the context, functions, place, time and situation is present without our conscious awareness of it. Gombrich (1956, -68) emphasizes that we have great difficulties in separating *what we know from what we see* (or hear, feel, taste, smell ...). Or as Nørretranders writes (1991) *we know more than we know,* meaning that our subconscious knowledge is considerably larger and more influential than we consciously know. These two views contribute to a wider understanding of the difficulty in separating the direct, aesthetic-sensuous perception from the cognitive, intellectually reflected consideration

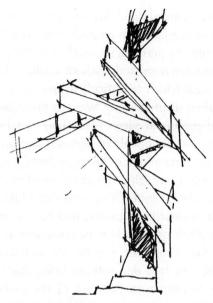

Fig. 6. Judischer Museum, Berlin by Arch. D. Liebeskind (B. Cold).

and assessment. It is, however, in the ability to separate these from each other that we find the difference between lay people's and experts' judgements of aesthetic, environmental quality. The Norwegian philosopher Bø-Rygg argues that we are *aesthetically mature* when we can separate our own emotional, aesthetic attraction or abhorrence from *the aesthetic quality* of a phenomenon. This aesthetic maturity is the basis for passing qualified or professional judgements on aesthetic phenomena.

If we are to pass on such a qualified judgement we need both an understanding of our own aesthetic relation to the environment and of the importance of acquiring an aesthetic repertoire which enables us to compare one phenomenon with many others of the same type. Such a repertoire also enables us to recognize when something mediates new ideas and images and therefore requires a different approach and awareness than when we make comparisons (Fig. 6). Building up a large repertoire is a professional necessity, and as well as being open and curious, we need to train and use emotional empathy and intuition, especially when being confronted with new phenomena. The idea of an elevated, knowledgable, open and curious aesthetic critic is that he or she has both empathy and considerable knowledge without being governed by personal sympathies or antipathies, or is at least able to distinguish between them and aesthetic quality. This description of a perfect critic is an ideal which is difficult to live up to because even experts encounter difficulties distinguishing between professional, cultural-ideological and personal-emotional views. This may not be a problem, however, as long as these views are openly recognized, mediated and can be discussed. Some of the best critics of our architect students' graduate projects may value the quality of a project highly, but at the same time they may be happy that it is not going to be realized. This means that while the professionality and even the talent mediated in a project may be evident, the kind of architecture on the chosen site or context is not desirable at all. Problems might arise, however, when people or experts are convinced that their aesthetic judgement is the only true one without being able to explain the judgement criteria. This brings us to the core of the problem, because architecture as an artistic phenomenon is not a question of democratic and rational agreements, but of artistic talent, aesthetic empathy, intuitive knowledge, contextual feeling and considerable knowledge of the art of building. Social scientists might object to this statement, as they might not accept that architecture is an aesthetic-artistic phenomenon and rather point out that it is a social-behavioural and instrumental-physical phenomenon which should be agreed on in a cooperative process of designers, clients and users. This statement may also be true if we concentrate on the present users' comfort and satisfaction, while the architecture-as-art-statement may be more true when we deal with aesthetic quality, artistic value and beauty in a wider temporal and cultural perspective. This should not be understood as if architecture is pure art, because it is both art and instrument, and a psychological-aesthetic, social-cultural and physical-instrumental phenomenon.

Well-being and health

Researchers and theoretians within the trans-disciplinary field of environmental psychology investigate and try to understand the physiological, psychological, emotional and behavioural relations and interactions between man and the physical environment. The interest in this volume is centred on research, theories, ideas and reflections within environmental aesthetics, on people and their aesthetic preferences and beauty, and their sensation of well-being and health. The definition of health is here quoted from Lawrence's essay: "*According to the World Health Organization health is a state of complete physical, mental and social well-being and not merely the absence of disease or infirmity. ... it is a state or condition that is defined in relation to the constituents of all the environmental and human characteristics that make up the daily lives of people and the reciprocal relations between them.*" In his essay Arnulf Kolstad compares this definition of health with being happy.

We might believe that humans are equipped with an intuitive feeling of what supports a successful relation between their well-being and health and the aesthetics of the environment. The problem is, however, that the originally instinctive feeling of this natural relation may have been suppressed or overcome by cultural norms and social conventions, and a lack of individual self-understanding and confidence have left the responsibility to specially empathetic often artistic experts to explore and mediate aesthetically the intuitive feeling of well- or bad-being related to the environment.

As a reaction to the view that knowledge and professionalism are the best basis for qualified judgements, Goleman's book *Emotional Intelligence* (1995) is interesting. He points to the importance of understanding the role of the emotions for our behaviour and decision making. Direct sensuous, aesthetically pleasurable or unpleasurable experiences and emotions related to the environment are rooted both in individual motivations and conditions and in the individual and collective *subconscious field,* while assessments, criticism and professional judgements of aesthetic quality are dominated by intellectual, rational and philosophical theories and ideas related to *the conscious field*. Well-being and health may therefore be approached and understood as a dynamic person-role-place-time action and a culturally influenced relationship including sensuous perception, emotional cognition and intellectual considerations moving between the subconscious as well as the conscious field.

We all know, consciously and subconsciously, what well-being is and how it feels. The present situation, the past and expectations of the nearest future highly influence the relationship between the environment and the feeling of well-being. Environmental research tries to overcome this complex approach by implementing *preference studies* to investigate the degree of common human, cultural and individual preferences related to certain situations and places, for instance schools, offices, homes, hospitals and places in urban and natural environments, hypothesizing that people feel well when they are surrounded by an environment or environmental elements they like or prefer.

In the empirical research on environmental aesthetics many experiments have been implemented to separate the direct, aesthetic-perceptual preference from cognitively considered preference and assessment. It appears, for instance, that people generally react spontaneously and positively, without any consideration of nature and natural elements in the environment. That is interpreted by the social scientists R. Ulrich (1983) and Kaplans (1992) as an aesthetic perception with deep roots in the evolution of man, which has led to an aesthetic, common "preferenda" introduced as a theory by Appleton (1975). Not all environmental psychologists agree on the existence of a "preferenda", but they do agree that cultural norms and individual conditions are the main roots to aesthetic, intergrated preferences and that also human biology somehow counts.

Beauty and well-being
Whatever belief we may have of the origins of aesthetic preferences, our aesthetic experience and knowledge have their roots in sensory perception. The aesthetic perception of beauty begins with a sensory stimulus, is emotionally recognized and cognitively processed either as a phenomenon which fits in with categories already recognized as beautiful, or as a new category of beauty which should be created. There is, however, a tendency to omit an aesthetic, direct perception or a reflection which requires awareness and engagement, but rather, "with a simple glimpse" to state what one likes or dislikes in accordance with one's established knowledge structure and conceptions. This reaction may be caused by our modern busy behaviour, an instrumental attitude to time and quality, too many impressions or the lack of ability and willingness to "look upon the world as if it were new". Instrumental day-to-day behaviour in an urban environment appears to

Fig. 7. Hagia Sophia, Istanbul (B. Cold).

prevent aesthetic awareness, and hence a pleasurable aesthetic experience, opposed to the diversionary behaviour of tourists or vacationers taking great pleasure in environmental beauty (Heath, 1988).

We have learned that certain buildings, natural phenomena and works of art are beautiful, they are pictured in our textbooks, postcards and tourist posters. They belong to a cultural-historic convention and a stated canon which everybody within "civilized society" should know and appreciate (Fig. 7). Such "a canon of beauties" can be the worst enemy of experiencing beauty because convention does not demand a direct and dynamic engagement and awareness, which is the basis for discovering and experiencing beauty, and the feeling of intense well-being. The paradox is that *a real beauty experience* can not be ordered, neither can we be certain that it happens if we are not prepared or have learned to search for it, to see, listen, move, smell or taste carefully. The culturally approved beautiful works, which have survived throughout history and become "classical", were also dependent on being perceived and discovered as something extraordinarily attractive in their time or rediscovered in another time by somebody with a "nose", empathy, under-standing, position or power.

Gadamer discusses the nature of the beautiful in his essay on "The

Fig. 8. Summerhouse in Portør (1950ᵗʰ) by Arch. Knut Knutsen.

Relevance of Beauty" (1986). He refers to *"how the alps were described in travel diaries in the eighteenth century as terrifying mountains whose ugly and fearful wildness was experienced as a denial of beauty, humanity, and the familiar security of human existence. Today, on the other hand, everyone is convinced that our great mountain ranges represent not only the sublimity, but also the exemplary beauty of nature"* (p. 30). He further states that *"we see nature ...with sight schooled by art. Hegel rightly grasped that natural beauty is a reflection of artistic beauty, so that we learn how to perceive beauty in nature under the guidance of the artist's eye and his work"* (p. 31). It is an interesting and fascinating suggestion that artists are *discoverers* of beauty, and that, in eighteenth and nineteenth century nature-imitation art, environmental beauty had to be discovered and interpreted by artists to create a basis of a common cultural and aesthetic perception and hence develop knowledge of the beautiful.

Architects believe that their task is to develop such knowledge by creating aesthetically pleasurable and beautiful environments. In his essay "The Mind of the Environment" Pallasmaa refers to Aalto who realized, after a stay at a hospital, how important carefully designed details and elements, and legible and comfortable environments with meaning and familiarity were for the well-being of patients, or for *man at his weakest*. Even if the average patient is not as sensitive to his environment as Aalto was, it is of great importance to listen to people with an empathetic awareness, because they capture something which concerns most people even if it is on a subconscious level. Generally, architects are trained and have developed a special sensibility for aesthetically high quality environments, and their task is to design pleasurable and artistically valuable architecture (Fig. 8).

The norms of beauty, if we accept Gadamer's view, are influenced by the abilities of artists as well as architects to be open and curious, perceiving, discovering or imagining and mediating unnoticed or new aesthetic qualities in such a way that both the observer and the creater are *seduced*. The concept of seduction is used by the Danish artist Willy Ørskov (1966) who argues that a work of art forces itself upon the observer with its sensuous and psychic "disrejection", that art is the art of seduction, not in the meaning of a "cynical seducer", rather that the artist as creator must be a seduced observer him- or herself and that the observer must want to be seduced.

How can we understand the phenomenon of beauty, timeless beauty, *artistic and seductive beauty* and *fashions* which become popular, loved and preferred and then after a short while are totally rejected as boring or even ugly? Perhaps one difference is the intention and aim of the creator, or of the social-cultural processes behind him or her and the expectations of the public, both mediated implicitly in the creations, artefacts or environments, and explicitly in the presentation and distribution of them. Fashion is expected to live briefly, art and beauty to live long. Fashion creations, be they clothes, artefacts, prefab-homes, colours or textures, are partly the result of market analyses of what people like and buy, having "a good nose" for what people secretly long for, and partly the result of the will and talent to create an aesthetic longing for beauty, status, well-being or happiness through convincing advertisements with only one intention, to sell and earn money. A fashionable creation is meant to be a tempting "dish to buy, consume and digest", and when the hunger rises again, there is a new fashion creation to acquire. Fashion can make us happy for a short while, very happy sometimes, because it strengthens our self-confidence and self-belief and makes us feel well in a social context. As soon as a fashion is not popular it loses its aesthetic and social value and the former feeling of well-being turns into a feeling of being outdated and *old-fashioned*. Fashions may also have a long life, for example blue jeans. Their original social and utilitarian purpose may change, and they turn into a tradition if the functional, aesthetic and symbolic qualities are united and correspond with or simply create a social-cultural image. A fashion can also be valued as art and end up in museums when the aesthetic-artistic quality is spectacular to the point of a time-expression, or

Fig. 9. Morton College, Oxford (B. Cold).

mediate an astonishing and sublime sense of timeless beauty. It is difficult to describe and clearly distinguish between the qualities of time-less beauty, beauty belonging to a culture, periodic style and time-fixed fashion (Fig. 9).

Following Gadamer's view, beauty may be found "everywhere", but it has to be discovered or imagined artistically in a dynamic moment by an empathetic, talented person who knows how to mediate in order to seduce the observer and him- or herself. In poetry, music, architecture and works of art, from cave paintings to water lillies and bicycle seat-handlebars transformed into an oxhead sculpture, prehistoric man, Monet and Picasso have succeeded in seducing themselves, observers and art critics because of the direct radiation of the artists' discoveries and ablity to mediate these into art.

However, not all art has beauty as its aim or means. Perhaps we can recognize works of art up to our time as having aimed at beauty to mediate spiritual, intellectual, emotional or sensuous ideas or discoveries. The art of our time may often be perceived as if it is fighting against beauty. The artists do not want or feel the need to mediate their intentions by utilizing beauty as a seductive language. Perhaps sketches and sketchy installations in their unfinished spontanous innocence are works which may give a promise of beauty without themselves representing a normative beauty.

In the book *L'idée de beau* Lacoste (1986) writes about beauty in the history of the art of painting. Many of his reflections may, without any difficulty, be transferred to architecture. He argues that due to the lack of contemporary firm criteria for beauty, we balance between a historically rooted attitude, preserving all works of art from the past and an attitude which rejects former art expressions when a novel expression turns up. The exception, he argues, is the cinema and movies which, as a new field of art in a state of innocence provide us with experiences of beauty, beautiful landscapes, actors and stories. As a new form of art, it has its legitimate right to present the happy beauty which most other art forms neglect.

This discussion has not proved or disproved that beauty and well-being are connected, it has rather tried to encompass ways of approaching the phenomenon beauty in order to understand its relevance for our well-being.

The Essays

The invitation

The essays have been written by social scientists and architects. They practise, do research, theoretical and empirical, write, edit and publish, nationally and internationally, and have been or are teaching at universities. Their work testifies to their enthusiasm, interdisciplinary interest, and cross-cultural and intimate knowledge of people-environment relations. As in society, social scientists generally deal with behavioural, social, functional, physical and psychological relations, while few deal explicitly with the environmental-aesthetic field. Knowing that aesthetics stems from sensory perception and cognition, the essay writers have integrated the aesthetic and well-being dimension in their professional work in different ways. The editor believes that the invitation to explicitly investigate and reflect on aesthetics and well-being in various people-environment relations provided them with the opportunity to do just this in an interesting way for the reader and the inter-disciplinary field of environmental-aesthetics.

The essays show the benefit of including many different ideas and perspectives in the discussion. The various approaches give us an insight into concepts such as place identity, multisensuous and emotional processes, geometrical order and controlled space, architectural plasticity, aesthetically real and virtual values, participative design processes, ethics in architecture, and beauty and happiness.

The essays' views on aesthetics and beauty, well-being and health

The essays display a wide range of views depending on their chosen approach to the subject. Some views, however, permeate all the essays.

Aesthetic perception and cognition of a place include not only visual features of a setting but acoustical, olfactory, tactile, kinesthetic, and non-verbal behavioural qualities that enable people to experience aesthetic objects and stimuli within a broad and coherent socio-spatial context. Western culture has emphasized visual aesthetics entirely, and consequently architects and planners have contributed to a sensory deprivation harmful to the physiological, psychological and social well-being.

There is no simple one-to-one relationship between well-being, health and the aesthetics of the built environment. Within the field of environmental psychology it is agreed that people-environment relations are interactive and that aesthetic experiences are integrated in all other experiences. Aesthetic needs consequently become part of all other needs. This integration means that it becomes problematic to separate aesthetic preferences and appreciations of environments or buildings from the actions and sensations that they generate due to the multidimensional nature of integrated sensuous-aesthetic experiences.

The essays also mediate specific views and enhance special aspects of aesthetics and beauty, well-being and health. In the following we provide the reader with an impression of the various views and approaches under the two headings *aesthetics and beauty* and *well-being and health*:

Aesthetics and beauty:
- The concept of aesthetics is ambiguous because it includes both direct sensory perception, which suggests a certain aliveness, and judgement and contemplation, which include norms of beauty.
- Aesthetic experience has three components, one biological, one cultural and one individual component, and all three should be taken into account because they represent three different domaims which should not be mixed. None of them can, however, explain the whole spectrum of human aesthetic behaviour on their own.

- Beauty and happiness are mutually infectious, and being happy may enhance the healing process.
- Beauty is dialectic, it requires a direct, dynamic-emotional engagement, and thorough knowledge and interest. Experiencing environmental beauty may be the starting point for understanding oneself and the places involved.
- Aesthetics and the norms of beauty form the mental order through which we organize our environment into a physical order. One of the things we find hard to bear is having our notions of order put in doubt.
- The cultivation of aesthetic values and aesthetic-environmental qualities on the community level may be undermined by the time and resource-consuming movement to virtual realities.

Well-being and health:
- Aesthetic well-being is dependent on a building's ability to enhance confidence in the well-known and encourage exploration of novel qualities.
- Spiritual and existential values projected into and mediated by objects and environments are the main concepts for enhancing long-lasting environmental qualities and human well-being.
- Healthy environments are distinct from the actual health of their occupants, and the sensation of well-being and health is different than the appreciation of an environment that contributes to this. Appreciation also has an intellectual aspect which involves understanding the qualities of imagination, crafts and endeavours that have gone into the act of creation.
- Knowledge of people's preferences, and the needs and wishes of the users are the basis for creating and designing aesthetically pleasant and healthy environments.
- The healing environment offers rich stimuli and considers man at his weakest. It helps in orientation, movement and use of space, as well as creating a feeling of security, comfort, meaning and familiarity.

Environments and places in the essays
The essays' different approaches help us to see the subject from many perspectives which take several directions and include a wide range of environments and places, such as hospitals, schools, Renaissance and Danish

allotment gardens, Norwegian agrarian landscape, housing and homes, urban buildings and public spaces, a Toscane village and Japanese traditional architecture, megalithic stone monuments and a cottage in Wales, Montreal, and virtual environments.

One question to ask is if the same psychological processes and reflections on aesthetic quality and environmental beauty apply to all these different environments. The answer is no. The difference may lie in the level of personal involvement in a place compared to the professional investigation and assessment of places. Being personally involved in a place entails an emotional relationship in which it is hard to distinguish between aesthetic qualities as such and a perceptual-emotional experience. Memories of events and people attached to a place influence our aesthetic judgement and throw a veil of love or hatred over it, if we are not able to separate our personal feelings from a professional, aesthetic quality judgement. This is one reason why lay people's and experts' judgements differ.

When social housing blocks are demolished, it is not because they lack beauty, but because the place is identified as socially unfit or dangerous for human life. It is important here to understand what the concept of a place can be, and we here refer to Canter's model of place identity (1977), the inter-play between *the physical attributes, the ongoing activities* and *the conceptions* of who is there, what should happen and how the surroundings should be. We hypothesize that lay people, for instance politicians, inhabitants or user groups, have a tendency to identify the unwanted activities and their concep-tions with the physical surroundings, projecting the software into the hard-ware, so to speak, and rather than intervene in and adapt to the difficult social-economic conflicts and conceptions, the buildings are demolished. This projection of a social-cultural environment on the physical environment is mirrored when activists fight for the preservation of socially well-function-ing but old and worn out housing areas, or the demolition of all the right buildings in a socially malfunctioning estate.

Canter's identity-of-place model shows us how difficult and perhaps absurd it is to separate aesthetic qualities from other phenomena when dealing with social-cultural environments. It also shows that well-being and health attached to a place involve more than environmental aesthetics. The differences in the psychological process can also be found in another model by Canter on *place role and place evaluation* (1991). We evaluate a place from our role in that place, whether we are a visitor, architect, investigator, caretaker, patient or student. It is the purpose of being present in a place which generallly guides the assessment.

The argument that the physical surroundings are only one aspect of several does not diminish their significance for our well-being and health, it just shows that there is no simple and direct relationship between them, rather it is complex and intertwined, which is also evident from the range of meanings the essays mediate.

Issues raised in the essays
- And do they break new ground?
The issues raised in the essays encompass a wide range of disciplines and professions: psychology, anthropology, physiology, philosophy, art, architecture and architecture history, ehtics and aesthetics. The special nature of the subject means that the issues dealt with are integrated and move freely across disciplinary and professional borders.

Canter comments in his essay that we are looking at the issue back to front when we ask how aesthetics and beauty might effect health and well-being. We should rather ask about the effects of health on aesthetics. Canter argues that our aesthetic perception is influenced by our purposes, conceptions, expectations and attitudes which in turn are greatly influenced by our personal health situation.

It may be important to ascertain how we distinguish between a general perception, cognition and assessment of an environment and an aesthetic one. An overall environmental assessment is not identical to an aesthetic perception. When dealing with an aesthetically pleasing perception, there is consensus among researchers that the pleasure is experienced through sight, sound and touch for their own sake, excluding other factors determined by interests, purposes or goals. One may then ask if an aesthetic sensory stimulus approach to well-being and health is too narrow, as Canter argues, as long as natural and man-made environments most often serve a great number of interests and goals, and our environmental perception is multifaceted. We most often experience the environment as a whole we like or dislike, involving emotions, feelings of identity, expectations, purposes and utilitarian goals.

Another relevant question to ask is if *the essays break new ground*. A spontaneous answer is no, not really, if new ground means that we have found something completely new. But they make us view or understand the subject in a more comprehensive, more inclusive and deeper way than many scientific papers have done. The primary advantage of the essays is that they make associations and integrate otherwise foreign issues and concepts to improve our understanding on emotional, spiritual and intellectual level.

User participation processes and guidelines or memory lists for overcoming the lack of understanding of people's wishes and preferences, teaching architect students environmental psychology in order to make them understand their own limited approach to environmental aesthetics, research findings on physiological and psychological well-being within this field, discussions on order and beauty and theories on the roots of aesthetic preferences are issues more or less known by those already familiar with environmental psychology and the subject. Others may find these issues important, especially when they are presented in well-written and lucid essays compared to much of the scientific, heavy presentations of research.

Breaking new ground is a rather ambitious endeavour. If we can talk about new ground it might be found in the choice of focus and concepts, comprehensive approaches, and in the interpretations, refreshing ideas and novel reflections on how to go about and understand the subject. This does not necessarilly mean that we have to agree with the statements and views. Nevertheless, they help us reflect, rethink and reconsider our own perspectives, and they offer insight on an essential and sometimes spiritual level.

In the following we introduce the essays through five main issues and comment on their ability "to break new ground".
- *Healthy environments and aesthetic qualities*
- *Spirituality, health and places*
- *Beauty and happiness*
- *Architectural plasticity and controlled order*
- *"Bridging the gap" between people and experts*

Healthy environments and aesthetic qualities
- Essays by Roderick Lawrence, Daniel Stokols, Rikard Küller

 The difficulty of transforming knowledge from the research field of environmental aesthetics into requirements and guidelines is recognized in all the essays. *Roderick Lawrence* argues in his essay "Housing, Health and Aesthetics: Reconnecting the Senses", that a multisensory approach to the understanding and planning of healthy environments is necessary, as opposed to the Western emphasis on vision. Aesthetic needs are not, as Maslow indicated, separate and relevant when all the other needs are satisfied, on the contrary, they are integrated and part of all the other needs. Therefore it is difficult to describe purely aesthetic needs and qualities, and they cannot be defined and described by absolute rules. Well-being and health are dynamic phenomena and people generally feel when an environment is harmful or supportive, not in measurable terms but in a subjective way.

Lawrence has identified eight classes of dimensions in the research literature pertinent to an analysis of interrelations between housing, people and health. He claims that well-being is a result of and depends on a satisfaction of people's needs and goals related to the built environment, and that the complexity of housing qualities makes it necessary to approach housing research multidimensionally rather than studying single factors (Lawrence, 1992).

The idea that aesthetic needs are part of and integrated in other needs, thus rejecting Maslow's decision to put aesthetics in seventh place, may open for a wider approach to and understanding of environmental aesthetics and well-being. This means that we have to take aesthetics into account from the first moment when discussing and creating satisfactory human environments. The attitude in planning and building bodies is traditionally that "the aesthetic finish" is a separate entity, comes last and can be added like a bunch of flowers on a table to make a nice atmosphere. The idea that aesthetics is totally integrated in all we experience, do and think may make us more aware of the necessity to learn about the aesthetic dimension and its significance for well-being and health.

Daniel Stokols argues that empirical studies on environmental preferences and well-being have primarily focused on individuals' cognitive and emotional states and not on dimensions indicating the well-being and health of communities and social groups. Stokols' own research has provided us with considerable knowledge of healthy environments (Stokols, 1992). In his essay "Environmental Aesthetics and Well-being: Implications for a Digital World" he leads us to speculate on what might happen with the aesthetic development of people and public places when the Internet and media offer, as they do today, a full package of visual, aesthetic experiences of virtually perfect and exciting places. Sitting comfortably at home, at work or in theme parks, we push buttons and communicate in virtual space instead of participating in real life's face-to-face community. Stokols emphasises that we need to implement empirical research because the problem is that we do not know if the consequences of individually preferred aesthetic-virtual experiences make us neglect the aesthetic imperfectness of real environments, real people and real aesthetic-sensuous experiences. The challenge is therefore to develop community programmes supporting cultural institutions such as museums, theaters and concert halls. As Kim Dovey also pointed out, the more virtual and unreal the environment becomes, the more we need real and aesthetically stimulating places which inspire public participation and involvement.

The fear of the effect of virtual reality and information technology on the well-being of individuals is not new, but the reflection on what may happen to well-being at the community level is more rare. The awareness of the difference of perception and cognition in a real and a virtual world is important. The possibility of choosing exciting experiences while sitting comfortably is fascinating especially for young people curious about the world and themselves. Perhaps familiar, unreal or artificial media, such as literature, movies, televison and records are in danger of extinction, while the interest in real and virtual realities will grow and survive. Perhaps our knowledge of our own imperfection as persons in imperfect environments makes us wish to be accepted by other imperfect individuals in imperfect environments, and that a dialogue between the happy state of virtual perfectness and real imperfectness is a way of combining "looking at" with a "living in" society.

In the essay "The Architectural Psychology Box of Infinite Knowledge", *Rikard Küller* claims that when research within environmental psychology has succeeded in wresting from nature and culture the knowledge of some connections, there always appear to be new questions which require new knowledge. He compares this process with opening Chinese boxes, that each time you have just opened one, you discover a new box which needs to be opened and investigated to fully understand the subject. Even if results are attained and relations between man and environment can be proved physiologically, psychologically, socially and culturally, it is often difficult to explain why these arise and which consequences they have in the long run. Küller also claims that we are flooded by a surfeit of various scientific results threatening to drown both practitioner and specialist. He discusses three research subjects within environmetal aesthetics which he and his colleagues have worked on during a lifetime and from which they have attained valuable results: environments with and without daylight (Küller and Lindsten, 1992), colour design and the arousal of the brain (Küller and Mikellides 1993) and institutional versus home-like surroundings for the well-being of patients with senile dementia (Küller, 1991). It is very encouraging that one who has worked all his life within the aesthetic field of environmental psychology emphasises an anti-deterministic, open and critical view on giving clear explanations on complex people-environment relations, even if society longs for simple explanations for why we feel good or bad, or how a healthy environment should be designed. Nevertheless, his research findings show that it is possible to improve the physical environment significantly to the benefit of people's well-being.

Spirituality, health and places
- Essays by David Canter, Kim Dovey, Juhani Pallasmaa, Kaj Noschis

The issues in these three essays involve spiritual and existential values and their roles as mediators of the social-cultural and spiritual processes that created them.

It is a paradox, *David Canter* argues in his essay "Health and Beauty: Enclosure and Structure", that we search for a connection between well-being and the aesthetics of the built environment when we know that people feel more attracted to natural elements than to built ones. Canter claims that we have to distinguish between aesthetics and comfort and that there are differences between the sensation of well-being and health and the appreciation of the environment that may contribute to this. He reflects on the early cultures' first fundamental architectural act, such as marking a spot "by placing an upright stone as a point in the landscape", and making places of *identification, specification and enclosure* in the landscape. Their significance for the well-being of the people were dependent on how well these places mediated the purposes of the social-cultural processes, which also include the quality of imagination and the endeavours that have gone into the act of creation. Canter discusses if these three concepts may be aspects of human existence and their manifistations may be interpreted as universal forms originating from evolutionary or social-cultural processes. Modern societies are more complex than the prehistoric, nevertheless, to have a positive influence on well-being and health our places are equally dependent on mediating social-cultural and spiritual relations, which in turn is a result of how we look upon ourselves, a view also shared by Pallasmaa in his essay. Canter points out that the aesthetic response is an interaction of emotions, expectations, purpose and function, and that its strength lies in integrating these in the mind.

Canter's scientific publications highlight the necessity to understand the complexity of man-environment relations in real-life situations. His choice of place and *place identity* as a key concept describing the interaction between people's actions, conceptions and the physical environment has helped us to better understand the conditions for creating better physical places (Canter, 1977).

Canter's emphasis on the importance of the "quality" of the social-cultural processes behind historic monuments makes us reflect on the quality of the processes behind contemporary monuments and environments. The deep admiration, enthusiasm, wonder and love which generations have perceived and projected into these huge historical stone monuments indicate that "their message has been understood".

Museums, textbook authors, the media and the tourist business have recognized our need for an aesthetic, emotional and intellectual approach to the past by opening for a direct sensation, emotional identification and an intellectual understanding as well as an admiration of the endeavours and skills behind the work. Today we are not certain of the purposes or the social processes behind these aesthetic monuments. They are mythical and from these myths we imagine or "feel" the spiritual forces of the places. This means that the success of architecture as signficant for well-being is dependent on whether intentions, purposes, aims, wishes, hopes and passions, originating in each of us and integrated in the social-cultural processes are mediated and perceived as existentially relevant for people, not only in a materialistic sense but rather in a spiritual sense.

In his essay "The Aesthetics and Place" *Kim Dovey* intergrates feeling at home, being familiar with, feeling safe and secure, having control, participating and being responsible for environ- ments into an overall concept, which he calls *"healthy places"*. He asks if it is possible to design healthy places. He is inspired by Heidegger's terms "living in" and "looking at" as conditions for understanding that healthy places are related to both terms, the direct, practical and emotional as well as the distant, theoretical and contemplative. Healthy places are signifi- cant because they "generate, celebrate and sustain life", "they heal in the sense of making more whole", and they hold authenticity, a concept Dovey earlier has analysed brilliantly (Dovey, 1985). Dovey contends that aesthetics as a concept should retain its ambiguity as to both direct sensory perception and the study of beauty. It is important to keep the dialogue alive because aesthet- ics is based on a fruitful complexity of ideologies of beauty and the forces of sensations and experiences. Part of the task for architectural aesthetics is to ensure that the architectural discourse becomes a discourse about life and the aesthetics of everyday real environments. This becomes even more important the more we simulate life and inhabit virtual space, as Stokols also argues in his essay.

The concept of healthy places as dynamic social-cultural and physical- formal representations of life and death, emotions and conflicts, questions the conception of creating harmonic, static and ideal places, if this means that they become stiff and dead rather than lively and temporarily chaotic. This is a relatively new and postmodern idea in architecture and a difficult one to grasp because it breaks with the ideas in architectural history of harmony, balance, classical beauty and stable structures. It is, however, a necessary concept to consider and discuss.

 In his essay "The Mind of the Environment", *Juhani Pallasmaa* argues that a weak point in the culture of architecture is that ugly and beautiful environments are results of both negative and positive intentions and values of the architects and builders because man simultaneously builds the image of himself and the world. These intentions and values are both on a conscious and subconscious level. The conscious aspects, such as architectural style, symbolic meaning and manifistations of social institutions, are less crucial for our well-being and health than the subconscious structures and meanings expressing existential motives such as hope, wishes, fears and anxieties. Behind our behaviour and aesthetic preferences there are subconscious bio-cultural layers rooted in our biological past. Environments which are considered as good and friendly are always in harmony with these archaic instinctive reactions. The bio-evolutionary view is shared by many of the essays, even if it is still a controversial concept amongst experts.

In his book *The Eyes of the Skin* (1996), Pallasmaa points out the one-dimensional Western cultural approach to aesthetics which totally estimates the visual aspect of the environment, an observation also made by Lawrence in his essay.

The importance of the existential content of architecture compared to the stylistic conventions, the consciously expressive forces and functional norms is an important issue to discuss today because of the new interest in the formal, stylistic and expressive forces of architecture. The impact and significance of architecture for "cultural well-being" lie in its capacity to mediate existential values. Pallasmaa claims that our bodily sensuous and existential knowledge is superior to our possibility of rational perception and analysis. Emotional intelligence has become a subject of scientific interest just recently. We recognize traditional architecture as valuable and contributing to people's well-being. The dilemma implies that tradition can not be owned or inherited, it has to be created by each new generation. Attempts to create a logical tradition on a conscious programme have not succeeded because they lead to one-dimensional and sentimental interpretations. As Canter points out in his essay, the social-cultural processes behind the art of building have to be spiritual and authentic to mediate values and well-being. Attempts to revive traditions from the past because we feel comfortable in such traditional environments easily acquires a comfort-commercial and pseudo-emotional nature, an issue also discussed by Dovey (1986).

Within architecture and psychology it is rare to focus on a concept, such as "the unknown" when discussing environmetal aesthetics. *Kaj Noschis* does that in his essay "Aesthetics in the Built Environment and its Influence on the User". It is, however, important to think in this direction in order to understand why we appreciate, want to experience, collect, exhibit, strive to create aesthetic and beautiful objects and make them significant in our daily and ritual behaviour. The unknown out there and in ourselves is an existential and spiritual question which is very seldom related to the discussion on environmental symbolism, craftmanship and our need for emotional comfort, safety and well-being. The same need to connect with the unknown may also lie behind the beauty projected into human-created fine arts and architecture today and through-out history. Well-being then becomes the result if the human endeavour succeeds in creating and experiencing beauty.

Beauty and happiness
- Essays by Arnulf Kolstad, Birgit Cold, Perla Serfaty-Garcon
The essays discuss beauty as a subjective, emotional aspect of well-being, a general sensuous-aesthetic stimulus and a cultural concept.

In his essay "What Happens if Zeleste Becomes an Architect? Development of aesthetic preferences and their influence on well-being and health", *Arnulf Kolstad* wonders why his four-year old daughter dresses in pink, gold and silver on her birthday, radiating happiness and a beauty which is captured not least by her father, making him feel happy. Beauty and the feeling of being beautiful radiate happiness in an infectious way, he argues. From the moment we open our eyes we learn about the social and physical environment and automatically combine sweet, good feelings and nourish actions with aesthetic sensations which develop into preferences. He asks if being happy and satisfied makes people more healthy, but does not believe that simple rules of aesthetics cause good health. On the other hand, there are indirect effects between beauty and well-being because a positive mood may influence our health in a good manner, even enhancing healing processes. Being surrounded by a beautiful environment may also increase our self-esteem, making us feel more valuable because we identify with the environment.

The infectious nature of a person's happiness from experiencing being beautiful or being surrounded by beauty is a convincing explanation of the coherence between happiness and beauty. This may also explain the success of commercializing fashions within "prefabricated homes and clothes" by means of happy faces and families. One might ask if beauty also exists without making anybody happy and if unhappiness also is infectious in a way which makes us experience otherwise pleasant surroundings as ugly. We may ask how much the emotional reactions and the qualities of an environment are mutually infectious. The well-known and old experiment presenting a friendly face with various backgrounds showed that people's judgements of the person were influenced by the background.

 It is not possible to understand the concept of beauty separated from the context, nor is it possible to penetrate it in a purely rational way. This is what *Birgit Cold* discusses in her essay "Beauty". We may argue that beauty is an old-fashioned term inherited from historic times when rich and well-educated nobles were surrounded by artists, architects and craftsmen, eager and capable of providing beauty as a celebration. Is it possible today to speak of beauty, and programme and design it intentionally, or is beauty a happy result of successful processes? Beauty appears to have a "core of qualities", a certain amount of balance and order, as advocated by Schjerup Hansen in his essay, and an excitement which is thrilling, making us wish to explore and renew our experience further with the object or environment. This is close to the above-mentioned preference concepts of the Kaplans (1987). We also experience environments as beautiful on the basis of knowledge and interest, we learn to listen and to observe, and we are emotionally attached to individual experiences from childhood, which means that the experience of beauty has evolutionary, culturally-learnt and individual-emotional roots.

Beauty is multidimensional, it is a relation between properties of the environment and our senses, mind and knowledge. Time, place and role factors influence the experience of beauty. Trivial and instrumental activities in familiar surroundings make us more or less unaware of both ugliness and beauty.

Knowing Gadamer's hypothesis that beauty has to be discovered and mediated by empathetic artists before the public learns to appreciate it, we may learn that it is the task of the artist, architect, planner or designer to discover "beauty" and mediate it in a way which makes people experience beauty and happiness. It appears as if this process of discovery and mediation can not be promoted rationally and intellectually, but develops in a fusion of subconscious-artistic and conscious-intellectual forces. Which means that beauty and happiness, or well-being, can not be ordered nor created by conscious processes alone.

 The essay by *Perla Serfaty-Garcon* "I Live in a Beautiful House, on a Beautiful Street in Beatiful Montreal: Notes on Well-being and the Experience of Place Aesthetics" tells a story about love of "Mediterranean beauty" as a home base from which she assesses, appraises and understands other places and herself. She succeeds in poetic terms to describe physical aspects of the environment, and she examines aesthetic qualities of times during the day and life, spoken words, and activities and people in different places related to her experience of well-being and beauty. Mediterranean beauty is especially precious and touching in arid areas and surprising when experienced in the North. It has personal roots in childhood and constitutes familiarity also related to other countries, climates, places and people with respect to the awareness and appreciation of beauty.

Beauty becomes a phenomenon equally related to the atmosphere of places as to the person experiencing it. Bearing this in mind it is encouraging to read an essay written by an experienced researcher highlighting the essence of aesthetic awareness and multisensuous experiences as interacting, childhood-influenced, mood-inspired and social-related phenomena. It shows with great conviction the difficulty of performing reasonable research on separate, aesthetic matters, trying to isolate certain aspects of a total experience. One way of making us more aware of these interactions is to ask people to tell their personal stories on aesthetic experiences or ask researchers to write essays as we do here.

Architectural plasticity and controlled order
- Essays by Ann Westerman, Jens Schjerup Hansen
In built environments we find a certain recognizable order, geometrically controlled or topologically arranged space, structure and plasticity in exteriors. In her essay "Buildings Imaged as Bodies", *Ann Westerman* describes her research findings of men's and women's preferences for building facades with different plasticity (Westerman, 1976). The identity of a building and its ability to enhance confidence and be a source of enjoyment are important conditions for preference. She hypothesizes that on a subconscious level we associate a building or parts of a building with different parts of the body. Children love to crouch in small nooks and sheds imagining their safe stay in their mother's womb, men are fascinated by hollows, intruding openings and spaces imagining penetrating a woman's body, and women are equally attracted by salient, conspicuous parts, such as balconies, towers and pillars imagining a man's body. These "body images" are discussed as an explanation for the preferences of different forms of plasticity in building facades. Her hypothesis is that a balance between the feeling of *safety* in the well-known in our own body, and the promise of *excitement* when making new discoveries of the body of the other sex, makes us unconsciously image buildings as bodies. This "safety-excitement theory" may be compared with the evolutionary preference theory of the Kaplans (1987) referred to above. Coherence and legibility creating a safe feeling of control, and complexity and "mystery" creating excitement, are here key concepts for an environmental understanding and encouragement to exploration.

The idea that we image buildings as bodies is daring and also fascinating. It is, however, not possible to prove or disprove this idea scientifically, nor is this the purpose. It is a hypothesis which makes us wonder, reflect and want to make assessments in order to explore the idea. Westerman shows that both men and women prefer a certain plasticity with both "in and outgoing elements" above smooth facades. This may give us an understanding of the love for ornamented, profiled and plastic architecture from the past and present, and the disapproval of modern smooth architecture, which hides "the body of the building", leaving no images.

 Jens Schjerup Hansen argues in his essay "Aesthetics, Order and Discipline" that what we find delightful and beautiful amounts to culturally conditioned order. One of the most difficult things for people to endure is having their sense of order put in doubt. We are thoroughly permeated with "a controlled order" generated by our fascination with perspective space. He presents an interesting perspective on the history of the Danish allotment gardens influenced by the Renaissance norms of controlled order and the bourgeois ideals of what was and still is "nice and tidy". These two ideals continue to influence the style of the small gardens, originally meant to give workers and the abject poor an extra source of food and the possibility of getting away from unhealthy surroundings, physically as well as socially. Schjerup Hansen doubts if the concept of controlled order, which he also finds very clearly used in the huge Nazi-parades demonstrating the mental control of the collective spirit, will continue in modern society with its indisputable individualistic character. The growing focus on the values of individual freedom and the persistent criticism of the built environment from the sixties could be an indication of an emotional break with controlled order.

This issue is important to consider when observing the individualistic, uncontrolled and accidentally located buildings invading the landscape around towns and cities. Just as uncontrolled, and turning into a mess of stylistic and pseudo-traditional elements, are commercial urban areas with buildings designed as special advertising signs for the companies that occupy them. At the same time there is a renewed interest, not least in the UK, for the patterns of controlled geometrical and symmetrical order in both urban and landscape planning inspired by historic places and monuments, presumably as a nostalgic longing for the easily recognizable and well-known beauty experienced in classical buildings and Renaissance gardens. Schjerup Hansen shows us that controlled space may agree with the wish for mental order. The powerful impact of a geometrical symmetry creating a totally controlled space has been utilized throughout history by emperors, totalitarian regimes and influential persons and bodies to impress and discipline individuals and the masses, to legitimate a power system, and also with the intention to create harmonious, friendly and predictable environments, as Palladian architecture. It is the combination of the proportional system of order in itself and the situational and social meaning put into it which creates pleasure and well-being or intimidating horror and impressive fear.

"Bridging the gap" between people and experts
- Essays by Aase Eriksen, Byron Mikellides, Sue-Ann Lee, David Uzzell, Einar Strumse
These essays deal with how architects, researchers and theorists communicate with architect students, other professionals, builders, users and the public. If this communication is appropriate and facilitates understanding and mutual respect, it may improve the learning, planning and architectural processes, and hence the aesthetic quality and common well-being.

 One architect who has developed and consequently employs a user-participation process in all her architectural works is *Aase Eriksen*. Her background is both as an architect and an educationalist. In her essay "Creating Aesthetic Built Environments through the User Participation Process", she describes three of her architectural works which are based on user participation processes developing and communicating the knowledge, wishes and preferences of groups of users, including children. Architects seldom take the trouble to listen to children to understand their needs and wishes and observe their behaviour in order to transfer this knowledge to architecture. User-participation processes are the basis for creating a functional and pleasant architecture, she argues.

According to the users' views and public evaluations, she has successfully incorporated these qualities in her works. Few architects are able to develop and implement pedagogically user-participation processes and incorporate the obtained psychological and social knowledge of the users directly into the design. Her works, however, are not just as highly regarded by the architectural society. As Mikellides points out, user-friendly architecture does not win first prize, rather the winners are those with the greatest architectural originality. The best architecture, however, may be original, pleasant and user-friendly.

 To create a basis for understanding and utilizing environmental and architectural research findings, it is important to develop interest and knowledge on the educational level. *Byron Mikellides* and also Sue-Ann Lee, who both teach environmental psychology to architectural students, emphasize that it is important that students keep an open mind, establish an attitude and respect that built and natural environments may have an effect on people's well-being and health. They argue that good architecture is created from an empathetic knowledge of the needs and wishes of existing and future users. In his essay "Reflections on the Concepts of Aesthetics, Health and Well-being", he stresses the importance of developing environmental-aesthetic knowledge during the first years of architectural education. Knowing about human needs is the first educational step, understanding their implications and roots is an important second step, while transfoming this understanding into architecure is a demanding third step which requires empathy, aesthetic sensitivity and talent. He introduces high quality architecture and natural environments as excursion and training targets for studying aesthetic concepts such as "synchronic and diachronic rhyme", rhythm, balance and harmony.

His reflection on whether research and teaching within environmental psychology has helped at all to improve the quality of environments is an important reminder of the aim and purpose of this field. Mikellides shows with great understanding of the architect students' commitment, that the main purpose of teaching environmental psychology in architectural schools is to find a way of developing a fruitful interplay between *"a psychological eye and a creative hand"*. In his earlier book *Architecture for People* (1980) Mikellides has highlighted this subject by presenting essays written by renowned professionals on how they *bridged the gap* and developed architecture which people appreciate.

 Sue-Ann Lee presents a critical review of architectural styles and ideologies such as Arts and Crafts, the Garden City movement and Modernism in the essay "Chuck out the Chintz? Some Observations on Aesthetics, Well-being and Health". No single style or ideology has been able to satisfy the functional and psychological-aesthetic aspects of the human environment. Only a deep understanding of the interplay of these aspects can create the basis for designing healthy and pleasant environments. It is impossible to arrive at a final conclusion on how to create ideal human settlements and buildings. If one, however, develops an inclusive attitude towards research findings, theories and human approaches within environmental psychology, there is a basis for a more sustainable and ecologically sound development.

Neither Mikellides nor Lee is optimistic in their analysis of the results of teaching environmental psychology to architect students and communicating this field to architects. It appears as if most architect students are interested in the subject, but architect teachers and practising architects do not spend time and effort to learn about people's preferences and understand the roots to them. This social-science field, the scientific-professional language, the experimental research and quantitative methods presented in the literature, the focus on single aspects and the failure to communicate a comprehensive and multidisciplinary integrated view of complex people-environment relations may be reasons for the scarce interest and utility of research findings and knowledge by architects, planners and builders. The essays, however, show different approaches to improved understanding and procedures. In recent years professionals within environmental psychology have become more aware of their obligation to communicate their knowledge in a more understandable and engaging way. This volume of essays is one attempt to share ideas and knowledge with people and other professionals.

 In the essay "Conversations on Aesthetics", *David Uzzell* describes the communicative gap between design professions, conservation groups and the public. This is illustrated in fictive conversations between persons representing different roles and views. The dialogues are based on interviews in a research project examining which design criteria different groups consider important for assessing the visual impact of buildings. The dialogues give a vivid and informative insight into the procedures, problems and beliefs in the understanding and communication about aesthetic criteria. Uzzell explains how the design of visual criteria within the project developed into a concentration on process-based criteria, formulated as a memory checklist, rather than on judgement criteria, determining whether a building is "good or bad". Instead of giving "right" answers, it formulates appropriate and relevant questions to be considered in each part of the planning and design process, and thus becomes a systematic list, or *aide memoire*, of criteria, supporting a dynamic procedure. The demand of the architect or developer becomes to justify the decisions made at each step of the design process.

These conversations illustrate in a keen and humorous way different actors' attitudes, perspectives, interests and understandings of aesthetic quality and beauty. Of course there is always a risk that such checklists may develop into fixed images and solutions shared by the controlling groups. On the other hand, they may direct communication in the design process by facilitating which questions are important to consider in the various steps of the process. This may be an improvement of the traditional programme and design procedure, especially when the users are involved in the process.

 Einar Strumse is inspired by Kaplan's reasonable person model in the essay "Reasonable Persons and their Preferences". This is a model for understanding the communication between experts and the public. Experts obtain insight into people's visual and spatial assessments and preferences by implementing procedures based on giving the public relevant and understandable information and opening for their expressions of multiple needs, not taking for granted that people desire the maximum quantity. Strumse has concentrated his research on Norwegian agrarian landscapes to investigate how different built features are assessed aesthetically (Strumse, 1996). It is important to understand the aesthetic qualities of the cultivated landscape because of the frequent neglect of aesthetics in most of the technical built environments, which we find evidence for in modern farming, road planning and electricity poles. He argues that environmental design often is dictated by fashion and designers' own environmental preferences and pragmatic aspects, such as costs, than by knowledge of human perception, preferences of the public and criteria for people's well-being. He discusses the aesthetics of the natural and built environment, referring to the concepts used in the preference model of Kaplan & Kaplan.

Strumse points out that the designer profession has neglected the public's

Fig. 10. Dragvoll, University of Trondheim in Norway by Arch. H. Larsen (B. Cold).

aesthetic preferences in the agrarian Norwegian landscape and that the most "criminal", aesthetic mistakes are caused by the lack of will, effort and knowledge of planning the landscape aesthetically, which we may agree with. The lack of aesthetic knowledge, however, on the part of the public, farmers, politicians and municipalities is considerable. Observing the new pseudo-stylish prefabricated housing-supplements tacked on to existing traditional farms does not convince us, that the preferences of farmers or building authorities, responsible for the aesthetics of the countryside and agrarian landscape indicate that they have any clue of aesthetic values. In Norway many of the municipalities have very few, if any, professionals with aesthetic knowledge, something which also becomes evident when assessing the agrarian landscapes, especially around the cities in most countries. It is high time to be aware of the aesthetics of the agrarian landscape irrespective of who is at fault. A positive dialogue between experts and the public is necessary to obtain more aesthetic solutions in the future.

Our message and hope
The many different approaches and perspectives in the essays illustrate the variety in this field of knowledge. Trying to understand and communicate the core of relations between aesthetics, well-being and health is far from simple. The essays are a lucid and inspiring attempt at getting closer to the feeling and understanding of these relations. We hope the readers will enjoy the essays and that they may be inspired to contribute to further development of the theme, both practically and theoretically (Fig. 10).

References
Appleton, J. (1975). *The Experience of Landscape.* Wiley, London.
Canter, D. (1977). *The Psychology of Place.* Architectural Press, London.
Canter, D. (1991). Understanding, assessing, and acting in places: Is an integrative framework possible? In T. Gärling & T. Evans (eds). *Environmental Cognition and Action. An Integrative Multidisciplinary Approach.* (191 - 209). Oxford University Press, New York.
Cold, B., Kolstad, A., Larssæther, S. (eds) (1998). *Aesthetics, Well-being and Health, - Abstracts on Theoretical and Empirical Research within Environmental Aesthetics.* Norsk Form. Oslo.
Dovey, K. (1985). The Quest for Authenticity and the Replication of Environmental Meaning. In *Dwelling, Place and Environment,* ed. D. Seamon & R. Mugerauer, Martinus Nijhof, The Hague.
Gadamer, H. G. (1986). Part I: The relevance of the beautiful. In R. Bernasconi (ed). *The Relevance of The Beautiful and Other Essays.* Cambridge University Press, USA.
Goleman, D. (1995). *Emotional Intelligence.* Bantam Books. New York.
Gombrich, E. H. (1956, 1968). *Art and Illusion.* Phaidon Press Ltd, London.

Hargittai, I. & M. (1994). *Symmetry, A Unifying Concept.* Shelter Publications, Inc, California.

Heath, T. F. (1988). Behavioural and perceptual aspects of the aesthetics of urban environments. In J. L. Nasar. *Environmental Aesthetics. Theory, Research and Applications.* (6-10). Cambridge University Press.

Kaplan, S. (1992). Environmental preference in a knowledge-seeking, knowledge-using organism. In J. H. Barkow, L. Cosmides & J. Tooby (eds). *The Adapted Mind. Evolutionary Psychology and the Generation of Culture.* Oxford University Press.

Küller, R. (1988). Environmental activation of old persons suffering from senile dementia. In H. van Hoogdalen, N. L. Prak, T. J. M. van der Voordt & H. B. R. van Wegen (eds). *Looking Back to the Future. Symposia and Papers* (133 - 139). Proceedings from the 10th conference of IAPS, Vol. II, Delft University Press.

Küller, R. (1991). Familiar design helps dementia patients cope. In W. F. E. Preiser, J. C. Vischer and E. T. White (eds) *Design Imtervention. Towards a More Humane Architecture.* Van Nostrand, New York.

Küller, R. & Lindsten, C. (1992). Health and behaviour of children in classrooms with and without windows. *Journal of Environmental Psychology,* 12, 305 - 317.

Küller, R. and Mikellides, B. (1993). Simulated studies of colour, arousal, and comfort. In R. W. Marans and D. Stokols (eds) *Environmental Simulation: Research and Policy Issues.* Plenum Press, New York.

Lacoste, J. (1997). Idéen om det skjønne. Trekk fra estetikkens historie. [The idea of the Beautiful. Features of the History of Aesthetics]. Forsythia. *L'idée de beau,* Paris 1986.

Lawrence, R. J. (1992). Housing and health: A complex relationship. *Archives of Complex Environmental Studies (ACES),* 4 (1-2), 49 - 58.

Mikellides, B. (ed). (1980). *Architecture for People.* Studiovista, London.

Noschis, K. (1994). Rummets betydelse i vårdmiljön (Swedish). [The importance of space in care environments]. In *Kultur ger helse.* Nordisk konferens 1994, Esbo, Finland.

Nørretranders, T. (1991). *Mærk verden.* (Danish) [Mind the World]. Gyldendal, Danmark.

Pallasmaa, J. (1996). *The Eyes of the Skin. Architecture and the Senses*. Academy Editions, Academy Group Ltd, London.

Stokols, D. (1992). Establishing and maintaining healthy environments. Towards a social ecology of health promotion. *American Psychologist*, 47 (1), 6 - 22.

Strumse, E. (1996 a). *The Psychology of Aesthetics: Explaining Visual Preferences for Agrarian Landscapes in Western Norway*. Doctoral dissertation, University of Bergen, Norway.

Ulrich, R. (1983). Aesthetic and affective response to natural environments. In I. Altman & J. F. Wohlwill (eds). *Behaviour and the Natural Environment* (Chapter 3). Plenum Press, New York and London.

Westerman, A. (1976). Estetisk värdering av byggnadsexteriörer (Swedish) [On Aesthetic Judgement of Building Exteriors]. Doctoral dissertation, KTH, Stockholm.

Ørskov, W. (1966). *Avlæsning af objekter og andre essays* (Danish). [Reading of Objects and other essays] Borgens forlag. København.

Health and Beauty:
Enclosure and Structure

David Canter

*Do the ancient monuments of upright stones mediate
something essential to us and our well-being?*

Dear Birgit

How thoughtful of you to ask me to contribute to your set of essays on the influence of environmental aesthetics on health and well-being. One's early ideas as well as the colleagues who are interested in them, are like childhood friends (it is over 20 years since I wrote *The Psychology of Place* and quite a few years since I finished the development of it in the *Facets of Place*, although that has only just been published). Their visits, though sadly these days more often virtual over the internet than in reality, are always welcome. For it is always a delight to pick up the conversation again, apparently at just that point where it was broken off some time ago, when we thought it would continue sooner than it has. But as the conversation unfolds you see that things have changed more than you realised. It is difficult to get back to the fresh enthusiasm of yesteryear. Yet as the conversation develops, hopefully, new excitements emerge to replace the old.

Sitting here in this hidden Welsh valley, I am looking across a small, rain swept, lush green field, to the dense, silver-grey, leafless trees that enwrap a steep hill. The paths through those trees lead up across the auburn bracken to the blue-grey rocky outcrop that is called in Welsh *Carn Ingli* ("the hill of angels"). Thinking about my experience here as a basis for writing to you about built environment and health, it is tempting to see architecture and the aesthetics, which grows out of the creation of places, as a profound paradox. For the most obvious aesthetics is the naturally occurring one: a beautiful view, an attractive woman, a pretty flower. It is a common experience, strongly supported by empirical studies, that the major distinctions people draw between places is whether they are natural or man-made. Invariably the natural is preferred to the man-made. We even undertook some studies recently of people's views of materials, like steel and plastic and again the major distinction that emerged is whether the materials were thought to be natural or synthetic. So, if we all enjoy the natural and it provides the benchmark for the beautiful, the creation of a building is a step away from that natural attractiveness towards the built which is inevitably a step towards the ugly. The paradox therefore lies in the search for the aesthetic significance of a building that undermines what may be beautiful by moving away from the natural.

Thought and feeling

Yet would I appreciate the view of *Carn Ingli* so much if the heating in my cottage did not work, or if the rain gusting past the window were blowing in my face? Maslow was, of course, the person who did most to propose that there is some hierarchy of needs, with the more spiritual and less functional needs built upon the satisfaction of the more lowly. I have never been convinced by this proposal for many reasons. I think two of the most telling are that the supposedly distinct "needs" interact. The delicious taste of a simple apple when it is eaten at the top of the hill opposite, after the rugged exercise of climbing up there, has similar aesthetic qualities to a carefully prepared sit-down meal in a grand restaurant. The experience may be modified by what happens before or after it, but the actual nature of the experience itself may have similar properties. This really relates to whether there exist some "pure" emotions that are then labelled to take on different meanings, as many psychologists believe. So whether I feel elated or anxious when I get to the top of the hill will depend on whether I see a storm coming to cut off my path down again. The physiological reaction may be the same for both feelings but it is the interpretation I put on my circumstances that creates the different emotions.

This has the implication that even the fundamental distinction between emotion and thought quickly becomes confused. There can be no pure emotion or, for that matter, no pure thought. So the idea of a ladder of needs that you climb up ignores the fact that the interpretation of the "higher" needs is always available to you. You might be starving in a dessert and not really interested in the view but that does not mean that you will be blind to its awe inspiring qualities. This was illustrated recently when one of the persons rescued from the Estonia disaster recalled that they had talked about the beauty of the night when they were shivering in their life rafts.

Beyond the fact that the reactions to unfulfilled needs obviously interact, the second major problem with any reductionist theory like Maslow's is the related difficulty that human feelings are obviously not uni-dimensional, whereby we feel one thing at a time. The observation in the Gospel according to Matthew, that man does not live by bread alone, is merely one of the earliest references to the inherently multivariate nature of human experience.

Aesthetics versus preference

The mixture of emotions and cognitions within experience is really at the heart of the aesthetic response. The psychological literature, particularly in the study of architecture, is usually very confused about this. I remember an old and revered lecturer, at Strathclyde University's School of Architecture in the 60s where I first started, criticising my "post-occupancy evaluations". In those days most schools of architecture had at least one central European emigré whose Viennese accent was worn as a badge to demonstrate his sensibilities and ward off the prevailing functionalism. When I began to study the meaning of buildings he said to me "Now Canter, at last you stop ziss building psychology and start *architectural* psychology!"

He was arguing that the preferences and evaluations that people have for their surroundings may be emotional reactions but are not aesthetic reactions. I have had similar comments from teachers of musical appreciation. They say that although you can delight in a piece of music, the full appreciation has an important intellectual component. Knowing, for example, that the second motif is merely an inversion of the first adds a frisson to the enjoyment. Recognising that the jazz improvisation on Autumn Leaves has taken a phrase out of Summertime enriches the excitement of listening.

What I am leading to here is that there are two stages in our thinking that need to be clarified before we can even begin to consider architectural aesthetics and health. First, we must distinguish between aesthetics and comfort. Is a warm bath after a day roaming the hills in the rain an aesthetic experience? Is the smoky smell, and crackle of a log fire enjoyed whilst sipping a good malt whisky? The loose fold of golden curls falling on a woman's smooth, white neck? Are these to be compared with listening to a late Beethoven quartet or looking upon Picasso's Guernica? Can I enjoy the pattern of stones over my cottage fireplace although I know the builders never mastered the skill of preventing the smoke blowing into the room? Can I appreciate the power of the concept of Frank Lloyd-Wright's Guggenheim museum, although I know it is extremely limited as a place to hold exhibitions?

How much can the appreciation of a creation be separated from the actions and sensations that it can or may generate? With buildings this problem is complicated by the fact they never exist merely as objects, as abstract entities devoid of any meaning, possible or actual use. This generates the prospect that the appreciation of architecture is the ultimate aesthetic experience. It is always both an intellectual understanding and a direct sensation. Perhaps this is how we should search for the influence of building aesthetics on health and well-being?

I squeezed a lot of ideas into that last paragraph, Birgit, so let me go over them again a little more slowly. I want to draw a number of distinctions. They are all aspects of the distinction between aesthetics and preference, drawing attention to the fact that aesthetic reactions are not the same as the conventional "evaluation" of buildings, or studies of how much buildings satisfy "user needs". This, I'm afraid, does resurrect the separation of appreciation from fitness for function, but then I think the idea that aesthetics was merely a representation of function was a very short-lived idea in architecture. Even at its height it was more of a visual style than a mechanical response to the use of buildings.

I guess that your search, Birgit, for aesthetic effects on health is a hangover from those heady days of the international movement and "functionalism". This was probably the most destructive phase that architecture has ever gone through. It pretended to ignore the distinction between buildings as abstract objects that may be appreciated for their formal qualities (although we may have some difficulty in defining what these qualities are) and buildings as receptacles. This is like appreciating the squat yellow jug sitting on the dresser behind me for how well it captures the whole expression of an object for containing and delivering a liquid (its "jugness"), as opposed to appreciating how much it holds or how well it pours. But buildings (and jugs) can be appreciated for a whole variety of reasons that has nothing to do with what they hold. It is only if we believe that their function, in a simple usage sense, captures all that is relevant to their aesthetics that we look for a direct relationship between the building and health.

There is an important distinction between the sensation of health or wellbeing and the appreciation of the environments and settings that may contrib-ute to this. There may be many indirect routes from the physical environment to our well-being and there will certainly be many non-environmental influences on our well-being, so there will never be a simple one-to one relationship between a building and health, except at the edges of physical impact when discomfort moves to danger. Therefore whilst it may make sense to think of a building as inherently "healthy" that view will always be distinct from the actual health of its occupants.

There is at least one more distinction that emerges when we think about buildings and health. Illness does not seem to be just equal and opposite to health. We can specify the lower limits of comfort and indicate when discomfort will start and injury follow. But by just reversing the trend we do not appear to guarantee health or even pleasure. High levels of noise, for example, are clearly deleterious, as are light or heat. We know that by going to these extremes we will produce illness and reduce pleasure. But the same is true for low levels of noise, heat or light. They can be deleterious too.

Space appears to operate differently. Low levels are bad, but are high levels bad or good? Of course, what we are exploring here is the idea of optimum levels, just enough, but not too much. Yet the problem with all that is that the optimum is a moving target. The silence of the Welsh countryside at night can frighten many city dwellers and would be quite inappropriate in a Liverpool night club.

But, as I said, this is all fraught with the architectural paradox. Natural phenomena, as appealing as they are, do push beyond the limits of acceptability, so humankind has always striven to pull these limits back into the envelope of comfort. This adds a further complication. The moment that there is any obvious human endeavour involved, whether it be the way the hedge opposite me has been cropped, or the iron age fort that sits on top of *Carn Ingli*, there is a recognition of the effort, craft or skill that goes into the endeavour. This recognition is different from the appreciation of the significance or power of the finished object. I think this is one reason why an aesthetic response is not merely preference. It is not merely emotion. It includes some understanding, however vague, of the human skills and qualities of imagination that have gone into the act of creation.

Purpose not function
It seems to me that the one way to understand the relevance of architectural

aesthetics to health is to look more closely at the *purpose* of architecture and to distinguish this from its function. To my mind function emerges out of the mechanics of use. It is part of a materialist view that puts human activities in the here and now, in pride of place. Purpose by contrast always has an eye on the future. It recognises that there are unfolding objectives that shape people's lives. I am tempted to paraphrase the oft quoted aphorism from Churchill here. We shape our lives and then they shape us.

This means that architecture is always a statement now about what the notional use of a building is, but also an expression of the aspirations (or lack of them) of all those involved in the building process. Design cannot help but look to the future (even if it does this by looking at the past) at the same time as it shapes the present. Architecture is one of the ways that we all become time travellers.

The most elementary architectural act thus carries many layers of implications about the location in which it occurs, about the present and future use of the building and about the people who are creating it. This is how it helps to define the place it helps to create, location, use and people, reflecting the elements of physical attributes, activities and conceptions that go into making places.

Moments in architecture

I am fascinated by the neolithic remains that are scattered around this corner of Wales. They may be an accident of its separateness from the main developments across Britain. They may have been especially dense here and thus a few have survived. Or it may even be that the local materials are especially hard wearing. Similar structures are, of course, found throughout North Western Europe, but there are few places where they are so dense. So, whatever the reason, scattered through the hills of Pembrokeshire are many stone monuments that, for me, capture the essence of what architects attempt to achieve. By looking at the three basic moments in architecture that they illustrate I do think that we can get a better understanding of how building has its relevance and influence.

These monuments are thousands of years old, some estimates put them at least between 5,000 and 3,000 years old, certainly on a par with the pyramids of Egypt, and much older than the *druidic* myths that surround them today. There is very little known about the social processes or daily activities that energised the people who put up these structures. What is known is greatly confused by the layers of meaning that later generations have given these elderly objects (not unlike the confusion that arises when we consider a warehouse that has been created from a disused church). But what seems certain now is that these structures were erected with great care, both in terms of the selection of the location and to ensure that they would be stable over long periods of time. They are therefore worthy of very careful consideration.

- Moment one: Identification

One set of objects that I consider to be architecturally most primitive, and that may turn out to be the oldest, are those structures known as standing stones' or *menhirs* (Fig 1).

These are solitary stones, sometimes three or four metres high that are set deep into the ground. The stones themselves were carefully selected, usually being roughly rectangular, or triangular, in section so that one side may be a metre wide with the other less than half that. There is even some evidence that they may have been selected or shaped to taper a little to the top. There is archeological evidence, also, that some form of human ashes are buried underneath some of these megaliths, indicating at a minimum that they were considered spiritually significant.

In his important book on the history of psychology Leslie Hearnshaw points out that psychology as a systematic study must trace its routes to those earliest times of human existence when people first buried their dead. Burial indicates the recognition that the person is and was more than a mere physical form. Respect for the person who enlivened the body requires that the body be respectfully disposed of. If the physical carapace was all that mattered then it would be discarded not buried. So, human remains add to the significance of any location. I think the message must be that this is true whether the remains are actual physical bones or ashes, or tribal memories of what happened there.

In other words, this first architectural moment is one of identification of a place. The architectural statement points to the location and declares it as being of significance. This is the most fundamental architectural act. The

Fig. 1. "Bed Morus", Newport.

marking of a spot. A one dimensional point. But although the geometry can be considered one dimensional the significance is multi-faceted. Meaning is impossible unless it is a part of a network of other meanings. No word can be defined by simple cross reference to one sign. Meaning derives from the culture of which its language is part.

These standing stones are of little more than curiosity value today (although perhaps not surprisingly the old myths are kept alive by those seeking a "new age"), but the effort that went into erecting them must indicate that they were of great importance in their time. Well-being must have derived from the fact that they designated culturally significant locations in an appropriate way. So this is the first way in which architecture promotes health, by identifying places appropriately.

This is a way of providing focus on an otherwise undifferentiated landscape. It is an essential component of any creative process. Rudolf Arnheim argues that all structures have a focus:

"psychologically as well as physically, every structure is focused on a center. ...each component of the whole has its own capacities and idiosyncrasies, and the art of obtaining perfect functioning consists of placing and employing them in such a way that their role is in keeping with the free display of their nature".

"The Split and the Structure", 1996, page 7.

In the case of neolithic standing stones, points in the patterns of meaning that the land shared have been articulated by their placement. The stones must have brought together cultural and topological understanding and have given it a precise centre, thereby allowing other processes to grow and evolve.

- Moment two: Specification

Putting two standing stones in a line takes them beyond the particular point and indicates more clearly some reference beyond the location of either one. Avenues of such stones, as at Carnac, in Northern France, where there are thousands of such stones forming eleven avenues, imply routes to other places. They reach out for other connections. Thus for my present argument they can be seen as a transition phase, perhaps more related to planning than to architecture. But something very interesting happens if the ends of these avenues connect. Then the solitary stones change their significance. They no longer indicate a point in a landscape. They specify an area. The role of the architecture changes from designation to localisation. What is most curious is that in these neolithic structures the area so defined is typically circular, the archeological remains being known as "stone circles" (Fig. 2).

This is the next great moment in architecture, when an area is specified. Shape and size of the location now carry significance as well, not just *where* it is. It is now possible to recognise when you are inside or outside the significant area. Meaning attaches to where you can enter it and how large it is. So there is a much greater possibility for investing the place with meanings. A new level of significance is possible. People may be forbidden from touching a *menhir* but they are always in its presence if they can see it. But it is possible to be *excluded* from a stone circle.

The circle reflects social division. Either different people are allowed in to those who are not, or the same people are different when they are inside to when they are outside. There was almost certainly some astronomical signific-ance to these constructions, but at the very least this must have meant that astro-nomers could wield almost as large resources 5,000 years ago as they can today with their telescopes sent to look at the moons of Jupiter. But whether the space was created for a Cabalistic priesthood or the technocrats of the day (or

Fig. 2. Aster Callanish 1, Lewis.

both) it is still clear that this development in architecture was there to distinguish an area in some way that reflected distinctions between and/or within people.

The health of such an architecture would depend on the health of the social processes of which it was a part and how effectively it reflected them. The evolution and development of these stone circles and the period over which they were constructed certainly indicated that they were created by a stable society that could devote considerable resource to what was clearly not an entirely utilitarian use. The function of these stone circles may be a complete mystery, but we can glean some idea of their purpose.

These considerations also lead me to emphasise that when considering the contribution of architectural aesthetics to health we have to try and specify which aspects of health we consider relevant. The aesthetic response mixes thought and feeling, function and purpose. I would even claim that its power comes precisely because it leaps these barriers of the mind. As a consequence we must search for its relevance to health in how it helps to heal the paradoxes of identification and specification. The neolithic stone circle has an entrance and an orientation but it has only one "side". It is a continuous wall.

The place it defines has no corners and thus is difficult to differentiate further, it is all quantitative aspects of its centre, infinite gradations from its one focus. It is the purest form of built place. Modern society is far more complex (as is our current understanding of the heavens) so our spaces need to reflect a more complex pattern of social relationships and relationships to what we regard as the spiritual. But it is in how well they do that their contribution to health lies.

- Moment three: Enclosure
However, the way in which built places identify locations of significance and specify the social processes that are part of the purpose of those places are not the whole story. There is a crucial third stage in architecture, when the gourd becomes a jug.

One important facet of this is revealed by the fact that from our earliest consciousness humankind has found it essential to produce aesthetic artefacts. There is even some evidence that music as we know it goes back many thousand years. Certainly painting and other marks of a symbolic nature are contemporary with the origins of *homo sapiens.* Indeed, there is a real sense in which modern science is a direct descendant of the early cave paintings. Science is based on the manipulation of abstract symbols. The origins of such symbols must have confused what we now regard as the distinct realms of science and art. They captured mood and spirit whilst also creating the abstraction that allowed comment and thought. In architecture the selection of the stones to place had aesthetic implications, but beyond the *menhir* and the stone circle a huge leap occurs when one stone is placed on top of others, a *dolmen* (Fig. 3).

These constructions are clearly associated with burials and are usually referred to as burial chambers, wherever they occur, as far away from South West Britain as Syria and Japan. They introduce the third element of architecture, enclosure, when all three dimensions are articulated. By adding a ceiling the place is defined even more closely as an entity that is only within the bounds circumscribed by its builders. Indeed, the building *is* the place in a way that earlier constructions were not.

At this stage a subtle change occurs. What was a position on some mental

Fig. 3. "Lanyon Quoit", Cornwall.

map of significates becomes an object that can be considered independently of its geographical locus. Building is born, but it never quite loses its contact with its origins in the identification and designation of a location. The power of this place now gains something from our awe at the capabilities of the people who built it. A new level of meaning becomes powerful, the authority and patronage of the architects themselves. The place gains added significance from our relationship to the people who constructed it. What the place tells us about them and their relationship to the use of the place adds to the quality of our experience.

It is when we reach this third and most important moment of architecture that the question architecture has to struggle with becomes most clear. This is whether architecture is an aesthetic phenomena like all others. The question may be asked of any art form. Is ballet really part of the same class of experiences as painting? Is listening to music akin in any way to reading poetry? What of the beauty of an elegant mathematical equation, or the admiration we might have for a well wrought argument? Then there is the appreciation of craft and skill. How far is that really from aesthetic appreciation?

The Soviets would not tolerate the decadent world of jazz and pop music, but they supported folk music as a reflection of the spirit of the working people, so keeping jazz and pop alive in camouflage during those deadening days. The crafts in the Soviet Union were the areas in which modern art forms of all sorts were allowed to flower, due to the belief that art devoted to a function was a mere craft and therefore worthy of a materialist society.

Like the Nazis, the Soviets also held the confused view that art could be cleansed of unwanted foreign influences, that pressures on it could be limited to ones that were local or historically appropriate, what we would today call "politically correct". But, paradoxically, these reactions of totalitarian states show the perceived power of all those influences, beyond the merely functional, that go into creating what is often called a "style". The meaning is carried in how the design problem is solved as much as in what the design problem is.

The profound mis-understanding that was inherent both in totalitarian reactions to art and in the naive rhetoric of the modern movement was to ignore the fact that any act of shaping, of giving form, of finding structure, requires a selection. This choice makes the act not just a skill but also an art. The capstones on *dolmens* are not just any stone of an appropriate size. Like the standing stones there is a preferred shape to them, a shape typically that emphasises the combination of their weight and their role as a platform. They are also placed on points of their uprights so that they often give the sensation of floating. Architects thousands of years ago could no more throw together a haphazard mix of components, ignoring the fine details, than they can today, especially if they hoped for another commission.

So a building tells us something about who has created it, or at least about the people who commissioned the work. The low roofs and small windows of the cottage I am sitting in speak of the humility and limited resources of the people who created it over a century ago. As a place to escape to and hide from the virtual reality of the modern university, these are the admittedly romantic qualities that are its attraction, and I would claim contribute to my well-being.

Where are the universals?

One other important question emerges from these considerations, especially given that I have deliberately chosen illustrations from as far back in architectural history as I can reach. This is the question of universals. I have had long e-mail debates with my colleague Amita Sinha about this. Schooled in Jungian psychology she is a firm believer in archetypes and the collective unconscious. Interestingly, these beliefs are fostered by her own Hindu background and her study of Indian architecture and landscape. This gives her the breadth of knowledge to show how many similarities there are in design solutions across the world's cultures. She has convinced me that there are certainly remarkable consistencies across time and place in the forms that buildings take and how those forms are related to social processes. The question really is whether these consistencies are, in the jargon of the day, "hard wired" or an almost inevitable product of human, *social* existence.

This, of course, is an old debate, that reverberates from Platonic ideal forms to present day evolutionary theories. It is worth, for example, reading Edmund Burke's "Essay on The Sublime and Beautiful", published in 1757, to see how little some ideas change. He argues that there are a number of physical properties that are inevitably beautiful, such as smoothness, sweetness, softness, smallness. However, even with this simple perspective he finds the need, as many have since, to argue for the power of words beyond their direct reference to objects:

> "*Certain it is, that the influence of most things on our passions is not so much from the things themselves, as from our opinion concerning them; and these again depend very much on the opinions of other men, conveyable for most part by words only.*"
>
> 1757, page 312.

This is all important when considering the fundamental source of well-being in design. If we regard some aspects of architecture as naturally responding to biologically based universals then it will be assumed that they will promote well-being in so far as the design accords with these universals. Research in this framework is the search for these fundamental influences on our well-being. However, if you see the relevance of building as emerging from a constructive transaction with the possibilities for identification, specification and enclosure, then research must explore the myriad varied ways in which these transactions are achieved and explore their successes and failures in relation to the purposes of those who create and use them. This will require an understanding of the role of "opinions of other men", not just a specification of the physical properties that are relevant.

A fascinating development of this idea is given in Simon Schama's monumental study of the cultural history of landscape in his book *Landscape and Memory,* published in 1995. He shows, through painstaking scholarship, that even such an apparently natural part of our physical world as the landscape is a product of a complex interplay between human cognition and environmental processes. He demonstrates that the landscape itself may be regarded in many ways as the greatest repository of human, personal and cultural memories.

Richard Sennett takes this approach one step further in his 1994 book *Flesh and Stone.* He argues that throughout history the whole shaping of cities has been a reflection of a culture's stance towards the human body. For example, to greatly simplify his subtle argument, the comfortable acceptance of nakedness for the ancient Greeks produced, or at least was reflected in, the openness of their monumental architecture. Mediaeval cities, in contrast, reflected a view of the body as made up of distinct organs which had higher or lower functioning, thus giving rise to city forms that created many distinct districts. The discovery of bodily systems, notably circulation of the blood, was part of a changing perspective that gave rise to the passion that the planners of modern cities have for moving people around.

There may be aspects of human existence that are always reflected in architectural aesthetics. As I have suggested, I would put my money on a) identification, b) specification and c) enclosure. But how these universals are manipulated to create particular forms is a consequence of cultural processes which themselves have their roots in the views that people have of themselves.

Control and health

So, Birgit, you asked about the effects of architectural aesthetics on health? Perhaps you can see from my meanderings above that I think you have the assumptions the wrong way round. You should be asking about the effects of health on aesthetics. Our state of being, the assumptions and expectations that we bring to any built environment, shape what we look for in it. These are encapsulated in the human purposes we have.

To achieve these purposes we must be aware of ourselves as distinct, personal entities, which is why the role of building in identifying a location is so significant. We need to have some understanding of what the actions are that may be housed, to which we may relate as social beings. This is why the ways in which a building specifies those places is important. But we are also aware of the forces that produce the enclosure that is the building and, in so far as they are appropriate to us, our well-being will enable us to relate to these forces.

I enjoy my escapes here to Wales because when I am here I have more control over my actions and feelings, but also because I have the possibility of building some connections with the landscape and its history. This is not just an abstraction, though. It has a direct influence on design decisions. The cottage is probably too small for many of the things I would like to do here, but I would be horrified at a development that did not keep what I see as the character of the place. Indeed, it is fascinating to discover that planning regulations require that any stone used in any additions to the building must actually be local stone, from within a few miles. A principle that the builders of the *menhirs* and *dolmens* did not always adhere to thousands of years ago.

We have a vision of an experience and seek to keep control of it through our design work. The health of the aesthetics that results is a product of the extent and variety of control that we can maintain, at the personal, social and cultural level.

But this control is driven by our thoughts and feelings. You see, I have tried to create the mood of writing from my cottage in Wales. Like most discussion this has been in words on paper. In fact, all the writing has been carried out 150 miles away, in Liverpool. Does that change your view of me, or of the cottage I have tried to paint in words? Where does your aesthetic reaction to the cottage lie now? How much of my health derives from the fact that that cottage exists? How much does my health make that cottage and its location an aesthetic experience?

With fond regards, David Canter

Sketches by the author

References

Arnheim, R. (1996). *The Split and the Structure.* University of California Press, Berkeley.

Burke, E. (1824). *A Philosophical Enquiry into the Origin of our Ideas of the Sublime and Beautiful with an Introductory Discourse Concerning Taste: And Several Other Additions.* A. Robertson & Co, London.

Canter, D. (1996). "The Facets of Place" in D. Canter (ed.) *Psychology in Action.* Dartmouth, Aldershot, 107-138.

Schama, S. (1995). *Landscape and Memory.* Fontana Press, London.

Sennett, R. (1994). *The Flesh and the Stone: The Body and the City in Western Civilization.* Faber and Faber, London.

Beauty

Birgit Cold

Has beauty become an old-fashioned, worn out concept?

Introduction

Beauty today appears to belong to "another time and another place". But beauty is nevertheless an important part of our everyday lives, even if we do not think about it consciously. Only when we suddenly become aware of something beautiful and smile, or we become thoroughly bored by ugly, accidental surroundings, do we realize that we long for a coherent, harmonious, and stimulating, beautiful environment. Just realizing the words we use when we spontaniously describe beauty, gives us a hint about what it is.

We have thus an immediate intimation that there must be a connection between the concepts health, well-being, aesthetics and beauty, but it is hard to unveil. It is unclear where the lines are to be drawn, where they start and where they end. Perhaps we should start with a positive perception of a relationship between the environment and human needs. Pleasant aesthetic-sensory perceptions of objects and surroundings which satisfied our basic needs may over time have devolved into preferences for these, and further developed into "a sense of beauty and well-being" connected with these. Evolutionary theory that says our preferences are connected to environmental qualities which helped early man to survive, may, in a modest way, be used to argue for a socialized development of a sense of beauty during childhood's positive sensory and social experiences. During maturity, however, people generally change or develop their childhood's sense of beauty into a more "sophisticated", culturally-influenced and individually-learnt sense of aesthetic quality. Nevertheless, when confronted with our childhood's favourite beauties many of us recognize a warm feeling of forgotten beauty-experience.

We may also consider if well-being and health are underpinnings for experiencing beauty, as David Canter suggests in his essay. The answer may be twofold, beauty makes us feel more happy and good health makes us more fit to sense aesthetic qualities and beauty.

During medieval times, beauty equalled truth and a radiation of godliness was mediated by bright colours, gold and gildings (Fig 1). Perhaps beauty and truth, as ideas or unattainable concepts, have always inspired art and that beauty springs from a longing to unite beauty and truth. Even if it may be hard to discern, perhaps such yearning for beauty and truth may also be the foundation for today's fine arts and architecture. Well-being and health thus

Fig. 1. St Mark's Cathedral, Venice.

may pertain to experiencing a "corner of this truth". Following the historic ideals of beauty through changing styles and fashions, it appears that the idea and, hence, experience of beauty mainly is conditioned by culture and the times, and that aesthetic well-being follows in the wake of ideals of beauty. However, there may be certain features in objects and surroundings which we may believe can be linked generally to human preference and environmental well-being and which also may constitute the core of the perception of beauty. We may find or interpret these features in nature, in microcosmos such as ice crystals, flowers, leaves and the human body and in macrocosmos such as the moon, stars and the universe. Structures, patterns, rhythms, and symmetries are qualities we often recognize in what we find beautiful, as well as dualities, such as order pared with variation, fitness with small surprises, harmony balanced with minor irregularity, planned work with improvisation, originality with a certain familiarity, human endeavour with artistic nerve, symbols of the existential with spiritual values, and "femininity and sweetness" complementing or contrasting masculinity and potency. As demonstrated in this list of qualities we indicate that beauty is not absolute and perfect, neither in nature nor in human-made objects. Industrial products, on the contrary, may be perfect and nevertheless lack this undefined slightly varied beauty; or is this a purely romantic idea over-emphasizing the human touch of imperfectness?

We find the fascination of symmetric order systems, in nature and transferred to human-made objects and spaces throughout history, in early cultures and in sophisticated ones. In their book *Symmetry. A Unifying Concept* (1994) the Hungarian biologists I. and M Hargittai[1] argue that: *"beyond geometrical definitions there is another, broader meaning to symmetry - one that relates to harmony and proportion, and ultimately to beauty."* They add that *"when all materials on symmetry are assembled in a book, a fascinating theme emerges, that symmetry is a unifying concept."* They contend that while the sciences, the humanities and the arts have drifted apart over the years, with a growing trend towards specialization within physics, chemistry and biology: *"symmetry, however, can provide a connecting link"*, and *"the bridging ability of the symmetry concept is a powerful tool - it provides a perspective from which we can see our world as an integrated whole"* (p.xv) (Fig. 2).

These statements are interesting insights from scientists specializing in molecular structure research. The symmetry of molecules, invisible to the naked eye, was the impetus that directed their attention to the symmetries of the visible world. Symmetry may be a quality which is deeply rooted in human perception, not necessarily a perfect geometrical symmetry, but rather a balance which makes us feel well. It is quickly perceived, easy to read in the environment and recognizable and understandable. Architectural styles, and also a great deal of anonymous architecture, are generally based on symmetric compositions. Modernism, on the contrary, looked upon symmetry as the source of conventionalism and traditionalism and an obstacle to creating modern dynamic environments. The early days of modernism practised, nevertheless, a refined and artistic balance inspired by abstract, cubistic

Fig. 2. Todaiji Temple in Nara, Japan.

painting. We find this balance strongly represented in Dutch architecture from the twenties of the De Stijl movement. Symmetry and balance appear to be key characteristics associated with beautiful artefacts and architecture. Is the recent deconstructivistic, chaotic "hand-granade architecture", with bits and pieces sticking out everywhere, just a passing phenomenon, or does it express a longing to artistically demonstrate a fragmented, meaningless and "up-to-date post-world"? Is today's beauty to be discovered in chaos, which also is shown to consist of symmetric structures?

We may reflect upon these ideas, and upon questions on how to define beauty, if it is at all definable, where beauty springs from the work, our minds or both, whether beauty can be created consciously as an objective or may be a result of successful processes, whether experiencing beauty can be ordered like a ticket to the opera, or whether beauty today is a useful concept at all.

Defining beauty
Immanuel Kant defined aesthetic perception as a direct sensory perception, disinterested and unaffected by ideals, functions, emotions and intentions. If

this state is attainable and environments are perceived aesthetically equal by persons from different cultures, it then follows that there may be a general human, aesthetic perception which is not significantly influenced by cultural learning. A number of preference studies have demonstrated that nature and natural elements, landscapes offering good overview and places for refuge such as large trees, and the presence of water, appear to have general meaning and relevance for human well-being across cultures. When these qualities are transferred symbolically to built environments, it appears that people prefer spaces with an overview which offer the chance to withdraw into niches and nooks, roof overhangs and collonades or loggias as transitory zones, and built places with plants, fountains and running water (Fig. 3). This may be a simplified description of general environmental preferences, nevertheless, it is a reminder of generally pleasurable qualities and characteristics which many cultures appreciate and agree on.

We may say that people generally have a great deal of wanderlust and enthusiasm for experiencing foreign countries' special nature phenomena and architectural monuments, such as mediaval towns, cathedrals and mosques, antique temples and edifices, and unique constructed environments, such as the aquaducts and the pyramids. We may ask if the various cultures perceive a unified beauty and well-being, or if they have totally different perceptions and emotions related to their own nature and built inheritance: Are the Norwegian fjords and waterfalls, for example, perceived aesthetically differently depending on culture, or does nature beauty call upon more general perceptions and feelings of admiration and pleasure as assumed in evolutionary theory? On the other hand, we may perhaps realize that such experiences of beauty are products of a common cultural learning. Perhaps, as Hans Georg Gadamer claims (see the introduction to this volume) beauty in nature, and perhaps beauty as such, has to be discovered and mediated by empathetic and artistic persons before we, the public, are able to perceive and emotionally relate to it. Conventions and ideals taught in schools and used in the various media have presumably created a global cultural perspective on beauty. This concerns naturally architecture and the arts which are distributed to cultures all over the world.

In the cult book *Zen and the Art of Motorcycle Maintenance* from 1974,[2]

Fig. 3. Canale Grande, Venice.

Robert Pirsig writes that quality has two sides, one static, safe, familiar and recognizably experienced, "classic" quality, and one dynamic, immediate, new and emotionally perceived, "romantic" quality. The former ensures continuity, the latter change. Traditionally we ascribe beauty the classic quality, while an aesthetic and direct perception of quality is dynamic and romantic, in the sense of being emotional, and may break with predominant ideals of beauty. An aesthetic experience of quality is a natural part of the perception of beauty, but we do not necessarily find a perception of beauty in any aesthetically qualitative perception. Beauty may be understood as a confirmation of aesthetic quality related to a person's history of experiences, confirmed cultural ideals and general human perceptions. Valuable objects and buildings, which have withstood the passage of time, and contemporary ones valued by experts within a field, have become culturally protected monuments, a cannon, which is identified as being beautiful. We find them in books, films, postcards, videos, and of course on the internet and, thus, an institutionalized beauty may become a confirmation of something "we know is true".

Antiquity's ideals and the classical ideals of form may appear to be such "truths" which have had a recurring influence on the art of building throughout history. Alberti in *The Ten Books of Architecture*,[3] presenting and systematizing Vitruvius' treatise, Palladio in *The Four Books of Architecture*,[4] and more recently David Watkin in *A History of Western Architecture*[5] have all propounded classical ideals (Fig. 4). Watkin emphasizes *the validity and vitality of the classical language of architecture, as opposed to the conception that architectural forms are grounded in the spirit of their particular age, so much so that it is impossible to reuse them in other contexts and ages.* Why is this language so attractive even today? We may be attracted, on an aesthetically direct level, by the Pythagorean-Platonic theory of numbers, the "cosmic ratios" of proportions and details, both rich and simple, always creating a symmetrically ordered and well-structured entirety. This is presumably transformed from rationally balanced wood structures.

There is, however, a considerable distance between claiming that classical ideals are very enduring, perhaps fundamental, to actually copying them. For many of us who have been educated and still work within the functionalistic-aesthetic ideals of modernism, it is impossible to be elated by a direct transfer of classic elements to modern architecture. We do not accept that ideals of beauty from past architectural styles can be transferred directly to modern construction elements, such as prefabricated antique concrete columns, architraves and window framings. We demand a rational link between function, form, materials and construction, place, way of living, knowledge and skills, an authenticity which, good or bad, is perceived as ideals of our times and hence genuine. Nevertheless, it is undeniable that all the architectural styles since antiquity, also functionalism, have aspects of the classic ideals of order, not necessarily as transferences but rather as transformed systems of order. Le Corbusier created a microcosmic system of order based on the human body in action, Le Modulor, which is inspired by the Renaissance microcosmic-human system of order.

Kim Dovey[6] writes that authenticity and genuineness do not only apply to antiquities and alien countries, but also to the acquisition of a directly involved and vital relationship with day-to-day environments. Furthermore, he underlines that the yearning for authenticity is a sign of a profound crisis between man and his environment, that the pursuit of what is authentic and

Fig. 4. San Andrea by Alberti, Mantua.

genuine in itself creates a suspicious and investigative attitude to the surroundings. We do not become involved before we know it is worth our while and we will not be cheated. This attitude prevents us from acting directly in relation to our environment as living, curious persons. We are also more easily fooled by copies increasingly more skillfully produced, thus making us even more suspicious. Hence we must ask ourselves where the line is drawn between what is authentic and what are reproductions. These have become a rather integrated part of our industrialized environment, whether in art, applied art or architecture. It may then be tempting to claim, that as long as we perceive that something is a reproduction, a replication of the original with the intention of transferring the meaning, we may enjoy it without feeling that we are being cheated. Could we then say that a "good replication" is what one can discern as an "honest reproduction", while a "bad reproduction" is an exact and "dishonest copy" complete with patina and the lot, whether we are speaking about an antique temple, a baroque row of houses or a painting? Post-modern architects, for instance Robert Venturi, James Stirling and Aldo Rossi, are not copying but rather quoting and transforming classical elements sometimes in an ironic and joyful way. The replication of classissicm today may be based on the idea that people become proud, feel important and happy when they believe that the meaning and status of classical ideals are transferred to their surroundings and hence themselves. Perhaps architects are strict and puritan, out of tune with the public, when believing in architectural honesty, authenticity, originality, truth and so forth, when people (the clients) do not care if they are being cheated or not as long as they can choose to surround themselves with things and environments which give them a feeling of dignity, celebration, historic atmosphere, picturesque scenery and sweet dreams of glory. People appear to be happy, feel better and perhaps healthier when they are able to surround themselves with emotionally "true fakes" whether classical, peasant style or neo-something. Why do architects and artists continuously try to express their own time, when most people prefer expressions from the past?

The art and architecture of our times are not necessarily ideals of beauty, rather an explorative longing for something unpronounceable, transcendental and true, which questions the accepted ideals of beauty. Each era presumably searches for its own authentic expression of beauty exemplified through the talented and empathetic works of its artists. The wish to release the creative subconscious powers and watch what happens seems to be strong in our times. This was quite apparent in a television programme in 1996 featuring the Danish artist Per Kirkeby, where during a period of more than a year he painted and commented upon a large winter picture. Each time he had painted something we, the audience, liked, and which he himself also liked at the time, a good light or a beautiful colour, the very next day he felt compelled to remove and vanquish "the beautiful". Perhaps he was counteracting his own longing for the beautiful as a convention and continuity, wishing to create a new and more "true content" breaking with traditional expectations.

In what is new and transcending we may perceive a dynamic quality or novel beauty which may be completely impassable and incomprehensible for the man in the street, but which artists and art aficionados have sensitivity and knowledge to "grasp" and understand, and which in time may become the general experience of beauty. If architects and artists did not search for a different and novel beauty, cultures would stagnate and slowly die for want of aesthetically stimulating renewal.

Does beauty reside in the work, the mind or both?
Surroundings can not be considered neutral with man projecting his emotions onto them, just as man can not be considered an instrument of reception for the qualities and features which are built into the environment. By giving names to objects and the world around us we try to create and freeze an image of them to distinguish them from all other objects. In all names and images there are over time some characteristics which are retained and others which change. The characteristics which we immediately perceive without consideration or reflection, such as the patterns of order, contrasts and hierarchies, structures and forms creating simple readable fitness to utility may be the most durable, while those that demand reflected and closer observation and assessment, knowledge and interpretation are those that change over time and which are closely connected to culturally based meanings and ideals, norms and fashions. Or is it the other way round, that the meaning of an object or environment, on both a subconscious and conscious level, offers a considerably larger resistance to change than the immediately perceivable characteristics do? It appears as if we as educated persons are more trained to use and rely on our knowledge of the world than on our immediate, sensuous-aesthetic perception of it. We have to bear in mind, however, that in our everyday lives, all the environmental qualities are interwoven in a total experience, and we do not separate the utilitarian and symbolic qualities from the aesthetic.

Yi-Fu Tuan writes in his book *Passing Strange and Wonderful*[7] that *"only when explorers entered the High Plains and the Rocky Mountains, after the 1870s, did rocky and barren scenes enter the American consciousness as in their own way beautiful"* (p. 146). Is it such that beauty is present everywhere, in

micro- and macrocosmos and it is up to us to discover it? This is a phenomenological attitude which might be a tempting place of refuge when reflecting
upon beauty in works or in our minds. However, we need somone to draw
our attention to these everyday beauty phenomena. Artists in all professions
do this, within architecture, pictorial art, film and theatre, music and literature. They have a sensitivity in their perception, ideas and works which reveals
beauty to us. Thus, it is the relationship between the artists' sensitivity,
imagination and skills mediated in the works, and the ability of the audience
to perceive and recognize it, that constitutes beauty.

Beauty as the aim or as the result
Beauty was not the primary objective of functionalism, nevertheless it
became the result in the best, most artistically successful examples. Primo
Levi in his book *The Periodic Table* describes a generally functional, simple
and rational ideal which he believes has been a motivation power for man
throughout time. He compares the beauty of a chemical structure (Fig. 5)
with the beauty of architecture (Fig. 6): *"The structure makes you think of
something solid, stable, well linked. In fact it happens also in chemistry as in
architecture that 'beautiful edifices', that is, symmetrical and simple, are also the
most sturdy; in short, the same thing happens with molecules as with the cupolas
of cathedrals or the arches of bridges. And it is possible that the explanation is
neither remote nor metaphysical: to say beautiful is to say 'desirable', and ever
since man has built he has wanted to build at the smallest expense and in the
most durable fashion, and the aesthetic enjoyment he experiences when contem-
plating his work comes afterwards...the true beauty, in which every century
recognizes itself, is found in upright stones, ships' hulls, the blade of an axe, the
wing of a plane"* (p. 179). The bridge and the cupola used by Levi as examples
are generally built on constructive rational principles which are also symmetrically constructed, similar to what we find in the building blocks of nature,
as mentioned above.

The beauty described by Levi is in keeping with Martin Heidecker's
concept of "zuhande", where quality lies in an obvious relationship between
man and the surroundings in everyday life, compared to those things that are
"vorhande", present without filling an obvious role in life. The difference thus

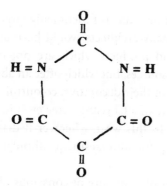

Fig. 5. Chemical structure of alloxan.   Fig. 6. Villa Rotunda by Palladio, Italy.

exists between objects and surroundings which have an obvious meaning in their presence and part of life, in contrast to "meaningless" objects which fill up the voids of space and mind. Looking around us a fundamental human wish or need appears to be to give objects and surroundings a "meaning", a symbol content, to adorn surfaces, to place one's personal stamp on construc-tions and to enjoy completely "useless" things, decorations, superfluous frames and decorative ornaments. The aesthetic-emotional side of what we dub art may be a result of such a human need and thus a completely indis-pensable part of life. It is tempting to interpret the great monuments and art of previous times not only as manifestations of power, spirit and skills, but also as expressions of a general human need to create and be surrounded by stimulating, lavishly decorated, multicoloured and ornamented objects or surroundings.

Douglas Porteous writes in his very comprehensive and fascinating book *Environmental Aesthetics*[9] about P. F. Smith's perhaps slightly speculative, neuropsychological explanation of our need for more than good instru-mental objects and surroundings. Smith claims that we are equipped with a nervous system which consists of the neocortex (the new brain) with the left hemisphere, logical and rational, and the right hemisphere, intuitive and creative, and in addition the limbic system (the old brain), which reacts to and processes emotions, including what is colourful, lively and glittering. He maintains, that all three parts of the system need stimulation if we are to feel well and exploit our potential. We may not be quite as functionally targeted and "sober" as Levi and Heidecker, and many architects would have us. It appears that man wants surroundings and products which are not only optimal in a perspective of function and resources, but which offer an abundance of playfulness and creative pleasure in their decorative, colourful and even glittering aspects. Think of the pleasure of a Christmas tree even in the most super aesthetically designed homes. In this wish, wherever it derives from, we may discern an obvious yearning for pure aesthetic stimulation, which may also be a longing for beauty.

The beauty of a city is generally a result of a mixture of conscious planning, human manipulation and "random events" which have occurred and been built throughout history. Irrespective of how we regard beauty, it is extremely difficult to point out what exactly creates it. In the essay *Aflæsning af objekter* [The Conquest of the Spectator],[10] Willy Ørskov contends that there is an ambiguity in art with a conscious side comprising illusion, persuasion, professionalism and bluff, and a subconscious side which is naivety, faith, directness and inspiration; and in the experience of good art there is a total fusion of these two sides so that no ambiguity is felt. This way of understanding good art may also be valid for beauty, that a fusion of these two sides gives us a basis for creating and experiencing beauty. We may wonder whether the conscious side primarily produces and experiences a beauty content which corresponds to ideals and visions, while the subconscious side makes a work aesthetically and sensuously stimulating and unique. This is of course impossible to answer because, as Ørskov argues, it is the fusion of these two sides which characterizes the experience of good art and which creates it.

We are charmed when we hear stories of the composer, the author or the architect who worked in a state of "flow", where ideas flowed freely and merged with knowledge and skills. In his book *Om kreativitet og flow* [On Creativity and Flow],[11] Georg Klein refers to Mihaly Csikscentmihalyi, who describes "flow" as a state of complete concentration which is followed by a euphoric sense and a perception of complete focus. It may be the mixture of knowledge and skills, direct focus and inspiration which in a state of "flow" creates art and also beauty. Only the best are blessed with the ability to combine these sides; they have a repertoire of professional knowledge to draw on, as well as openness, curiosity, creativity and presumably a mixture of megalomania and humility. Still we can not truly distinguish art from beauty, just state that art is not always perceived as beautiful, but beauty is often perceived as a piece of art.

Can perception of beauty be "ordered"?

When travelling with architect students on excursions a funny thing happens. Setting a programme full of prime examples of good architecture we, as enthusiastic teachers, expecting our students to be enthralled by perceptions of beauty, often to our surprise do not see enthusiastic signs of appreciation in our students.

Do our expectations and the fixed programme paralyse the students; have they been satiated prior to their encounder with important monuments of architecture? Feedback often tells us that on days when students were left to their own devices, to decide for themselves what they wanted to see, they had the most wonderful experiences when they saw something that really aroused them, thus giving them the best day of the whole excursion!

Is it impossible to go to a museum and have a really fantastic experience of beauty if the visit has been planned in advance through minute preparations? On the other hand, tradition would have it that offering background information is useful in order to fully enjoy and understand what we are experiencing. However, on discovering art or architecture we have never seen before, perhaps a sculpture reminding one of Marino Marini's works (Fig. 7) or a town house from the nascent stage of modernism, it is as if we personally have created a relation between great art and ourselves. In a way we become responsible for the existence of what is beautiful. Perhaps this is the "responsibility" which cannot be ordered, but which has to arise of itself.

This self-discovery may also come about in the experience of "unfinished" art, through the sketch, the outline of the sculpture, the scaffolding of a building or ruins. These "sketches" hold something immediate and alive, where the impression of being on the way becomes an expression of life itself. Perhaps beauty is not necessarily the accomplishment but the promise, that something is coming about, that it is experienced as alive and open to further

Fig. 7. Sculptures by Marino Marini.

fantasy, as if the artist or builder, in the quest for perfection, has left his or her work for a minute, leaving us to interpret and complete it.

Perhaps environmental beauty primarily has something alive about it, as in nature, thus it is fleeting in its character, such as a sunset, or the morning light through diaphanous curtains, or the outline of the city against a leaden sky; that beauty should not be sought in what is permanent, but in the mutable, in the immediate; that art and architecture are not created as something beautiful, but that at certain moments they may be experienced as beautiful. Thus we might say that perceptions of beauty are difficult to "order" and perhaps easier to attain in a state of spontaneity and voluntariness.

Is the concept of beauty old-fashioned?

The idea of beauty may be "used as the launching pad" for active efforts to keep, improve, repair and innovate, whether as a continuity of accepted values or as the starting point for a complete break with these. Or are we rather concerned with historic "footprints", either conserving or creating them, than beauty? What are our concerns with during the creation of new architecture, what inspires us and makes us as architects work far beyond normal working hours and profitability?

Is it so that the beauty created today must be understood pragmatically as connected to time, place, situations and to everyday surroundings, conditions and actions? Or is it rather an ideal concept similar to truth and goodness, that is something we strive for but which is unattainable? Perhaps beauty may have both an everyday pragmatic side and an ideal side which somehow converge?

The more the term beauty is used in this text the greater the need to ask whether it is alive today or whether it has become outdated and outmoded. It almost appears, when written and read, like an old-fashioned term more at home in a previous class society, where an upper class had time and money to cultivate beauty in music and art, to create stylish country estates, town palaces, parks and gardens, to decorate drawing-rooms and mirrored halls, dress in beautiful materials and colours, and adorn themselves with gleaming gems. Then beauty was part of life, and today it is irrelevant. Or is it? I believe that it is not because we have a constant longing for something which we could call "beauty". We have to discuss it, to work with it, to find today's understanding of it in our everyday surroundings, in contemporary architecture and in fine arts.

However, it is not easy to speak about beauty in the arts because present artists do not claim to be seeking it, but rather fighting it. Beauty is cloying and a provocation to be conquered and combated, claims the artist Per Kirkeby. Artists and architects are rather working with sublimity than beauty with contrasts, tensions, explosions, surprises, rebellion, humour and irony, chaos and mysticism, and a few minimalists with quietness and purity. Beauty as a concept has been worn out, it is no longer alive. Or rather the concept of beauty has become shrouded in a fog of stylistic and conventional conceptions. This means that beauty has a built-in conservativism, a tradition which demands continuity, and beauty rarely or never is ascribed innovation, because this, by its very nature, constitutes a break with the acknowledged ideals of beauty.

A work of art in our times is not conceived as art, if it strives consciously to attain an acknowledged and well-known beauty. In the experience of good architecture in our times we find a beauty which is experienced as radiating empathy and interpretation of a task, a place and culture, in the sense of contributing to something essential to the times.

A study of the comments juries made over a period of 25 years of judging wood architecture[12] (Fig. 8) showed that the most frequently used terms in order of priority were *wholeness* with harmony and balance (Fig. 8a), *originality* (Fig. 8b), *belonging in its location* (Fig. 8c) and *sophisticated simplicity* (Fig. 8d). Not one word about beauty. We might, on the other hand, interpret these concepts as a whole which describes beauty. We need a cluster of qualitative characteristics in order to encircle and mediate our understanding of beauty.

When we turn to literature within environmental psychology on aesthetic preferences, we rarely find the word beauty. Terms describing the perceived qualities of what is preferred are used, as for example coherence, order, complexity and affection. When the aim is to classify and analyse individual phenomena in a preference, this approach may be more useful than to ascertain whether overall they constitute the foundation of beauty. Scientifically the concept of beauty may be too comprehensive and therefore troublesome,whereas in a humanistic perspective it may be absolutely essential.

In his book *On the Aesthetics of Architecture*[13] Ralph Weber states that there are two conditions for aesthetically successful form [here beauty]. The first is that *"the best condition for perceptual segregation occurs when an object permits the formation of perceptual wholes ... The more the overall structure of a percept ... tends toward pregnant form* [figural regularity] *the stronger its impact in aesthetic terms will be"* (p. 130). The second determinant of aesthetic value is related to an object's ability to arouse perceptual interest, *"that it possesses a minimum of structure, yet not so much relative complexity that it causes the brain's biological capacity to process information to be overtaxed. A state of*

Fig. 8. Twenty-five years of the Norwegian awards for wood architecture.

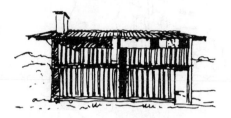

8a, wholeness with harmony and balance,
1966. (Private house, Lysaker,
Arch. K. Lund and N. Slaatto.)

8b, originality, 1973.
(Museum. Hamar, Arch. S. Fehn.)

8c, belonging in its location, 1975.
(Private house, Bergen, Arch. C. Bjerknes.)

8d, sophisticated simplicity, 1971.
(Student Community, Bergen,
Arch. J. Djurhuus and F. Fernes.)

sustained perceptual interest would be the most aesthetically satisfying state" (p. 130). Here the foundation for a successful form or for beauty is described as a mixture of its ability to be perceived as holistic and its ability to arouse interest. This conclusion is also found in much of the scientific empirical literature within environmental aesthetics.

This discussion has shown that today beauty is seldom used as a single qualitative concept, rather it may be understood, implicitly, as a unifying concept including a number of qualities, but never the same qualities, as described above. This means that we must be more specific in our descrip-

Fig. 9. Pitigliano, Italy.

tions of beauty, and that the term beauty somehow is interpreted as being insufficient or giving associations to a static conventional concept which many feel is old-fashioned. I feel, however, that it is a challenge to revive beauty as a concept in order to be more consciously aware of our need for it, in all its shades of meaning.

A personal experience of beauty
We may approach the concept of beauty by also asking ourselves what we perceive as beautiful. Therefore I wish to describe two of my experiences of beauty to ascertain what they consist of. My experiences of beauty in architecture are tied to "strangeness", to what has surprised me, made me become quiet and smile, creating a profound wonder, curiosity and happiness, while also, I must admit, being a confirmation of my architectural ideals.

In Italy in the southern part of Tuscany you will find a number of medieval cities built on volcanic tuff, places such as Pitigliano, Orvieto, Sorano and Sovana. These cities give me a bubbling sense of happiness. When approaching them, seeing how they stand as man-made, edged "crowns" at the top of weather-beaten mountain massifs, seeing the incredible contrast

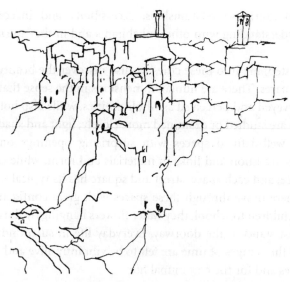

Fig. 10. Sorano, Italy.

and also the link between the surrounding dramatic landscape with gorges, forests, grass and vine-covered valleys, and the unified, though varied buildings, then I become happy (Fig. 9).

The beauty lies in the clarity and the contrast between nature and culture, between the growing, resplendent greens, the torn mountain hills and the man-made buildings as town walls. These are characterized by displacements, different roof formations, arches, ledges and cavities, and window openings in various rhythms and sizes which ensure that the walls are legible as habitations for people. Side by side with these clear and discernable differences between nature and culture we also find context and similarity, as the man-made elements appear to have grown naturally straight up from the rock, side by side and on top of each other. Just as we read the "needs" of plants for nutrients, light and shadow and for reproduction in an ecological system, what has been built may be read as the need of the inhabitants for protection against invaders and undesirable climatic influences, and the desire for overview, view and light. The ability of the inhabitants to optimally utilize the local resources has created solutions which exploit materials, building sites, neighbourhood relationships, accessibility and inaccessibility in a mutual understanding with other inhabitants and in the "spirit of the place" (Fig. 10).

When stepping into these cities we also discover the beauty of the streets and the squares. There are human dimensions in the sense that these squares can be surveyed and perceived as whole entities, while also holding surprises when they are studied or examined more closely; light and shadow, order and variation, well-defined spaces with surprising openings onto views and landscapes, tradition and links in materials and form, while each house has its own face, and each space, street and square has its typical features. People who live here move through these spaces with great confidence, they shop, they take children to school, they water flowers hanging by the entrance door, or they just stand in the doorway. Everyday life in surroundings that have withstood the ravages of time are felt to be vibrantly alive and right, both for private lives and for the communal life.

As is apparent from this description, it was no longer adequate to restrict oneself to just visual aspects. It was important to include the total experience of the town from the outside as well as from the inside, and not only as a "picture", but as a living organism. Nevertheless, there is no hiding the fact that the picturesque experience dominates strongly.

Another important perception of beauty for me stems from traditional Japanese building and gardening art, interior decoration, food and serving, and the writing signs which I feel are the most beautiful expressions of communication, even if I do not understand what they communicate. The traditional architecture mediates a cultural beauty of constructed art, both inside and outside. There is an incredible mastery of space and light, of structures, materials and details, of transitions between outside and inside and of perfection and irregularities balanced in an seemingly intuitive yet conscious way. I experienced an artistic tension and nerve, which demonstrated a complete professionality while also exhibiting a playful, capricious improvisation. The incredibly sophisticated simplicity also offered variations, surprise and variety (Fig. 11).

In trying to understand why these two examples have given me such experiences of beauty, I believe that both hold a seemingly perfect balance

Fig. 11. Japanese building tradition.

between place, culture and resources as a means of architecture and a profound knowledge of how to attain an inevitable beauty, without lavish and superfluous means. They represent a functionalistic ideal in a broad sense, encompassing not only functional needs in a utilitarian sense, but also the other needs which make us function as humans, such as emotional, intellectual, sensuous-aesthetic and spiritual needs.

The experiences of beauty described here are those of a visitor, a visitor not quite intimate with the culture which created the art of building, nor a part of the customs and culture of the place. Could this then be called a "pure aesthetic experience" in the Kantian sense?

This is perhaps where the dilemma lies, that such experiences are perceived from the outside, in a comfortably relaxed, non-instrumental state. If we participate in the trivialities, we would perhaps be blind to such perceptions of beauty, which means that perceptions of beauty may require a certain distance. We see beauty only when we are not "involved" and know too much about the state of affairs, about the efforts, shortcomings and random circumstances behind them. We perceive beauty only when we "take time out" and become a visitor or guest. Perhaps the everyday experience of beauty creeps in as an integral part of all the sensory and emotional perceptions and is stored on the subconscious level, only being retrieved to the surface when we receive "visitors" who draw our attention to things we know well, but which we do not "see" on a daily basis and are aware of. On the other hand, we may perceive things and people we love as being beautiful.

As indicated by the above it is not easy to distinguish the immediate qualitative aesthetic perception from a more cognitive experience of beauty. But why distinguish the one from the other? In order to study, analyse and understand a phenomenon, we must separate, exclude and purify the individual components and relations, and then reassemble them again. This is not the way it is in real life where we mix up everything, the aesthetic, emotionally expected and unexpected impressions, the intellectual and the spiritual. We move from one aspect to the next, we let ourselves be carried away by a mood, a melody, a particular light, the charisma of a person, and we are aroused by a sudden impression or confirmation of a vision. Afterwards, everything may then be included in a total experience where everything has contaminated everything. The beauty of a place is linked to a piano piece by Beethoven, with the view, with the food and wine, and with the persons with whom we discussed aesthetics and beauty.

Perceptions of beauty become integrated collections of aesthetic, social, cultural and emotional impressions in the context of a place and a situation which, in a "magic" moment, merge and reinforce each other. From this situational perspective beauty becomes a result of multi-dimensional relationships which may be created everywhere and which we ourselves are responsible for. Thus beauty depends on our aesthetic sensitivity, knowledge and ability to create and rejuvenate it.

From a non-situational perspective, beauty may be a result of aesthetic processes of linking the experience, knowledge and "production" of beauty together. Aesthetic preferences are probably influenced by early man's survival related to environmental characteristics, and further developed by each culture's and period's sensitive, knowledgeable and skilful people. Today man-made beauty to a great extent is institutionalised; it is analysed, described and evaluated by aesthetic experts and it is produced by aesthetically well-educated professionals within crafts, industry, architecture and the fine arts. We may conclude that there are various "kinds of beauty", a situational, a subcultural, a cultural-periodic, a historical, and a contemporary artistic-experimental beauty. To experience any kind of beauty, a mixture of awareness, curiosity and sensitivity is needed and to create beauty these must too be combined with aesthetic knowledge, artistic skills and creativity. First of all, however, we should recognize that beauty is a source of pleasure and happiness and gives a feeling of interdependence with the sourrounding world.

All figures are sketches by the author

Notes

1   Hargittai, I. and M. (1994). *Symmetry. A Unifying Concept.* Shelter Publications, Inc., Bolinas, California.
2   Pirsig, R. M. (1974). *Zen and the Art of Motorcycle Maintenance.* Bodley Head, Great Britain.
3   Alberti, L. B. (1485). *The Ten Books of Architecture.* London 1955.
4   Palladio, A. (1570). *The Four Books of Architecture.* New York 1965.
5   Watkin, D. (1986). *A History of Western Architecture.* Barrie & Jenkins, London.
6   Dovey, K. (1985). The Quest for Authenticity and the Replication of Environmental Meaning. In *Dwelling, Place and Environment,* eds. D. Seamon & R. Mugerauer, Martinus Nijhof, The Hague.
7   Tuan, Yi -Fu (1995). *Passing Strange and Wonderful. Aesthetics, Nature and Culture.* Kodansha International, London.
8   Levi, P. (1985). *The Periodic Table.* Michael Joseph Ltd, Great Britain.
9   Porteous, J. D. (1996). *Environmental Aesthetics, Ideas, Politics and Planning.* Routledge, London.
10 Ørskov, W. (1966). Aflæsning af objekter og andre essays. [Reading objects and other essays], Borgens forlag, København.
11 Klein, G. (1990). *Om kreativitet og flow* [On Creativity and Flow], Brombergs Bokforlag AB, Sverige.

12 Cold, B. (1990). What is good architecture? Discussion of modern and post-modern views. In P. Haluk, V. Imamoglu, N. Teymur, (eds).*Culture Space History. Symposia and Papers.* IAPS 11/1990. Vol. 3. Faculty of Architecture Press, Ankara (65-77).

13 Weber, R. (1995). *On the Aesthetics of Architecture. A Psychological Approach to the Structure and Order of Perceived Architectural Space.* Ethnoscapes Series: Current Challenges in the Environmental Social Sciences. Avebury, Ashgate Publishing Limited, England.

The Aesthetics of Place

Kim Dovey

What are "healthy places" and can they be designed?

The term "aesthetic has long had a certain ambiguity as referring to both sensory perception and the study of beauty.[1] The first of these suggests a certain aliveness to our sensory environment, based on the Greek root *aisthesis*: "to perceive." Hence the opposition to the *anaesthetic*. The second and much more recent meaning suggests the use of our senses for judgement and a certain contemplative distance from our world. Hence the opposition to the *unaesthetic*. I suggest that one of the tasks for an aesthetics of the built environment is to maintain and revive this ambiguity. This is because the built environment is both a world in which we are immersed and a world to which we bring our contemplative judgements. The latter use of the term predominates but it has a tendency to reduce the built environment to representational text. It asks the question about our judgement of a building or place, a question that is also an act of framing. Yet there is a prior "framing" within which this aesthetic question is asked, this is the manner in which built form "frames" our lives.

My interest is in this aesthetic of everyday life, an aesthetic which neither excludes contemplation nor the aesthetic impact of that which we have not framed for contemplation. I am aware of some problems of such a position, primary among them is that one cannot speak about such a world without framing it with the use of language. But before proceeding to problematize them, I want to explore some aspects of this aesthetics of everyday life.

As a graduate student I was attracted to phenomenology precisely because it seemed to offer an approach to architecture that was inclusive of the aesthetics of everyday life. For Heidegger, art and aesthetics are matters of dwelling. He distinguishes between two complementary modes of dwelling which can be described in terms of *engagement* with the world and *contemplation* of it.[2] The world and its aesthetic qualities unfolds through both our engagement with it and contemplation of it. The aesthetics of the built environment stem from a kind of dialectic between "living in" and "looking at". Yet for Heidegger "living in" precedes and provides the ground for "looking at". Such a view suggests a fundamental connection between issues of aesthetics and human well-being, rooted in the phenomenology of place experience. But this is not a cause/effect relation. The use of the word "place" and phrases such as "sense of place" and "spirit of place" reflects the attempt to appreciate architecture, urban design and landscape as lived experience rather than as objects in space. "Place" implies a certain "character" or "identity", however frustratingly intangible. A place is not an object or setting so much as a kind of interactive relationship between people and a setting together with a set of meanings that both emerge from and inform this experience and interaction. In this sense I believe that we may speak not so much of "good" places as of "healthy" places. I use the word "healthy" specifically to draw out the connotations of aliveness, wholeness of spirit and self-sustaining dynamism. Healthy places generate, celebrate and sustain life. They *heal* in the sense of making us more *whole*. I will briefly sketch a series of properties of such places.

Properties of healthy places

Most fundamental of these is the enabling of a strong sense of "being at home". There is not enough space here to outline theories of "home" experience,[3] but it is clearly not only about interior space, nor about dwelling in one place , and it is not a nostalgic and conservative return to the values and images of the past. Indeed the nostalgic aesthetic stems from the very opposite, the "homesickness" which was the original medical definition of "nostalgia". The experience of home is about ontological security and thus fundamentally important to human health.[4] The aesthetics of home is in many ways the most mysterious because it is the most ideological, the least conscious and the most deeply connected with human well-being.

Such a broad aesthetics of place extends to our more public world, urban places which can be construed as more or less "healthy". Healthy places often have a strong sense of cohesion or emotional connection between people and built form. The inhabitants feel identified with its forms and they share its meanings. Healthy places have a formal "character" akin to that of the life that grows and flows through them. Such public places are generally full of life, they are popular and sustain high levels of use. They can generate and sustain social cohesion.

Healthy places are not conflict free, places of bitter conflict can become important symbols of achievement. They are dependent on the vitality and diversity of social and economic relationships. Unhealthy places can emerge through the separation or exclusion of the aged, the disabled, the eccentric, women, the young and the poor from significant parts of the built environment. Healthy places are "transparent" in the sense that they create educational opportunities for the users to learn about the physical settings of their lives, the processes which create them and the ecology of which they are a part.⁵ Unhealthy places may be "opaque" in the sense that they obscure their origins, structures, processes and interactions in favour of an imposed image. It follows that a good deal of development undertaken with the rhetoric of a "sense of place", "spirit of place" or "home" may indeed be the opposite. Healthy places have a certain unique identity while remaining integrated with the larger places of which they form a part. It follows that healthy places cannot be mass-produced from a standardized design. Healthy places aid human orientation, we know when we are "there".

Healthy places are not static, they embody both cyclical changes (of behaviour, use, light and seasons) and irreversible changes (demolition, construction, new uses, new people and new meanings). Healthy places cannot be created instantly by designers, but grow and evolve through time with the assistance of designers, with the accretion of creative formgiving, and with the growth of identification and meaning. A great deal of the meaning of a place can stem from its sheer dynamism. Places which are frozen in a static state (conservation? museumization?) or are constantly maintained in a preferred image (sculpture? bureaucratic management?) may die. The exceptions are where the static image is consistently highly valued by the dwellers, where it engenders educative interaction and cohesion amongst them and a sense of continuity with the past.

Healthy places connect us with the past through their role as a repository for meanings and memories. They lend our lives a sense of continuity, order and stability. Healthy places become symbols of the experiences and achievements engendered within and through them, they show the traces of time and the interactions of the inhabitants. The forms of healthy places are often a collage of the individual and collective efforts of those who care about, rely on and are a part of them. Places may be unhealthy in this sense when they are constantly returned to an ideal condition, when they develop no patina over time, and when they do not show the traces of life.

Healthy places both require and engender the active participation of users in the processes of environmental change - the democratization of design. Healthy places change in response to changes from within, changes of occupancy, culture, lifestyle, size and meaning. Thus healthy places connect people to the future as vehicles for their dreams and hopes, by providing opportunities for their active and creative participation. They provide scope for the exercise of choice, power and control, whether personal or collective. Places may be unhealthy in this sense when they are managed at a distance or produced as commodities for consumption. Healthy places have a high level of autonomy.

The properties outlined above are akin to strands in a rope which may strengthen the meanings of place in varying degrees. They are also fundamentally problematic, healthy places very often embody contradictions. Since they are popular, they attract life and therefore money. Their commmodification may serve to exclude the very source of their own creativity. If there is a meta-property which sums up these properties it is that healthy places thrive not only because they embody creativity in their design but because they awaken and nourish the creative impulse in those who use them. Healthy places reconnect us with our past, with each other and with our physical world. Healthy public places can help to counterbalance and shatter private alienation.

Framing places

Having said all this I want to return to the ambiguity between an aesthetics of everyday life and of contemplative judgement. While it remains my concern to resist an architectural aesthetic which is limited to the contemplation of form, there is no way around issues of representation. As Heidegger understood, language is the "house of being". There is no simple return to the "things themselves". While architecture cannot be reduced to text, architectural aesthetics requires forms of textual or discourse analysis. This is because we not only dwell in the homes and places of everyday life, but in a world of discourse, and this includes the discourse of "home" and "sense of place" - places are "framed". These questions were awakened in my work by a paper I wrote in the early 1980s on the "quest for authenticity".[6] Here I was trying to interpret the proliferation of simulated meanings in the built environment, coupled with the attempt to eradicate it. Thus I explored the meanings of shutters which do not shut, fireplaces which do not burn, beaches in the desert and pseudo-vernacular housing projects. More and more meaning seemed to be coupled with less and less significance. These proliferating simulations are ever more apparent and I am still trying to cope with this unleashed can of worms. For now I will sketch the paths of a few I have followed.

The quest for authenticity is nothing more than the desire for the "real". Yet like the "real thing" it is easily confused with its representation. I would resist those like Baudrillard who suggest that there is nothing more than a sea of representations, nothing outside the text. But I would similarly suggest that anyone who suggests that there is any direct and unproblematic aesthetic engagement with an undistorted nature or archetypal meaning may also be deceived.[7]

Aesthetic images have the power to tell stories and awaken dreams in us - dreams of power, status, security, harmony, health, wholeness, fun, dynamism, liberty, nature. I have been inspired by the work of a range of aesthetic theorists including Barthes, Benjamin and Bourdieu.[8] The early work of Barthes is a compelling account of the power of formal imagery to construct myths, false stories or truth effects. Benjamin helps us to understand the dream-world of mass-culture, spaces of consumption and the modern urban realm. Bourdieu has countered the Kantian notion of aesthetic autonomy, exposing class roots of aesthetic distinction in forms of symbolic capital. The complexities here are overwhelming since all aesthetic discourse is fundamentally ideological and therefore ripe to the appropriations of various forms of power.[9]

The questions for me have moved somewhat from place experience to its discursive construction. Thus I began investigating the experience of home as seen through the dream constructed in the model home and its advertisements.[10] These models are, in my view, one kind of window into the phenomenology of domestic space. But this is no longer an unproblematized phenomenology of place. The advertising is based upon market research, but it also builds upon and constructs these values, ideologies and myths. I became similarly interested in why we continue to produce very tall buildings. They cause considerable aesthetic damage to the everyday life of the streetscape and they are functionally obsolete. Such city forms are also part of a dreamscape accessible through the window of advertising discourse.[11] Thus while architects blame the public for their nostalgic housing choices, and the public blame the architects for oversized buildings, they are all enmeshed in larger discursive formations.

I cannot pretend to have resolved any of these issues. In many ways I now see things more in terms of tensions and oppositions than of truths.[12] Primary among these tensions is the one between issues of place experience and its textual critique, which has been playing out a gentle dialectic in my mind for years. It is one of those interminable conflicts where, although the arguments seem mutually exclusive, I am unable to adopt one without reconsidering the other. I would maintain that both sides of this argument are valid and necessary, but that neither is sufficient for an understanding of the aesthetics of architecture. What if there are powerful universal archetypes of place experience, but that experience is at the same time subject to powerful ideological control? How do we reconcile a belief in the importance of place experience with the proliferation of packaged imagery as commodity?

If place experience has a fundamental connection to human well-being, as I suggested earlier, then the commodifications of place may be seen as a colonization of everyday life. This is what Habermas argues is the "system" colonizing the "lifeworld".[13] In its extreme forms it may be a kind of reverse psychoanalysis wherein our subconscious is exploited and stripped of depth. The experience of "home" is packaged and framed as the desire for a certain "home" is constructed. The mass-market manipulations can become the colonization of our emotional life by the forces of economic or political power. The architectural and spatial experiences that have most potential to connect us to our world are colonized and placed in the service of power, privilege and profit. A part of the dilemma is that it is fragmentation, homelessness, dislocation and alienation in everyday life that generates demand for a packaged and commodified dwelling experience. Our seduction by the pseudo-meaningful further reproduces this system. The commodification of space and of everyday life distorts, undercuts and fragments the aesthetics of everyday life.

I have no conclusions or answers to this conundrum other than the suggestion to keep both sides of this dialogue alive. And the tension between the built environment as "place" and as "text" is a close parallel to that between the aesthetics of everyday life and the aesthetics of contemplation with which I began this essay. The aesthetics of place has no autonomy from the struggle for privilege, power and profit. Yet the denial of the fundamental importance of place experience in our lives seems equally flawed. My plea is not for a middle ground between these opposing positions, it is for a sustained and rigorous dialogue between them.

There is a tendency within architectural discourse to reduce aesthetic attention to architecture solely as text. Hence the focus on unbuilt work, the pure text in the gallery where such an aesthetic really comes alive. Good design often comes from such work, yet this preciousness in aesthetic discourse both reflects and reproduces a discounting of the aesthetics of everyday life. A part of the task for architectural aesthetics is to ensure that architectural discourse becomes a discourse about life. The design of the built environment is vital because it is the invention of the future. And that future will be at once lived in and more and more saturated with text and simulation, we will inhabit more "virtual spaces". Does this mean that the aesthetics of place and everyday life become less important? Not at all, indeed there is evidence of the opposite. The virtual stimulates the quest for the real. Yet this is a highly problematic world we are entering. The aesthetics of the 21st century will be interesting indeed.

Notes

1 Williams, R. (1976). *Keywords.* Oxford UP, New York, pp. 27-28.
2 Heidegger, M. (1962). *Being and Time.* Harper & Row, New York.
   See also: Dovey, K. (1985). The Quest for Authenticity and the Replication of Environmental Meaning. In *Dwelling, Place and Environment*, (eds) D. Seamon, & R. Mugerauer, Martinus Nijhof, The Hague, pp. 33-50.
3 Dovey, K. (1985). Home and Homelessness. In *Home Environments* (ed) I. Altman, I. & C. Werner. (1985). pp. 33-64, Plenum, New York. Despres, C.

(1991). The Meaning of Home, *Journal of Architectural and Planning Research*, 8 (2), pp. 96-11.

4   Giddens, A. (1984) *The Constitution of Society*. Polity, Oxford. Saunders, P. & Williams, P. (1988). The Constitution of the Home, *Housing Studies*, 3 (2), pp. 81-93. Dovey, K. (1990). Refuge and Imagination. *Children's Environments Quarterly*, 7 (4), pp. 13-17.

5   Much of this paragraph owes a debt to: Lynch, K. (1981). *A Theory of Good City Form*. MIT Press, Cambridge.

6   Dovey, K. *The Quest for Authenticity*, op.cit.

7   Baudrillard, J. (1983). *Simulations*. Semiotext, New York.

8   Barthes, R. (1973). *Mythologies*. Paladin, St Albans. Buck-Morss, S. (1989). *The Dialectics of Seeing: Walter. Benjamin and the Arcades Project*. MIT Press, Cambridge. Bourdieu, P. (1984). *Distinction*. Routledge, London. See also: Dovey, K. (1995). *Architectural Design*, Profile #114, pp. 36-41. Place/Power.

9   Eagleton, T. (1990). *The Ideology of the Aesthetic*. Basil Blackwell, Oxford.

10 Dovey, K. (1994). Dreams on Display: Suburban Ideology in the Model Home, in S. Ferber, C. Healy & C. McAuliffe (eds) *Beasts of Suburbia: Reinterpreting Cultures in Australian Suburbs*, pp. 127-147. Melbourne University Press, Melbourne. Dovey, K. (1992). Model Houses and Housing Ideology in Australia. *Housing Studies*, 7 (3), pp. 177-188.

11 Dovey, K. (1992). Corporate Towers and Symbolic Capital, *Env. and Planning B*.

12 Dovey, K. (1993). Dwelling, Archetype and Ideology, *Center*, v.8, pp. 9-21.

13 Habermas, J. (1979). *Communication and the Evolution of Society*. Heinemann, London.

Creating Aesthetic
Built Environments through
the User Participation Process

Aase Eriksen

*How do participatory processes including children
influence architectural projects and our well-being?*

Building an environment which is both functional and aesthetically pleasing is a difficult task for any architect. Often the architect faced with a new project may feel he or she has recourse for ideas only in the technical and aesthetic knowledge gained from architectural school, or his or her own "taste" developed over time, or in the limitations created by budgets and clients' demands. But an important source for aesthetic as well as functional suggestions is a group all too often ignored in the planning process, that is, the *users*, those children and adults who will work, learn, play, rest and live in the buildings and spaces the architect creates.

In designing any environment, the architect should keep the users in mind. It is possible to combine the users' wishes with the professional's knowledge and thereby create an environment that the users will find both functional and pleasing. To do this, the architect must seriously listen to what the users say they want; indeed, the users (or future users) should be made part of the planning process itself. An environment that reflects the users' needs and wishes - which takes into account their notions of color, texture, variety of spaces, and so forth - will be an environment in which the users feel good because they recognize their own ideas in the architect's interpretation. As a result, they will use and protect the built environment more because it is, in part, their creation.

Most of this article is devoted to looking at some specific architectural projects in which the users, including children, took part in the planning and design process. These projects are all in Denmark, and include a school, a children's hospital wing, a meeting space for a foster children's institution, and the National Children's Museum of Denmark. First, however, it is important to clarify our understanding of the built environment and its roles in our lives, and then to look at the user participation process which allowed the users of these buildings and spaces to affect their environment in active, positive, aesthetic ways.

The built environment
The built environment is architecture in its broadest sense – the cities, streets, houses, schools, parks skyscrapers, bridges and bars that we build and the spaces that connect them. It frames our actions and in many ways determines

the shape of our lives. It affects us every moment, even though that effect is often unconscious. The setting may direct our actions, as we follow a path or a hallway, or it may prevent them, when we come to a wall or must knock on a door. The setting may lift or depress our moods, whether we are exhilarated by the beauty of a fount in a park or feel confined by a horizon which stops abruptly at the housetops across the street.

Indeed, our entire lives are given as much to interacting and coping with the built environment as they are given to interacting and coping with other human beings. As infants and children we explore a limited environment that gradually enlarges from the space of the crib to the entire house, the route to school and the classroom. As we grow older, our mobility increases and our world expands, from our neighborhood, town, or city to foreign places experienced in travel. With age, our environment often narrows again, limited to our town, community center, or senior citizens home. That a sense of place is extremely important to us is indicated by the intense memories of pleasant and unpleasant spaces that linger throughout our lives.

Because the built environment is so important in our lives, we need to learn more about it. This education may be self-directed, as the child learns to cope with obstacles such as stairs, or may take place in the more formal setting of a classroom, where the built environment provides rooms to measure, spaces to study for mathematical concepts, buildings for the understanding of history and neighborhoods and towns for civic studies. Built environment education should stress the development, first, of an *awareness* of surroundings (Fig. 1), senses, feelings, and needs, then, of an *understanding* of the functions and impact of the environment and, finally, of the *ability to use* the environment well and take action to change it to better satisfy our wants and needs.

The planning and design process for any architectural project invariably includes some built environment education for the participants. As the architect explores the possibilities for the project with the users and as the users think about their wishes for particular activities in the spaces being designed, the users learn about the built environment, that is, the form of a building's facade, the effect of light and shadow in a hall, the texture of the walls or

Fig. 1. Awareness of the surroundings.

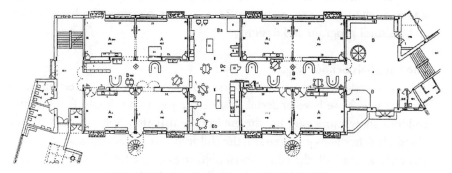

Fig. 2. First floor in the renovated schoolbuilding.

furnishings in a room. And, they come to understand why some of their wishes will work and others will not.

The user participation process

The user participation process we developed allows for the wants and needs of the users to be included in the final built environment. It is a process which has been used successfully in planning and designing environments in the United States and Europe, including schools, playgrounds, hospitals and museums.

The user participation process usually proceeds in four phases. Phase one is concerned with planning the process; on simpler projects, the architect may do this planning; on a more complex project, a committee may be established, consisting of all the representatives of the user/interest groups in the local community, institution or firm. Phase two is a group of meetings held with each of the identified groups of users, during which problems of usage, wishes, wants, ideas and suggestions are put on the table for discussion and comments, and then put into groups or lists of "activities" which will occur in the spaces being planned. Phase three is a series of "design-ins," where users plan and draw, sometimes based on the activities which have been listed and sometimes drawn in response to a topic, such as "draw a place of your dreams." A very important part of the design-in is the individual presentation and explanation of the content of the design to the rest of the group. This phase of the process usually elicits very concrete information about children's and adult's wants and needs. Finally, phase four of the process is the analysis of the activities, the drawings, and the presentations of the drawings by the leader of the process or architect. This analysis becomes the basis for the architectural program and design.

The Hirtshals School (Fig. 2)

The value and usefulness of the process described above can be seen in many projects which we have undertaken over the years. In schools, for example, children show more care for the environment if they help create it. In the Hirtshals School design program, the children's wishes and needs were taken seriously, along with the educational objectives of the teachers. The children felt a very strong need for a variety of spaces in the school, such as quiet

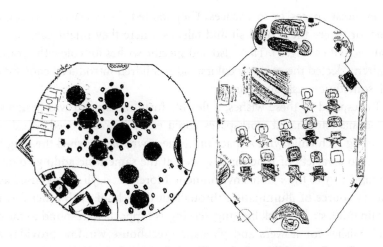

Fig. 3. Children's classroom designs illustrate the wish for a variety of spaces.

Fig. 4. A large birdcage.

spaces, noisy spaces, or soft spaces. They wanted places where they could be alone, or where they could sit and talk, or where they might participate in group activities (Fig. 3). They also had specific wishes for color: the youngest children selected the primary colors; older children introduced cooler colors and, sometimes, fashion colors.

To respond to these wishes, a flexible furniture system was designed so classrooms and shared workspaces could easily be rearranged. Wardrobes, providing each child with a space of his/her own, have turned the long hallways into a variety of functional spaces, at the same time adding color and design quality to the school environment. Moreover, daylight was used as the primary source of illumination throughout the school, with other forms of illumination, such as task lighting, serving as support. To respond to the children's wishes for flowers and plants, a greenhouse window provides each classroom with an indoor garden.

As a result of these design elements, the children say the school is now a happy place: there is sunshine, increased by the use of yellows and oranges; there are birds, for a large birdcage placed in the corner of the entrance hall to the school welcomes the children (Fig. 4) and creates a very different kind of arrival behavior; and there is a variety of useful and pleasing spaces. Also as a result, vandalism and destruction have virtually disappeared, in not only this school but every school project in Denmark or the United States where we have utilized the user participation process. When users have a stake in their environment, they protect it.

A children's wing at the Hillerød Hospital

Another instance in which users contributed significantly to the eventual built environment is in the children's wing at the Hillerød Hospital in Denmark (Fig. 5). Because the architect listened to children, parents and professional staff, the layout and design of the facility became very different from what one sees in most hospitals today. Aase Eriksen conducted a four-month planning process involving:

- participating with the professionals in their work during all shifts (participation observation);
- attending meetings respectively with children, parents, doctors, nurses,

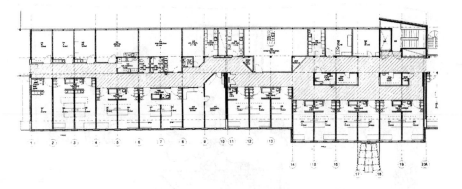

Fig. 5. Plan of children's wing at the Hillerød Hospital.

psychologists, social workers, educators and administrative staff at the hospital;
- attending meetings with children and their parents together;
- and wellcoming children's participation in "design-ins".

At the "design-ins" the children, through drawings, expressed their needs and wishes in relation to visits to an ambulatory area as well as to a hospital stay. They drew their pictures and interpreted them in informal sessions in their rooms, in the playrooms and at special "design-in" events to which children and their parents were invited (Fig. 6). Parents talked about their needs and wishes in the children's rooms or in the waiting rooms (Fig. 7).

The outcome of the process was a mixed collection of children's drawings, a list of "wishes" from the children, sets of comments from children, parents and hospital professionals, and our own observations. The next step in the design process was to analyze all this material, to find the common as well as special needs of the children, parents, and professionals, and develop design principles which would take all these needs into account.

From this participatory process came ideas for furnishings, colors and decorations of children's rooms (such as flowers and other illustrations on the ceilings), improved layout and design of the different workspaces used daily by the nursing staff, and even changes in the doctors' work: for example,

Fig. 6. Children's pictures of their wishes.

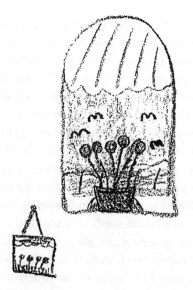

Fig. 7. Parents' wishes in the children's rooms.

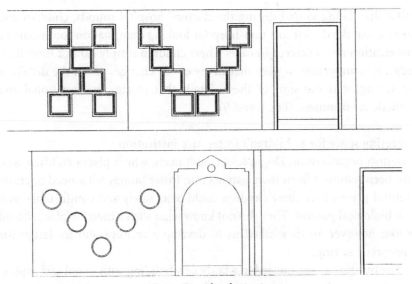

Fig. 8. Corridor decorations.

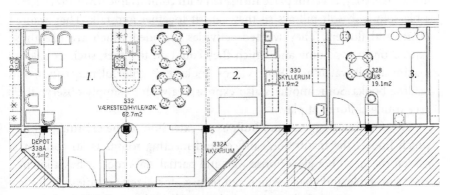

Fig. 9. Detailed plan of Children's Hospital.
1. Living room/playroom for parents and
children. 2. Sleeping cots for visiting babies. 3. Conversation/examination room.

rather than being visited during the doctors' hospital rounds, children and parents visit the doctor in a non-hospital-looking examination room called a conversation room (except in cases where children simply cannot leave their beds). It is important to note that many of the changes are in the details of the setting; it is the sum of these details that creates the functional and aesthetic environment (Fig. 8 and 9).

A meeting space for a children's foster care institution

A Danish organization, Døgnplejeformidlingen, which places children who have been removed from their parents into foster homes felt a need to create a central place where these children could meet safely and comfortably with their biological parents. They did not know what such a meeting place should be like, however, so they asked us to develop a concept and to design the appropriate setting.

The institution was housed in a fairly new building with a cool and sophisticated interior design, with architect-designed furniture and lamps. It was a place in which the clients - children and their parents who have lived in homes for people with severe problems - did not feel comfortable. Thus it did not support or promote the healing and well-being of the child and its parents.

And what did these children and their parents want? They wanted a home-like, cozy, cheerful place furnished with comfortable furniture, such as a big sofa with soft pillows so they can sit together and talk. They wanted plants and flowers. They wanted activities provided which are like those carried on in the home and which they could do together, such as baking, making food, watching TV or videos, looking at colorful magazines, and reading books. Some mothers also expressed a wish to simply observe their very young children at play.

The addition designed and built as an extension to the existing building which houses the institution's offices and meeting rooms is, in concept, a garden room, with a glass house wall and partial glass roof. It has a kitchen area, with table and chairs which can be used for many activities. There is a cozy corner with a sofa, bean bag chairs, a coffee table, and TV. And there is an open area with a table which converts into a sand box for younger children. Much of the area is covered with a soft carpet, whereas the kitchen is

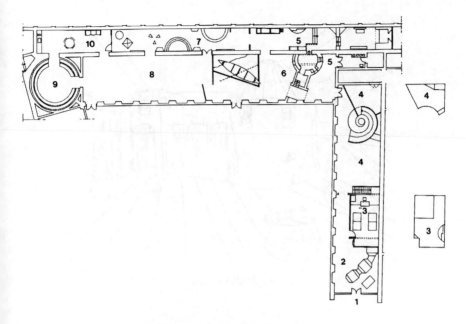

Fig. 10. Plan of the Children's Museum.
1. entrance. 2. "Recent times".
3. "Industrialization".
4. "The connection between Denmark and the outside world".
5. "Middle Ages - life in the castle and on the building site".
6. "Viking times - trading center". 7. "Games down through the ages".
8. Children's theater and other activities.
9. film. 10. personnel.

covered with linoleum. Another important part of the meeting area is a light and cheerful bathroom with facilities for changing diapers.

The new addition has now been in use for almost two years with great success. Everybody wants to meet in this room and it is fully booked for the next year.

The National Children's Museum of Denmark

The National Children's Museum is another illustration of an aesthetic envi-

Fig. 11. Medieval castle.

Fig. 12. From a tower one gains an overview.

ronment which influences the users' well-being (Fig. 10). It has become an enormous success, and children return several times, expressing their pleasure there. In fact, the Children's Museum drew 65% of all visitors to the National Museum in the first two years, and of these, 30% were adults without children. After more than four years of use by hundreds of thousands of visitors, nothing has been destroyed or taken.

Children from different parts of Denmark actively participated in the design of the museum. We conducted a series of "design-ins" in which the children, through their drawings and presentations, told us what *they* wanted to see and do in a museum of their own, which like the National Museum depicted "the old days". The result was enough suggestions for contents and activities to fill several museums!

The permanent exhibit of the museum is a journey back through time. Beginning with the present, the children and accompanying adults travel back through various periods of Danish history to finally reach the Viking period. The design concept involves using different architectural forms, colors, and light textures to create a variety of special experiences on different spatial levels. Some of the architectural forms are familiar ones, such as a medieval castle (Fig. 11); others are more abstract, yet they relate to the time period or theme being displayed in the room. These abstract forms provide visitors with shifting views, and with the pleasures of moving in many differ-ent ways and directions. The children are able to climb up a ramp and down a ladder, to crawl under an object, through a tunnel, and into a tower, or to stand above the area and gain an overview of all the activity settings (Fig. 12). All valuable *original* objects are kept close for viewing (display cases consist primarily of glass shields), but copies of the original objects are at-hand, and can be touched, manipulated, carried, used and arranged around the activity setting.

Conclusion

These examples clearly illustrate the value of the user participation process in the design of the built environment, both in terms of function and aesthetics. They are also proof of the built environment's influence on the well-being and health of children and adults, not only in the ways in which the users protect these environments, but also in the positive manner in which they tell others about them. It is in the sum of the details, functional and aesthetic, that pleasing and supportive environments are created.

What Happens if Zeleste Becomes an Architect?

Arnulf Kolstad

Does beauty support happiness and happiness health?

Why does my four-year-old daughter prefer pink coloured dresses, silver shoes and gold rings with pink jewellery? Why is she so happy when she puts on her pink robe, radiant rings, chains and earrings? Does her happiness and increased well-being have anything to do with her visual perception at all? Does she really prefer to look at pink colours, gold and tinsel? Does she like to know that she is wearing a nice robe when other people are looking at her? Why just pink, silver and gold? Does she relate the pink to something she knows is attractive? Is she consciously aware of pink as the colour of her sex, that culturally it is an expression of femininity? These questions came to mind while I was watching my daughter Zeleste at her birthday party when she turned four. I took part in her immediate pleasure and happiness and noticed that my own mood was infected by her enthusiasm. I once more realised that things, or more precisely, aesthetic elements in the environment, are important for man's well-being. From watching other people, especially children, and noticing my own emotional responses, I understand very well that the quality of the environment influences mood and happiness. But do the physical surroundings also influence Zeleste's and my *health* as well?

This experience on her birthday was of course not the first time I noticed that aesthetic elements directly or indirectly influence my thoughts and emotional states. Generally, I feel like most other people, more comfortable in environments I find aesthetically pleasing, and which give an impression of quality and hospitality. There is, however, a kind of tautological argumentation saying that aesthetic pleasure makes us happy. What we *define* as beautiful is often what increases our well-being. A feeling of happiness is a criterion for what is pleasant and preferred in the environment. (Happiness is used as another word for well-being or the feeling of joy. In this essay I do not make any point of marginal differentiation between such concepts.) In a pleasant and preferred environment we all feel more comfortable than in subjective unpleasant environments. Our preferences, however, are not similar.

What I prefer and define as nice to wear or beautiful to perceive is different from what Zeleste prefers. The difference is more than an accidental variance between individuals or a result of the saying *"tastes differ"*. The difference in preferences between Zeleste and me is mainly a result of the difference in age, maturity and knowledge. Responses to and preferences in the environment change during one's lifetime as a result of normal psychological development, particularly perceptual and cognitive functions. The same aesthetic object is perceived and responded to in different manners, it releases different emotional and cognitive reactions depending on age and knowledge. My aim in this essay is to provide an explanation of differences in tastes and responses. Before discussing the development of preferences, I must say a few words about the *similarities* in a culture, and the principle of emotional infection.

Emotions and preferences are infectious

When I became delighted at Zeleste's birthday it was not an immediate outcome of watching her dress and tinsel. I definitely do not have exactly the same taste as Zeleste concerning colours and visual stimuli. I have to admit, however, that she looks beautiful and fulfils my prejudices and expectations . of a daughter at four when dressed in pink and gold. The sparkling, glaring ornaments and the pink robe made her happy, and her happiness infected me. The infectious character is an interesting attribute of mood states. Happiness and well-being are transmitted from one person to another. There is a *synergetic* effect when people come together and are subject to reciprocal impacts. The first conclusion therefore is that emotions and mood states are infectious.

This principle is important for understanding fashion and common taste. When something is looked upon as beautiful by somebody, this increases the possibility that other persons exposed to these preferences will react in the same manner. Other peoples' emotions influence my aesthetic preferences. This is the reason why there are common style and art tastes in a specific culture or society. There are, however, also individual variances, due to differences in age, experience and knowledge, and there are other principles for aesthetic preferences than the infection of emotions.

The meta-perspective of perception

At Zeleste's birthday party I did not react only in an emotional way, infected by Zeleste's happiness. At the same time I was *reflecting* on the pleasure she derived from the bright colours, and I was struck by the instantaneous relation between what she found beautiful and her happiness. I could not relate to her situation without taking a *meta-perspective*, using my knowledge about the quality and symbolic nature of the colours and jewellery she admired. My reaction to the colours, forms and visual stimuli was different from Zeleste's. The experience that day illustrates generally that not only are my visual *preferences* different from hers, I even *perceive* the surroundings and the build environment in another way than Zeleste does. Nor do I express the same spontaneous excitement.

When she is enjoying herself spontaneously as a result of perceiving something pretty in her environment, I am considering and dwelling on the aesthetic object and at the same time reflecting on my own reactions. I have a *meta-perspective*, putting the questions, asking the what's and why's: What does the visual stimulus mean? What does it symbolise? What could the alternative be? Does it remind me of something or somebody? Is it appropriate? How do I explain what I perceive? Even if this cognitive activity is not always conscious, environmental signs or cues release stored experiences, cognition and emotions in my mind. They start a cognitive process. Adults *associate* and compare when perceiving aesthetic surroundings. Our reaction is therefore different from a child's spontaneous perception. Children *respond* to their environment, adults *evaluate*, give *meaning* and *construct* their physical and social environment in a meaningful way for themselves. Adults' perceptions are filtered through stored experiences before they are reacted upon. Emotional reactions, therefore, can never be spontaneous in the same manner as in infants and young children. Sometimes, but less often as we grow older, there are aesthetic and visual cues which do not fit into any experience or old category. We have to create new categories. New perceptions might also change what is already stored as knowledge, feelings and preferences related to a visual impression. But when we grow older we have to develop our preferences conciously through more knowledge, and elaborate a new language for perceiving the environment in a new manner.

When I notice, for instance, a beautiful building, I reason about the similarities to other buildings. I get associations to experiences that in one way or another are similar or comparable. When perceiving, adults activate and take into consideration their internalised value hierarchy, which is a synthesis of evolutionary, cultural and individual preferences, telling them what is good and bad, nice and ugly, and so on. Grown-ups have internalised standards or yardsticks for this evaluation and cannot disregard them when watching, perceiving, giving meaning to the environment, even if they can be modified as a result of new knowledge and another language and concepts. Zeleste, as a four-year-old child, does not have a large store of memorised experiences. She is responding in a more impulsive, immediate manner to the signs and symbols. As an adult, I am *reflecting* on them. These are two different ways of processing sensory data.

The development of aesthetic preferences
To explain why an individual has particular visual preferences, it is necessary to look at the *development* of preferences and how they change as a result of the mutual interaction between (1) instinctive, natural abilities; (2) social or cultural experiences and (3) individual peculiarities or particular experience. All these sources contribute to our preferences, to varying degrees, depending on age, maturity and experiences. The instinctive preferences are the most important up to Zeleste's age.

Instinctive preferences and evolutionary psychology
The perspective that sees environmental preferences as a by-product of human evolution has been growing in popularity. According to this view, human preferences have developed because they have been crucial to our survival as individuals and as a species. Put very simply, the evolutionary position states that individuals who "preferred" the "right" environments survived longer and reproduced more successfully than individuals who did not prefer them as strongly. These preferences, the theory says, are forwarded to a greater extent to the next generation. The tendency to prefer these same environments has in this way been passed on to us. We have therefore an inborn, genetic preference for whatever in our evolutionary history might have at one time helped us to survive. Research has supported the prediction that humans prefer scenes that offer "prospect and refuge". These preferences are said to be the remnants of successful evolutionary strategies that helped our ancestors detect and avoid predators and enemies. Children are said to

universally display a strong preference for playing in enclosed spaces, but also with the possibility of keeping an eye out for "the enemy" or predator.

Evolutionary interpretations of human aesthetic preferences are, however, still controversial. One problem is that instinctive, evolutionary reactions and behaviour are not expected to be conscious or even verbalised. The principle of evolution or "survival of the fittest" does not depend on subjective preferences. To be fit does not mean that individuals prefer in a conscious manner some environments instead of others. Making subjective preferences in an explicit verbal and deliberate manner presupposes the use of higher, not instinctive or lower psychological functions. The conscious, verbalised preferences cannot be inherited as a result of simple evolutionary principles.

When *adults* have preferences for particular visual elements or sights, this is of course not solely an expression of an inborn, instinctive tendency to prefer sceneries that are preferable from an evolutionary point of view. What characterises an adult is the ability *not* to be dependent on instinctive responses. The higher psychological functions which characterise the adult human being are only possible to the extent that instinctive mechanisms lose their directing function and recede into the background as a general substratum. When we are socialised in a society, and have acquired and internalised values and aesthetic preferences in a culture, have acquired a language and are able to reflect on the quality of the environment, then the spontaneous, subconscious evolutionary preferences such as Zeleste's, lose their grip. The conscious preferences are to be learned through socialisation in a culture. They belong to the higher psychological functions. Infants and children at Zeleste's age, dominated by an instinctive regulation of emotions and their preferences, are probably more influenced by common human forces and subconscious emotions than adults.

Are the lower psychological functions more emotional, does Zeleste express emotions more than cognition? It is difficult to distinguish psychological phenomena such as emotions and cognition. They are internally related and unified in a dynamic, mutual interdependent system. Emotions in adults are partly constituted by cognitive appraisal of events and thus depend upon cognition for their very quality. Zeleste's reactions are probably not based more on emotions, they are, however, based less on cognition.

Social and cultural experiences

Infants seek need satisfaction in an instinctive manner. But there is no reason to believe that there is a genetic inclination to prefer particular colours, forms or figures. Different forms, for instance if they are simple or complicated, symmetrical or asymmetrical have different effects and release different processes in the brain. The brain itself has no preferences concerning the geometrical form of the visual input. The brain has no limitation processing very complicated sense information. We "learn", however, very early to associate pleasure and satisfaction with particular colours or forms. When an infant is satisfied, for instance when being breast fed by its mother, it associates this pleasure with the sight of the mother's skin and symmetric face. The joy of being fed and satisfied is transferred to the visual sight of particular forms and colours, which are also found to be pleasurable. Tastes and preferences in childhood expand from the practical, contextual, non-linguistic experiences by means of the principles of conditioning and associations belonging to the primary or lower psychological functions characteristic of higher animals.

During socialisation we internalise values and preferences in a particular society and culture. We evaluate the environment, taking into consideration the criteria of nice and ugly, good and bad which exist in every subculture and society. There is partly, however, still an immediate, non-conceptual relation to the surroundings. Cultural values, norms and preferences are not necessarily formulated in a language. The biological/genetic predispositions, expressed in what sociohistorical psychology calls the *primary* or *lower psychological functions* assumed to dominate an infants' preferences, are gradually superseded by the *higher psychological functions*, characterising adult human beings' language and thoughts. The natural, spontaneous perception and associative, conditioned preferences in infants disappear in their pure form as the mode of reaction due to the acquisition of concepts and the possibility of combining language and thinking. The consciousness and the cognitive processing of environmental information reduce the spontaneous instinctive responses of external stimuli.

The built environment is also part of a *symbolic language* that has to be learnt. It gives meaning and has impact on our emotions and behaviour. In a church our mood is different from the mood in a circus. A graveyard expresses sorrow, not because we are born with a tendency to look at a tombstone in a sad or gloomy way, but because we are socialised in a specific culture. We have learnt that a tombstone signifies death and sorrow. Other signs and symbols express other mood states. They influence and release particular emotions and cognition due to a common cultural sign and a symbolic language. Children acquire this symbolic meaning and the accompanying emotions during socialisation into a particular culture.

Higher psychological functions
Higher psychological functions, including categorisation, cognition, memory and symbolisation, have a sociocultural character and foundation. Form and content are humanly constructed as individuals participate in social interactions. These social interactions determine the higher psychological functions, and therefore emotions, aesthetic preferences and tastes as well.

For an adult there is no instinctive preference for aesthetic, visual stimuli unaffected by experiences and concepts. The pre-language and immediate, instinctive responses of children are restructured when we are able to use the higher psychological functions. The lower, more spontaneous instinctive responses lose their primitiveness and take on social psychological features. They do not retain their original nature and simply coexist side by side with advanced higher functions. The primitive processes in animals and infants have therefore no analogy in human adults, even if some, for example artists and authors, are able to distance themselves from the common and popular ways of perceiving, and present reality in a personal, novel and childish way. Most adults with higher psychological functions are, however, unable to respond like infants and small children when perceiving . This is the price we pay for knowledge and maturity. Nevertheless, this does not mean that we as adults are unable to derive pleasure or enjoyment from our visual environments. Our emotional and cognitive pleasure do not necessarily diminish as a result of experience and knowledge. Our perception and experience are, however, different from the infant's immediate, conditioned, associative pleasure.

At what age does the spontaneous, passive *response* to the surroundings change to an active, cognitive construction? There is no sudden change, rather it develops gradually when children pick up the language and acquire a way of decontextual thinking. Their immediate response is gradually superseded by the higher psychological functions from about four to five years of age. I have followed this transition period in Zeleste's pleasure and explanation of it, gradually being able to reflect on and put words to her aesthetic preferences.

When I asked Zeleste on her fourth birthday *why* she preferred pink, gold and silver, she was unable to give an answer I found reasonable. She could not explain to me why these colours are so attractive to her, except to say they are "nice" and that "You have to understand that". On her next birthday, when she becomes six, Zeleste will probably be able to express her preferences in a language. But she will never be able to really understand why she likes or dislikes an object. That humans gradually are able to use words to express their preferences does not mean that they can disclose the mechanisms leading to their aesthetic feelings. They remain mysterious, as the Russian cultural psychologist Lev Vygotsky puts it: *"By its very nature, an aesthetic feeling is incomprehensible and fundamentally obscure in its evolution to the person experiencing it"* (The Psychology of Art, 1924).

Zeleste as an architect - what happens?

The same built environment therefore provokes and releases different emotions and cognition, depending on the person who perceives and gives meaning to the sensing. In ordinary daily life few people give priority to conscious reflections on their aesthetic environment. Only in a novel environment, such as, for instance, a hospital or an exotic country, will people pay much attention to the built environment. If they dwell consciously on the aesthetics at all it is done in everyday language. People generally lack concepts of professional reflection and find it difficult to state exactly why, for instance, a square, a building or a room gives rise to positive aesthetic feelings.

The professionals studying architecture and the built environment perceive and process the buildings and places in a different manner. They more often use scientific concepts and a specialised language, stating for instance that a building is *tasteful, harmonic, has a balance* or a *tension*. Lay people have to be trained to use this language that characterises the built environment. Part of the education as an architect involves using other concepts to be able to capture the environment in a more detailed, conscious and comprehensive manner.

Architects' preferences and tastes are normally different from lay people's, due to the same developmental principle explaining differences between infants and adults. Professionals have a broader experience and a deeper knowledge partly as a result of using other concepts and yardsticks. The "content" of their higher psychological functions is different. As an architect Zeleste would have used a professional language and she would hopefully have obtained richer and more exceptional associations when perceiving aesthetic elements.

Preferences, well-being and health

When watching the little bright girl and her sunny shining face on her birthday, I also wondered if her happiness made her healthier. Could it be that her laughter and happy mood, which was a result of the pleasure she got from what she looked at, also influenced her immune system? Does her happiness in general influence her health, or my health for that matter?

In fact I cannot really say. But I definitely felt good that day. The subjective, psychological well-being and happiness *seemed* to influence my body and mind in a healthy manner. From an everyday point of view it is of course difficult to reveal if my perceptions and mood have an effect on my health. A naive perspective would be that if I am "happy" because I am exposed to the environment I prefer, it also makes me healthier and less prone to illness. And in general: does being happy and satisfied and having good well-being make people more healthy? The answer depends on how health and well-being are conceived or defined. There is a close "relation" between health and well-being if "health" is defined according to the Alma Ata declaration. This manifesto gives a definition of health which is more or less identical to being happy and having good well-being. The "relation" is therefore a result of definition and not a correlation of different factors.

When defining health as the opposite of being *ill*, as something depending on physiological and biological processes and functions of the body, then it is harder to reveal the relation between preferences, well-being and health. It is,

at least, hard to reach a conclusion only by watching and noticing the immediate subjective responses. In this matter we need scientific knowledge.

The direct route does not work
There is no reason to believe that the visual cues or perception in themselves
influence health or illness. There is no *direct route* from aesthetic preferences
to health. What is beautiful from an aesthetic point of view is not always
healthy. My son Mathias spent two nights in hospital after he tasted the
yellow flowers and the green "peas" from the beautiful laburnum tree. The fly
agaric (the red amanita mushrom) also looks beautiful, but is poisonous. Our
aesthetic preferences cannot be trusted if we want to live a healthy life.

Particular colours and geometrical forms can release and activate particular physiological reactions in the body as a result of what they symbolise.
Red increases heart rates and *purple* slows down the rates. There is, however,
no reason to believe that this activation or slowing down of physiological
processes has any *general* or *direct* impact on health or illness. Colours,
meaning electromagnetic particles and light waves of different lengths, do
not have positive or negative impact on illness in themselves. Illness and
health are not influenced by the environment in such a simple way.

There is, however, an *indirect* effect. Beautiful environments increase our
well-being and positive mood, and this, in turn, influences our health in a
positive manner and enhances the healing process. As a social and health
psychologist, and not as Zeleste's father, I know this from textbooks and
scientific literature, which tell me that optimistic, happy attitudes about
yourself, other people and the world in general, influence some basic physiological and biological processes.

Laughter, as a sort of "stationary jogging", and a result of positive
emotions and pleasant experiences, increases respiration, heart rate and
blood circulation because this brings oxygen to the blood at a rate as much as
six times greater than during ordinary speech. Biochemical changes, including reductions in the stress hormone cortisol, have also been detected in
happy people. Salivary immunoglobulin A, which is thought to protect the
body against certain viruses, has been found to increase significantly in
people who viewed comedy videos. People who used humour to deal with

difficult situations in everyday life had the highest baseline levels of this protective substance. The therapeutic use of positive emotions to overcome illness has enhanced public awareness of the relatively new and exciting field of psycho-neuroimmunology. Emotions such as happiness give joy to our existence, and stress, illness and health are all entwined in this approach using humour to treat physical ailments. There also appears to be an immuno-logical suppression associated with downswings in pleasurable occurences, which leaves subjects vulnerable to the development of an infection in the presence of a virus. The pleasures of daily life have been found to positively affect mood and health.

There is also another *indirect route* to better health, namely to increase self-esteem by identifying oneself with high valued aesthetics. Health also depends on self-esteem and a feeling of being a worthy person. Beautiful environments also make us feel more valuable. The perception of ourselves, who we are, depends partly on the environment that we are part of. We define ourselves as a constituent part of the environment, and if the environment has a high value or status, this high value is transmitted to each individual who is a constituent part of this totality. This is the same principle as increas-ing self-esteem by social identification, which means attaining a better self-evaluation by identifying with social groups of high value. People with high self-esteem generally have better health and become less ill than people with lower self-evaluation.

Research in health psychology shows that surroundings that make people happy and satisfied, and give them high self-esteem, also make them healthy. This causality is well documented in health psychology, and is not only a subjective or intuitive feeling most people experience. It counts to be happy in environments you find pleasant and beautiful irrespective of whether you are a four-year-old or an expert in environmental aesthetics. What you perceive as pleasant depends on how the visual information is processed, and that will change in a systematic way during your lifetime as a result of acqui-sition of language, experiences and knowledge.

The Architectural Psychology Box of Infinite Knowledge

Rikard Küller

*How do we connect the research on single factors with an
overall view that everything influences everything?*

Introduction

The aesthetics of human-made environments, and the impact of those environments on people's well-being and health, are the topics of the field of research that I represent, namely "environmental psychology". Initially, in the sixties, this field was referred to as "architectural psychology" because most of its proponents originated in either of these two realms, one a traditional academic discipline, the other belonging to the arts and crafts. However, as a result of other disciplines being incorporated, especially medicine and the social sciences, the prefix shifted, and this also signified a widening of the focus of study to the environment as a whole. Still, for the present purpose, I will adhere to the original term (Küller, 1987).

To me, architectural psychology has been like mystery boxes. You open the first one, only to find another, perhaps slightly different, inside it. Just when you think you have found the final box, you may find that it looks exactly like the original one, and you will have to start all over again. Often that allegedly 'final' box even seems to be more complex, more difficult to grasp, than the one with which you started. I have spent more than 30 academic years trying to open some of the boxes of architectural psychology, and my belief in finding the final one has long since faded away. The solutions to scientific problems may not be as simple as we once hoped they would be. In all likelihood they may turn out to be infinitely complicated. Still, we learn something from opening boxes, and I will tell the reader about some of the things I have learnt.

The lightbox

Even if they believe that the universe works as a unitary whole, where everything influences everything else - the so called butterfly effect - scientists insist on dividing the environment into a number of different elements which they call "factors". Light is such a factor which I have studied in my research in architectural psychology. What is, to the physicist, a kind of electromagnetic radiation, to most ordinary observers means the opportunity to see the room with its objects, the building and the townscape or landscape surrounding it, to see other living beings or even oneself in the mirror. To humans, the visual sense provides the most detailed information about the "outside" world. From my viewpoint at a school of architecture, I dare say that architects share this priority. To them, the design of the visual world will be of the utmost, sometimes exclusive, importance. Yet, this is not what my research is about. Instead I have been focusing on the non-visual effects of light (Küller, 1981).

Sunlight, with its characteristic presence during daytime and absence during the night, has been of major importance for the evolution of life on earth. As a result, humans display the approximate 24-hour diurnal rhythm, involving not only wakefulness and sleep, but also body temperature and metabolism, and the production of different hormones. This "biological clock" is not as exact as one might assume. Keeping persons under constant, dark conditions has shown the "circadian" rhythm to be somewhat more than 24 hours, perhaps half an hour longer on average. Thus, for most of us the clock is somewhat slow. We are night-owls by nature, who find it easy to stay up at night and enjoy that extra hour's sleep in the morning. In order to remain synchronised with solar time, the clock has to be reset every morning, and daylight is the most important factor in accomplishing this adjustment (Boyce & Kennaway, 1987; Lewy et al., 1980).

The first light that reaches the eye in the morning will initiate a nervous process, which includes, amongst others, some small groups of brain cells known as the suprachiasmatic nuclei, as well as the production of a pineal hormone called melatonin. Whereas the production of melatonin is very low during the day, it increases in the evening, reaches a peak during the night and fades off in the early morning. Because of its nocturnal peak, melatonin is called a sleep hormone. It is known to affect the hypothalamic area of the brain as well as the pituitary, thyroid and adrenal glands. In addition to its rhythm-regulatory effect, melatonin has been found to affect the immuno-defence system (Arendt & Pévet, 1991; Brainard et al., 1988; Hardeland et al., 1995).

Another hormone, cortisol, produced in the adrenal cortex, has a diurnal pattern with high values during daytime and low values during the night. The highest level occurs early in the morning, possibly with a minor peak also late in the afternoon. The production is regulated by neurosecretion from the hypothalamus via the pituitary gland. Cortisol acts as a mobiliser of the organism. All kinds of strain, such as fever, pain, injury and psychological stress will increase the secretion of cortisol, and this will increase the organism's ability to cope with the situation. Cortisol, therefore, is often referred to as a stress hormone. One may say that, whereas the night is dominated by the sleep hormone, melatonin, the day is instead dominated by cortisol, and by other activity-promoting hormones (Hollwich, 1979; Linder et al., 1990).

Recent studies indicate that for persons living far from the equator, for instance in the Nordic countries, the production of the sleep hormones and of the activity-promoting hormones also displays an annual pattern. Our own research has shown that there may be a decline in the secretion of cortisol during the dark season. In one study, young children were investigated in their school environment for a period of one year. The children were situated in classrooms, some of which completely lacked windows and natural daylight. We found a systematic seasonal variation with more cortisol in summer than in winter, which in turn affected the children's ability to concentrate and cooperate, and possibly also their body growth and general health. However, the children in one classroom which lacked daylight deviated from this normal pattern. In another study, we compared the personnel working in subterranean military installations with personnel at regiments situated above the ground. The level of cortisol showed a substantial annual variation in the personnel working above ground, whereas the variation below ground was much less pronounced. The personnel below ground slept more, and they remained healthier during the winter than is normally to be expected in Sweden (Küller & Lindsten, 1992; Küller & Wetterberg, 1996).

Generally speaking, there seems to be a gradual decline in the activity-promoting hormone during fall and winter, followed by a strong rise in February, which levels off towards the summer. (This is for southern Sweden. Other climatic zones may show different patterns.) One thing we have learnt from our research is that most persons will benefit from daylight, especially during early spring. Without daylight and windows the rise in hormones becomes delayed, or does not occur at all. Therefore, daylight architecture is important for the mental health of people, and more so the farther to the north (or extreme south) they live.

However, when it gets very dark and the days become short, the biological clock may be upset, and such a disturbance of the basic diurnal pattern may result in fatigue, sleep disorder, depressed mood, and somatic disorders. Lack of daylight is considered to be the main reason for both midwinter lethargy and acute states of depression occurring during fall and spring, so-called seasonal affective disorders (SAD). Every year, about twenty per cent of the Swedish population suffers from moderate seasonal disorders, and another five per cent get seriously depressed. This large group would probably be better off , if they could avoid the seasonal variations in daylight by living either closer to the equator or under totally artificial lighting conditions. This poses new problems, amongst others about the quality of artificial light, but here adequate knowledge is lacking (Küller & Wetterberg, 1993; Lewy et al., 1987; Wetterberg, 1993).

Boxes of different colour
The psychologist who works at a school of architecture will learn much about colour, some of which is correct and some which is not. For instance, is it true that certain colours will promote certain emotions in all or most persons? Is it true that certain colours will make children more intelligent when used in the nursery, or make prisoners indulgent when applied to the prison cell? Is it true that some colours will have a therapeutic effect on persons suffering from certain diseases? Is it true that a room painted in warm as opposed to cool colours will speed up subjective time and cause a slight increase in body temperature? Actually, non of this is true. On the other hand, when certain colours are applied to the walls of a room and its furniture, this will affect the perception of the room, sometimes in a predictable way. From the sixties and onwards, our group spent considerable effort on studying such effects. Yet, we kept looking for deeper relationships (Acking & Küller, 1972: Küller, 1981).

Once again we have to turn to the brain for possible leads. About fifty years ago, knowledge began to emerge on the generalised effects of visual stimulation. A formation was discovered in the brain stem, which, when stimulated, seemed to affect the brain as a whole. Via this system, one brief but strong stimulus seemed enough to put the entire brain into a state of heightened arousal. For anatomical and physiological reasons this system became known as the reticular activation system. The need for such a system is obvious. In order to analyse a strong or complex signal, the brain needs to increase or redistribute its arousal. Thus, in a lively environment the brain's arousal is likely to increase and the organism suddenly becomes fully alert, which may be necessary for attention and perception. Whereas sudden or strong stimulation leads to increased arousal, monotonous stimulation may instead cause inhibition, rest or sleep. The reticular system also mediates certain responses of the autonomic nervous system, such as a change in heart rate or in the production of stress hormones (Kahle et al., 1986; Küller, 1991a; Luria, 1973).

Based on the theory of the reticular activation system, our research group in Lund, together with Byron Mikellides' group in Oxford, has investigated the possible relationship between colour and arousal. In order to measure the impact on the brain, physiological, so-called electroencephalographic recordings (EEG) were employed. In the waking brain, the components of the EEG referred to as alpha and delta seem to be highly responsive to stimulation from the surroundings. When a person is drowsy or relaxed, delta and alpha waves abound, but when the person is stimulated, for instance by light or noise, these slow, high-amplitude waves become attenuated, only to return when the person resumes the relaxed state. In addition, we used the electrocardiogram (EKG) in order to assess possible effects on heart rate, and seven-grade semantic scales to find out something about the subjective impressions in different rooms.

In one study, we compared two rooms, one with multi-coloured wallpaper, and the other painted all grey. In the colourful room there was a considerable decrease in alpha waves, indicating that the brain was aroused by the colours and patterns of the wallpaper. At the same time, the heart rate was lower in the colourful room, which meant that the increased attention led to a compensatory response in the autonomic nervous system. Those individuals who were most introverted showed the strongest defensive response, and had a reduction in heart rate by as much as ten per cent in the colourful room. If a person is highly aroused or stressed, this may be experienced as a loss of control over the situation at hand. Already from the outset our subjects reported feeling fully in control in the grey room. On the other hand, they had to spend several hours in the colourful room before they experienced control. More stress reactions became manifest in the male subjects than in the female ones (Küller, 1986).

Another study compared rooms with either warm or cool colorations. Again we used two rooms, but this time, one was painted red and the other blue. The colours had been equated for lightness and saturation, and special attention had been paid to the design of the rooms in order to make them look homely. Delta waves characterising a drowsy brain were more common in the blue room as were the alpha waves, indicating a more relaxed state, even if alpha did not reach full statistical significance. Thus, the brain waves differed in the predicted way, proving that red colours are more arousing than blue ones. Heart rate was slower in the red room than in the blue, which again may be understood in terms of a defensive response to overstimulation (Küller & Mikellides, 1993; Mikellides, 1989).

The results from these two studies warrant the conclusion that rooms decorated in a colourful way, especially with red colours, will cause higher arousal of the brain than rooms dominated by grey or blue colours. But where does this lead us? Which hues are to be preferred, how light and saturated should they be and how should they be combined? What about the differences we observed between persons with introverted and extroverted personalities, and between males and females? Again we are facing a number of new questions, new problems that were not foreseen. One plausible hypothesis is that colour is like background music. We may desire it when we are bored or relaxed, but when we wish to engage in serious thinking, we turn it down or shut it off completely. The implication would be to employ colour design in order to obtain desirable adjustments in the brain's arousal. For example, warm colours could be applied to add some extra arousal to a monotonous work-place, and blue colours could be used when we need to concentrate or be creative. But this is only guesswork, we really do not know. Not yet.

Boxes for dementia

In my last example, we will return from the laboratory to the real world. To be striken with a brain disorder is among the most terrifying things that can befall a person. Still, in old age this is very common. It has been estimated that one in every three or four persons who reaches the age of eighty will be stricken with senile dementia, most often varieties of Alzheimer's disease.

These patients suffer from severe confusion including deficiencies in memory, lack of initiative, obscured perception of time and space, and disability to think and speak. Their brains will deteriorate slowly but steadily, and no cure has yet been found that will stop or revert the process. Cerebrovascular dementia caused by cerebral haemorrhage or thrombosis constitutes another major group of patients. In addition to perceptual and cognitive deficiencies, they may have various neurological symptoms, including paralysis. As opposed to the former group, these patients are often completely aware of their situation, and this knowledge may lead to severe depression. However, both temporary and permanent improvements may occur. In addition, there are several other kinds of dementia which are much less prevalent (Annerstedt, 1995).

In two studies we have tried to create a more humane and homelike environment for patients with senile dementia than is usually to be found at geriatric hospitals. The first study took place at a large hospital in Malmö where we redecorated the dining room in one of the wards. Our intention was to recreate a dining room, as it may have looked in the thirties or forties when the patients were living an active life. The changes included the furniture, lighting, colour and table settings. Instead of serving the food on plastic trays, the patients were to serve themselves on porcelain of their own choice. The staff were to eat with the patients, who, as far as possible, would wear their own private clothing. We anticipated that these changes would activate the patients, make them feel more comfortable and help them to remember who they once were. The patients were studied both before and after the change by means of medical examinations, systematic observation and analysis of their dietary intake, and the results showed that changes even of this limited kind can be of importance. The patients became happier and more susceptible to social contacts and their dietary intake increased considerably (Küller, 1991b; Steen & Küller, 1989).

The ultimate aim was to be able to move geriatric patients to small, homelike units outside the hospital. To test this idea, two collective housing units were built when a large housing area in Malmö was being renovated. The units were designed to provide a high degree of familiarity and a homelike atmosphere. The style was the same as in the dining-room study, with furniture from the thirties and forties, and the decoration of the private rooms was based on interviews with the relatives of the patients. The outcome of this full-scale experiment was evaluated by studying the patients, first at the geriatric hospital, and then after they had moved to the collective housing units, and comparing them to a control group that remained at the geriatric hospital. The methods included thorough medical examinations, brain scanning, psychiatric assessment and systematic observation of each patient's behaviour. The patients who moved to the small units became much more active, engaged in everyday activities, and began to socialise with the other patients. One old lady who had not left her hospital bed for over a year began to get up in the morning, dress herself and make her own coffee in the shared kitchen. Other notable changes were the diminished use of diapers and sedatives, and the drastic change in the professional attitude among the personnel. Finally, and much to our surprise, the cost of care for this group of patients went down by more than half (Küller, 1991b).

Thus, by redecorating the nursing environment in a familiar way, and adapting the hospital routines to the demands of everyday life, it became possible to maintain the demented patients in a healthier and less confused state at a lower cost. However, again some new problems came to the surface. Because the small housing units lack medical resources, this type of long-term care will not be suitable for every category of patient, perhaps not even for all of those who are moderately demented. In designing for persons with senile dementia, not only the degree of the disease, but also the outlook for recovery, should be considered. For Alzheimer patients, the familiarity of the environment and the everyday activities may increase their comfort and security, and could also raise their functional ability. Persons with cerebrovascular injuries, on the other hand, must also be provided with the opportunity to practice their motor and intellectual faculties. Eventually, some demented patients will become exceedingly confused or aggressive. We must find, therefore, many different solutions rather than just one. Evidently, the process to design nursing environments according to the nature of the brain damage has hardly begun.

Conclusion

Briefly, I have described three lines of research in architectural psychology, in the introduction referred to as opening boxes. In the examples it became obvious that within each box there were other ones. The old belief that knowledge is limited and that everything will be revealed is not shared by today's scientists. Actually, one criterion of good research is that it should generate new questions and new answers. This may clash with the architect's legitimate need to get clear answers as guidelines for design. Unfortunately, what is true today may not be true tomorrow. Another troublesome fact is that not only are there too many boxes, but each contains too much and too detailed knowledge. Scientific results of the most varying kinds are overflowing, threatening to drown not only the general practitioner but also the specialist. There is an obvious risk that this mass of facts will hamper initiative and make practical decisions even more difficult tomorrow than they are today. Storing all this information stands out as a gigantic task, retrieving and using it calls for exceptional experience, common sense and intuition.

There are other boxes, we have hardly touched upon here, for instance the one containing subjective experience in an objective world. The British biologist and philosopher Nicholas Humphrey, who authored one of the chapters in Byron Mikellides' classic *Architecture for People*, has recently suggested a fascinating evolutionary solution to the subjective-objective controversy. Humphrey argues that whereas sensations, for instance in an earthworm, are direct approach/avoidance reactions to stimulation of the body surface, the primitive eye, which was nothing more than a light-sensitive cup in the skin, opened up a whole new world for perceptual analysis and predictions about an outside world. Consequently, the physical environment, from atom to universe, is a cognitive model based on stored perceptions, a model developed in the course of evolution because it enabled the beholder to survive. And that is all (Humphrey, 1993; Mikellides, 1980).

We also have the box containing aesthetics and beauty in the built environment. Neuropsychological research has shown that in the brain there are specific nerve cells, some of which will respond to either lines, edges, light, colour or movement, others that are capable of recognizing the human face or the body, and that these responses may be genetically determined. In a

Fig. 1. Capella dei Pazzi, Florence, 1446 by Brunnelleschi (B. Cold).

paper on the biological basis of aesthetics, Richard Latto recently claimed that: "Particular forms are aesthetically moving not because they reflect the properties of the world, but because they reflect the properties of our brains. Artists", he said, "are concerned with selecting from among the infinite possibilities which geometry offers those forms which will be most effective" (Latto, 1995, pp 68 & 69; Perrett et al., 1995) (Fig. 1).

Architectural psychology is a fast-growing field, drawing on many branches of research, some of which have been mentioned above. Its potential for application is now being recognised far outside the academic world. In many countries, architectural psychologists help to design, restore or evaluate landscapes, city centres, housing areas, shopping malls, offices, factories, schools and hospitals. Environmental psychologists have become involved in pollution control, assessing nuclear hazards and managing scarce resources. Some even assist the police in creating environmental profiles of rapists and murderers. Perhaps the discipline's strength and its future lie in the willingness of the architectural psychologist to become involved in the problems of everyday life in the real world (Axelrod & Lehman, 1993; Canter, 1994; Preiser et al., 1988; Stokols & Altman, 1987).

References

Acking, C. A. and Küller, R. (1972). The perception of an interior as a function of its colour. *Ergonomics*, 15 (6): 645-654.

Annerstedt, L. (1995). *On group-living care for the demented elderly. Experiences from the Malmö model.* Doctoral dissertation. Lund University, Lund, Sweden.

Arendt, J. and Pévet, P. (eds) (1991). *Advances in Pineal Research.* Volume 5. John Libbey, London.

Axelrod, L. J. and Lehman, D. R. (1993). Responding to environmental concerns: What factors guide individual actions? *Journal of Environmental Psychology*, 13: 149-159.

Boyce, P. and Kennaway, D. J. (1987). Effects of light on melatonin production. *Biological Psychiatry*, 22: 473-478.

Brainard, G. C., Lewy, A. J., Menaker, M., Fredrickson, R. H., Miller, L. S., Weleber, R. G., Gassone, V. and Hudson, D. (1988). Dose-response relationship between light irradiance and the suppression of plasma melatonin in human volunteers. *Brain Research*, 454: 212-218.

Canter, D. (1994). *Criminal shadows. Inside the Mind of the Serial Killer.* Harper Collins Publishers, London.

Hardeland, R., Balzer, I., Poeggeler, B., Fuhrberg, B., Uria, H., Behrmann, G., Wolf, R., Meyer, T. J. and Reiter, R. J. (1995). On the primary functions of melatonin in evolution: Mediation of photoperiodic signals in a unicell, photooxidation and scavenging of free radicals. *Journal of Pineal Research*, 18: 104-111.

Hollwich, F. (1979). *The influence of Ocular Light Perception on Metabolism in Man and in Animal.* Springer Verlag, New York.

Humphrey, N. (1993). *A history of the Mind.* Vintage Books, Random House, London.

Kahle, W., Leonhart, H. and Platzer, W. (1886). *Color Atlas and Textbook of Human Anatomy. Volume 3. Nervous System and Sensory Organs.* 3rd revised edition. George Thieme Verlag, Stuttgart, New York.

Küller, R. (1981). *Non-visual Effects of Light and Colour. Annotated Bibliography.* Document No. 15. Swedish Council for Building Research, Stockholm.

Küller, R. (1986). Physiological and psychological effects of illumination and colour in the interior environment. *Journal of Light & Visual Environment*, 10: 33-37.

Küller, R. (1987). Environmental psychology from a Swedish perspective. In: D. Stokols and I. Altman (eds). *Handbook of Environmental Psychology.* Volume 2, pp. 1243-1279. John Wiley & Sons, New York.

Küller, R. (1991a). Environmental assessment from a neuropsychological perspective. In T. Gärling and G. W. Evans. (eds). *Environment, Cognition, and Action: An Integrated Approach*, pp. 111-147. Oxford University Press, New York.

Küller, R. (1991b). Familiar design helps dementia patients cope. In W. F. E. Preiser, J. C. Vischer and E. T. White. (eds) *Design Intervention. Towards a More Humane Architecture*, pp. 255-267. Van Nostrand Reinhold, New York.

Küller, R. and Lindsten, C. (1992). Health and behavior of children in classrooms with and without windows. *Journal of Environmental Psychology*, 12: 305-317.

Küller, R. and Mikellides, B. (1993). Simulated studies of colour, arousal, and comfort. In R. W. Marans and D. Stokols (eds) *Environmental Simulation: Research and Policy Issues*, pp. 163-190. Plenum Press, New York.

Küller, R. and Wetterberg, L. (1993). Melatonin, cortisol, EEG, ECG and subjective comfort in healthy humans: Impact of two fluorescent lamp types at two light intensities. *Lighting Research and Technology*, 25 (2): 71-81.

Küller, R. and Wetterberg, L. (1996). The subterranean work environment: Impact on well-being and health. *Environment International*, 22: 33-52.

Latto, R. (1995). The brain of the beholder. In R. Gregory, J. Harris, P. Heard and D. Rose (eds) *The Artful Eye*, pp. 66-94. Oxford University Press, Oxford.

Lewy, A. J., Sack, R. L., Miller, L. S. and Hoban, T. M. (1987). Antidepressant and circadian phase-shifting effects of light. *Science*, 235: 352-354.

Lewy, A. J., Wehr, T. A., Goodwin, F. K., Newsome, D. A. and Markey, S. P. (1980). Light suppresses melatonin secretion in humans. *Science*, 210: 1267- 1269.

Linder, B. L., Esteban, N. V., Yergey, A. L., Winterer, J. C., Loriaux, D. L. and

Cassoria, F. (1990). Cortisol production rate in childhood and adolescence. *Journal of Pediatrics*, 117: 892-896.

Luria, A. (1973). *The Working Brain: An Introduction to Neuropsychology.* Penguin, London.

Mikellides, B. (ed) 1980. *Architecture for People.* Studio Vista, London.

Mikellides, B. (1989). *Emotional and Behavioural Reaction to Colour in the Built Environment.* Doctoral dissertation. Oxford Polytechnic (now Oxford Brookes University), Oxford.

Perrett, D., Benson, P. J., Hietanen, J. K., Oram, M. W. and Dittrich, W. H. (1995). When is a face not a face? In R. Gregory, J. Harris, P. Heard and D. Rose. (eds) *The Artful Eye*, pp. 95-124. Oxford University Press, Oxford.

Preiser, W. F. E., Rabinowitz, H. Z. and White, E. T. (1988). *Post-occupancy Evaluation.* Van Nostrand Reinhold Company, New York.

Steen, B. and Küller, R. (1989). Psychological and nutritional effects of redecorating the physical environment in nursing homes. In J. Wertheimer, P. Baumann, M. Gaillard and P. Schwed (eds) *Innovative Trends in Psychogeriatrics. Interdisciplinary Topics in Gerontology.* Volume 26, pp. 28-32. Karger, Basel.

Stokols, D. and Altman, I. (eds) (1987). *Handbook of Environmental Psychology.* Volume 1 and 2. John Wiley & Sons, New York.

Wetterberg, L. (ed) (1993). *Light and Biological Rhythms in Man.* Pergamon Press, Oxford.

Housing, Health and Aesthetics: Reconnecting the Senses

Roderick Lawrence

Is it possible to define the aesthetic aspects of the architecture which are important to our health?

Introduction

When I enter the local baker's shop, the variety of bread, croissants and pastries displayed on the shop counter, the smell of freshly baked dough and the display of posters about local associations and sports teams on the shop walls give me positive feelings. During the coldest months of the year the windows of the bakery are dripping with condensation and I cannot see the produce inside the shop. However, I can smell bread and pastries in the street before I enter. When I go further along the street to buy a pharmaceutical product, the antiseptic smell, the polished finish and artificial lighting of the pharmacy with everything for sale in its proper place contrast with the ambience of the bakery. Moreover, this pharmacy always smells and looks the same. My feelings about these two places are relative to each other, to my plans and my well-being on that day. I like to go and buy fresh bread on Sunday mornings. The local church bells provide the familiar resonant bearings that if I wait much longer the bread will no longer be warm and scented, and the loaves my family prefers may already be sold. In contrast to the predictability of the bell toll each Sunday morning, the strange quietness of the streetscape following unpredictable snowfalls in winter serves as a reminder that the aural dimensions of the built environment are an integrated component of my daily experience. This experience contrasts with the majority of academic research which does not account for the multidimensional nature of people-environment interrelations. Instead, the dominant approach focuses on a visual interpretation which does not adequately address integrated sensory experience, or the intended and unforeseen effects that the built environment has on human health and well-being (Fig. 1).

The above examples from places I regularly frequent illustrate that it is not easy to consider the visual dimensions of the built environment as being separated from their other dimensions which also involve the human senses. Nonetheless, this limited approach has become common in the Western world. Several studies, including Tuan (1982), show that from the 16th century, a consciously delimited social order based largely on social categorization and spatial demarcation has reinforced the importance of the visual dimensions of the built environment at the expense of aural, olefactory and tactile dimensions. In recent decades architectural discourse has been

Fig. 1. The interrelations between people and their environment are not just spatial, nor observable, but also (and indeed significantly) sensorial, cultural and metaphysical.

dominated by a concern about the visual appearance of the built environment. When architects, urban designers, researchers and policy decision makers make articifical distinctions between the visual and other dimensions of built environments they contradict the integrated way that the five human senses are used simultaneously to perceive and construe them, and attribute meanings and values to them. Consequently they contribute to sensory deprivation which can have harmful effects on physiological, psychological and social well-being.

Today it is commonly accepted that housing conditions influence the health and well-being of inhabitants. Nonetheless, amongst the numerous studies and overviews that have been published there is no consensus about the **nature** of the relationship between housing and health. Reasons for this lack of consensus relate to the complex nature of the subject and common theoretical and methodological approaches used to study it (Lawrence, 1993). Often these approaches ignore the integrated nature of the human experience of residential environments and how this experience is related to physiological, social and psychological well-being. This essay will discuss and illustrate how an improved understanding of the interrelations between housing and health can stem from the study of a wide range of material dimensions of the built environment, on the one hand, and numerous human dimensions, on the other hand. All these dimensions need to be studied using a temporal perspective that accounts for the integrated nature of human experience of built environments and the effects of this experience on health. In order to help achieve this goal a checklist is provided. This checklist presents indicators of housing quality which are related to people's experience and feelings of their residential environments and positive or negative impacts on their well-being. This approach leads to a concluding discussion about the relative importance of aesthetics in relation to housing and health.

Working definitions

In this essay, **health** refers to the physiological, psychological and social condition of human individuals, groups and communities over their life-span. According to the World Health Organization "health is a state of complete physical, mental and social well-being and not merely the absence of disease or infirmity." Health should not be interpreted only in terms of the absence or presence of infection, infirmity or morbidity. Rather, it is a state or condition that is defined in relation to the constituents of all the environmental and human characteristics that make up the daily lives of people and the reciprocal relations between them. Health is not a static equilibrium but a dynamic one that implies illness and disease if disequilibrium occurs. The ways and means by which people become ill are not wholly predictable. People feel when a room or building is supporting or harming their health and well-being. This means that the sick building syndrome is not simply measurable. It also includes subjective judgements with personal, cultural and bio-physiological dimensions that vary between people in the same society and over time (Burridge and Ormandy, 1993) (Fig. 2).

Housing evokes a range of images and concepts commonly related to the material and physical nature of one or more kinds of dwelling unit. Nonetheless, the meaning of "housing", like the meaning of "home", varies from person to person, between social groups and across cultures. Houses are commonly attributed an economic value, an exchange value, an aesthetic value and a use value, whereas in addition to these a home is usually given a sentimental and a symbolic value. All these values, as well as domestic roles, routines and rituals, are not simply expressed by individuals because they are acquired,

Fig. 2. The limited sensory dimensions of modern housing estates mean that people can feel detached from, and even hostile to their daily surroundings. This photograph was taken in a suburb of Melbourne, Australia. It is not unlike many so-called "model" housing projects built in numerous countries during the 1950s, 1960s and 1970s.

nurtured, transmitted, reinforced or modified by interpersonal communication.

The interrelations between housing, health and well-being are very different when viewed from the legislator's, the public administrator's and the resident's point of view. An ecological perspective enables the formulation and application of an integrated approach which can be applied to analyse the interrelations between housing, health and aesthetics from the viewpoint of individuals and groups in precise localities.

In this essay **aesthetics** pertains to the apprehension of things by all the human senses. The five human senses enable the cognition of any of the dimensions of residential environments in an integrated way. For example, the maintenance of building interiors, and the state or condition of outdoor space encompass numerous dimensions including the smell of animal litter or uncollected garbage, the appearance of graffiti and unkempt garden plots.

These dimensions influence human judgements and whether people have positive or negative feelings about their daily surroundings. When people lose their bearings in modern airports or administrative buildings despite sign-posting it is largely because they cannot rely on their five senses to reorientate themseves in a sterile interior. The restricted sensory dimensions of modern buildings mean that people can feel detached from or hostile towards their daily surroundings. This interpretation shows that alone, visual appearance, beauty or taste are insufficient to account for the interrelations between people and their surroundings. It also challenges a static interpretation of aesthetics based on rules of composition, proportion and order.

Theoretical and methodological principles

It ought to be more widely recognized that people do not just look at buildings, or perceive and experience them. Humans have the capacity to see, smell, touch, hear and taste specific constituents of their habitat. How people use their sensory capacities is not just determined biologically but also culturally. The built environment is an integral part of our livelihood and it can have multiple implications on human health and well-being, as shown by many authors in Burridge and Ormandy (1993).

The interrelations between people and the built environment involve biological, ecological and human factors. The latter include physiological, psychological and social dimensions. These factors and dimensions transcend the geographical scale of the building itself to include neighbourhoods and cities on much larger geographical scales. They also extend beyond the small scale of an individual or household to affect the occupants of buildings and other members of society. They surpass the temporal scale of the life-spans of people and building cycles because they include ecological impacts over longer periods. The following principles should be borne in mind.

First, the interrelations between humans and the constituents of their surroundings are manifested through a wide range of physiological, psychological, societal and cultural processes. These processes include sensations and perceptions (which animals also share) but also beliefs, doctrines, ideas and representations which are uniquely human and non-observable. *The interrelations between people and their environment are not just spatial, nor observable, but also (and indeed significantly) sensorial, cultural and metaphysical. Moreover, these interrelations are not absolute, nor static, but dialectical, and they are subject to change during relatively short and longer periods of time.*

Second, unlike other biological organisms, the sets of interrelations between human beings and their surroundings are characterised by both discursive and reflexive knowledge, including a recourse to symbols, particularly but not exclusively linguistic symbols. This characteristic is a distinguishing feature between anthropoid and human behaviour. It has important implications with respect to the human interpretation of built environments.

Third, the "human environment" can be distinguished from the "environment" of other biological organisms by its instrumental nature. Human products and processes transform the constituents of the environment in order to respond to prescribed aspirations, needs and goals that are defined both by individuals and human groups. Furthermore, it is necessary to distinguish between the environment that is perceived and used by people and both the micro- and macro-environments which human senses do not interpret without the aid of technological instruments. Although boundaries do not separate the environments along these different scales they do have different kinds of impacts on human activities, health and well-being.

The built environment can support or hinder the promotion of health; for example, by keeping the body in appropriate tempered surroundings that are not too cold nor too hot, and not poorly ventilated. In the absense of complete scientific data, people comment on the qualities of the built environment. Their comments concern a wide range of constructional aspects of the building envelope (lack of aural and thermal insulation); the size, shape and arrangement of rooms (for basic activities such as preparing and eating food); their environmental aspects (a sense of insecurity or a lack of privacy from others); and, last but not least, the internal and external appearance of buildings.

Not everybody suffers from dampness in the walls, the presence of formaldehyde, or mould spores in poorly ventilated rooms. Correspondingly, not everybody suffers from low levels of aural, thermal and visual insulation of the building. Nonetheless, today it is generally accepted that these may influence the health and well-being of people. In contrast, there is still little consensus about the impact of the appearance of the built environment on health and well-being. The visual dimensions of buildings are often considered only after practical problems have been dealt with. This custom is partly related to the fact that aesthetic dimensions are not considered as an integral component, but as an addendum. Too often they are considered to be subjective, difficult to measure and therefore not studied.

The relative importance of aesthetics

There are numerous studies of human needs and well-being which cannot be presented here. However, the contribution of Maslow (1954/1970) is noteworthy because it has been widely used as a reference for recent contributions on this subject. Maslow established a hierarchy of human needs that accounts for both conscious and unconscious human motivations and personality. This hierarchy of needs conforms to the list in Table I (next page).

This classification of basic needs by Maslow (1970, p. 54) "attempts to take account of the relative unity behind the superficial differences in specific desires from one culture to another". This hierarchical interpretation implies that the ordering of human needs is universally applicable and that the fulfillment of aesthetic needs only becomes important when the other six classes of need have been met. This interpretation contradicts the integrated one proposed in this essay. Bearing this qualification in mind, it is noteworthy that some contributions in the field of people-environment relations have proposed a hierarchy of needs they consider to be innate or omnipresent. Cooper (1975), for example, modifies the list of basic human needs which Maslow presents in order to establish a hierarchy of housing needs including:

1. Shelter
2. Security
3. Comfort
4. Socialization and self-expression
5. Aesthetics.

Consequently, shelter is considered a more basic need than security. This is a segmented not an integrated interpretation. Furthermore, what both these

Table 1 (Maslow, 1954)

Primary level	**1. Physological needs** (Homeostasis, food consumption, sexual behaviour).
Secondary level	**2. Safety needs** (Security; stability; dependency; protection; freedom from fear, anxiety and chaos; need for structure, order, law, limits ...). **3. Belongingness and love needs** (Stable affectionate relations with people and places, including homes and neighbourhoods ...). **4. Esteem needs** (Firstly, for strength, achievement, adequacy, mastery and competence; for confidence, independence and freedom; secondly, for reputation, prestige, status fame and glory, dominance, recognition, attention, importance, dignity and appreciation).
Tertiary level	**5. Need for self-actualization** (Individual differences are significant at this level). **6. Cognitive capacities** (The desires to know and to understand are the preconditions for the basic need satisfactions). **7. Aesthetic needs** (Need for order, symmetry, closure, system and structure).

kinds of need mean for residents in a specific context, and how they are related to human experience, is open to conjecture.

Interpretations of human needs, health and housing

In recent years it has become increasingly common for medical and social scientists and professional designers to address the "needs" of residents living in diverse kinds of housing (Cooper-Marcus, 1977). The word "needs" is used very loosely, so that distinctions between biological, psychological and cultural needs, on the one hand, and individual and shared needs, on the other hand, are rarely made explicit. Consequently, attention has rarely been given to resolving the conflicting or contradictory needs of different groups of people. This brief overview suggests that it is important to identify those dimensions which are pertinent for studies of the relations between housing, health and well-being in precise localities. These dimensions should include the human senses which help to provide people with bearings and to recall other localities. In principle, sounds lack a spatial definition, but church bells provide temporal bearings and a dynamic dimension to everyday life. Unlike visual appearance, odours do not give a sense of space because fragrances are diffuse. They arouse feelings of pleasure, well-being, nostalgia and revulsion. The tactile sense functions by means of the surface of the skin which is the largest human sensory organism. Unlike the plugged ear or the closed eyes, the skin constantly relates to the immediate surroundings of the human body. Collectively, the human senses serve to orientate the human body, to monitor and support human conduct, and guide people in daily life.

The preceding discussion and examples illustrate that the meaning and use of the built environment are not intrinsic to a set of aesthetic or physical characteristics. There are no **absolute** rules or orders that define the visual, aural, olefactory and tactile qualities of residential environments. The qualitative definition of housing should be understood in terms of the **contextual conditions** in which that housing exists. These contextual conditions cannot be limited to a study of the site and the availability of construction materials because they define and are defined by a range of architectural, economic, political, social and economic dimensions in a precise context at specific points in time. The remainder of this essay will present a checklist of these dimensions in order to promote our understanding of the relative importance of aesthetics with respect to housing and health.

Multiple dimensions of housing quality

Housing quality can be interpreted in many ways. Various approaches reflect the rationale and objectives of those who conduct or sponsor research and policy formulation. For example, studies on housing quality may be intended for the formulation and implementation of government housing policies, or academic research, or the dissemination of information to professional groups (such as architects or building contractors) and to the public. The purpose of defining housing quality may concern one or more of the following goals:

1. The assessment of aesthetic and/or functional values of residential buildings.
2. The identification of targets for upgrading or replacing the existing housing stock.
3. The allocation of housing loans and subsidies with the criteria: effective occupancy conditions, household income and expenditure.
4. Concern about the health and well-being of the residents in relation to the internal and external conditions of housing neighbourhoods.

There is a wide range of studies on the subject. Therefore it is not surprising that there has been little consensus about those concepts, means and measures used to define and assess housing quality. Each of these approaches examines a number of factors. However, it is rare for the studies to address or define a broad, integrated definition of housing quality which accounts for the three sets of approaches simultaneously. There appear to be no methodological reasons for this lack of integration. The aim of formulating an analytical checklist for the study of the qualitative aspects of housing is primarily to assist researchers in addressing the complexity of this subject by using the contributions of diverse interpretations in a complementary way. This checklist integrates the qualitative aspects and explains why some dimensions may need to be stressed or under-valued with respect to others.

From this perspective, researchers and practitioners can situate their approach, forcibly partial rather than inclusive, in terms of this reference model. Nonetheless, an important prerequisite for considering any example as a whole is the definition and comprehension of the component parts and the reciprocal relations between them.

An analysis of two hundred publications, in English and French, enables us to identify eight classes of dimensions which are pertinent to an analysis of the relationships between health and housing.

These dimensions concern:

1. Architecture and Urban Design
2. Housing Administration
3. Societal Factors
4. Household Demography
5. External and Internal Environmental Conditions
6. Ergonomics and Safety
7. Individual Human Factors
8. Residential Mobility and Choice

Although there are many studies which examine one or more of these classes of dimensions, it has not been commonplace to examine the interrelations between them in an integrated and interactive way (Lawrence, 1993). There have been numerous empirical studies that measure the residents' satisfaction with their home environment. Some studies have focused on specific needs, such as security, socialization and self-expression in the context of medium- and high-density housing. According to Zimring (1982, p. 153), when these needs are not met the consequences may be detrimental:

"At the public level, people have a need for social networks and for a sense of mutual caring and protection; when these networks break down, crime and vandalism may result. At the private level, individuals need solitude for self-reflection and intimate conversations to create and maintain personal relationships. When these needs are frustrated, intrapersonal costs may result: withdrawal, depression, illness."

According to Zimring and others, these physical, social and psychological consequences result from a process by which people attempt to achieve congruence between their needs and goals and what is provided by the built environment. It is now widely accepted that architectural variables are not determinants of individual or group behaviour. In a seminal discussion about the interrelationship between architectural and behavioural factors, Gans (1967) distinguished between "potential" and "effective" environments. The latter include integrated sets of cultural and sensorial dimensions that provide individuals with a framework for appraising whether personal and group needs have been met in diverse ways. Further research on this subject is required in order to improve current understanding of the impacts of housing areas on physiological, psychological and social well-being. This research should reconsider the function and purpose of the five human senses as an integral part of the human experience of residential buildings.

Conclusion

This essay has briefly presented a personal interpretation of the aesthetic interpretation of residential buildings. It is based on my own experience briefly illustrated in the introduction. This experience has provided the underlying framework for my past and ongoing research on housing, health and well-being in collaboration with the World Health Organization. My personal experience (too often taken for granted) and my research (too often separated from daily life) confirm that it is too restrictive to examine the interrelations between housing and health only through the study of cause and effect relationships between isolated dimensions, such as visual appearance, at a specific point in time. The integrated approach advocated in this essay is presented as an alternative. It requires further development and applications in the future if we are to enhance our understanding of the interrelationships between housing, health and aesthetics. What is at stake is important because we are rapidly constructing built environments in which deceptive appearance masks a lack of concern about the rich sensory dimensions of human life. This may not seem surprising given that we live in a world dominated more and more by images. Unfortunately, the consequences for our health and well-being have been largely ignored.

References

Burridge, R. and Ormandy, D. (eds) (1993). *Unhealthy Housing: Research, Remedies and Reform*. E. & F. N. Spon, London.

Cooper, C. (1975). *Easter Hill Village: Some Social Implications of Design*. The Free Press, New York.

Cooper-Marcus, C. (1977). User needs research in housing. In Davis, S. (ed) *The Form of Housing*. Van Nostrand Reinhold, New York, pp.139-170.

Gans, H. (1967). *The Levittowners*. Pantheon Books, New York.

Lawrence, R. (1993). An ecological blueprint for healthy housing. In R. Burridge and D. Ormandy (eds) *Unhealthy Housing: Research, Remedies and Reform*. E. and F. N. Spon, London, pp. 338-360.

Maslow, A. (1954). *Motivation and Personality*. Harper Row, New York (2nd Edition 1970).

Tuan, Yi-Fu. (1982). *Segmented Worlds and Self : A Study of Group Life and Individual Consciousness*. University of Minnesota Press, Minneapolis.

Zimring, C. (1982). The built environment as a source of psychological stress: Impacts of buildings and cities on satisfaction and behavior. In Evans, G. (ed) *Environmental Stress*, Cambridge University Press, New York, pp. 151- 178.

"Chuck Out the Chintz*"? Some Observations on Aesthetics, Well-being and Health

Sue-Ann Lee

How can we understand and deal with the aesthetic honesty of architects designing "natural and reasonable" objects and people's love of ornaments and chintz?

"A lot of people are fond of nature, many sleep outdoors occasionally, and people in prisons and hospitals long for the day when they will be free to enjoy the beauties of nature, but few are so shut away and isolated from that which can be shared alike by rich and poor. It's not imagination on my part when I say that to look up at the sky, the clouds, the moon and the stars makes me calm and patient. It's a better medicine than either valerian or bromine; Mother Nature makes me humble and prepared to face every blow courageously.

Alas it has had to be that I am only able - except on a few rare occasions - to look at nature through dirty net curtains hanging before very dusty windows. And it's no pleasure looking through these any longer, because nature is just the one thing that really must be unadulterated."

The Diary of Anne Frank, June 15th, 1944 (p. 218)

Introduction

I would like to share with you some observations on aesthetics, well-being and health culled from some years as an environmental psychologist teaching in a school of architecture in Britain. I will make these observations from 3 main perspectives although in reality they overlap; the architectural, the social/psychological and the educational. For the sake of brevity I will comment only on a few aspects of this wide ranging topic. My observations are from a British perspective and I am aware that there are different interpretations in other cultural contexts, which this collection of essays may well highlight. I will focus on the built environment of housing, and particularly on state housing, which raises particular issues in this context and which forms a large proportion of the British housing stock. I will also focus on aspects of aesthetics and well-being which are connected with housing residents' physical and psychological health.

I wish to follow a number of threads in this essay, some of which are evident in the passage above, written by Anne Frank after nearly two years in hiding. It shows for example; that she sees a strong link between nature and well-being; that nature is shared by everyone, rich and poor; that aesthetic aspects of the built and natural environment are important; and that perceptions and appraisals change over time.

My title comes from the recent advertising slogan being used on British television by IKEA, the Swedish home furnishing store. They suggested that British housewives should "chuck out the chintz" (throw out their patterned and ornate furnishings) and go to IKEA for some new, plain (but colourful) furniture and fabrics. The advertisement featured the women moving all their patterned items out of their houses and loading them into a builder's skip to be taken and thrown away. In contrast, IKEA's 1996 catalogue featured Anders Moberg, the President of IKEA, telling the reader how the organisation was built on a "waste not, want not" philosophy and talking about its responsibilities for the environment, policies of recycling and so on! I was surprised by the strength of my negative reaction to this advertisement. It grates, it stereotypes, it oversimplifies and it is arguing on the basis of style.

It made me think again about the emotional aspects of aesthetics and the long standing, heated debates over style and taste, particularly concerning the role of ornament. It also reminded me of a programme on British television a few years ago called "Signs of the Times" in which a number of individuals and couples were interviewed in their homes about their décor decisions and opinions of each other's choices. It showed more graphically than many academic papers how the built environment is both a mediator of, and also the product of social relationships, and in many cases it was profoundly depressing! There is no doubt in my mind that people, the lay public and designers, care about aesthetic aspects of the environment. But equally there is no doubt in my mind that this is a complex domain and that there are no easy absolutes or formulae to be found here.

I hope to show in the following observations that there are differences in the approach to aesthetics, well-being and health by designers who focus more on built form as a "container" of social processes and by social researchers who focus more on the built environment as the "context" of social processes, and that this difference contributes to the "gap" between designers and users which informs my educational observations at the end.

Architectural observations
For centuries artists, designers and architects have debated aesthetics. I shall confine my observations to two threads of debate which have had an impor-

tant influence on the aesthetics of the built environment of British housing today. The debate has focused on the role of ornament, nature and technology, in built form.

In Britain, following the Industrial Revolution, more than half the population was urban by the middle of the 19th century. In the context of the widely held belief at the time, that surroundings influenced mood and behaviour, there emerged both a growing dissatisfaction with the urban environment and a nostalgia for the countryside. Aesthetics, well-being and health were seen to be connected - albeit in a rather simplistically determinist way. People saw the move from the country as an aesthetic exchange - ugly for beautiful - and as an exchange of an unhealthy environment for a healthy one, and also in social terms as a kind of "fall" from the "natural order" to disorder and suffering (Williams 1973).

It is no coincidence that at the 1851 Great Exhibition "naturalism" dominated every branch of decorative art. Inside the house at this time, nature (often expressed through "exotic" plants and landscapes) was represented on the carpets, curtains, walls, and plates.

William Morris, the poet, craftsman, socialist and one of the founders of the Arts & Crafts Movement, was a strong exponent of the natural and by extension an enemy of mechanistic urban industrialism. He acknowledged that his handcrafted approach and pleas for direct experience of nature were mainly open to the rich, but he fervently believed in the aesthetic benefits of nature for all, and saw others benefitting through his wallpaper designs and chintz when they could not afford the tapestries. However, he did not follow the then current taste for "exotic" nature, his aesthetic, the version of nature that he promoted, was that of the fields and gardens of Britain in the Middle Ages. His work is important because it brought together both social and aesthetic objectives: "For Morris the question of suitable surroundings was "the most serious ... a man can think of; for (it was) no less than the chances of a calm, dignified, and therefore happy life for the mass of mankind" (Rees 1993).

Later in his life Morris's own perceptions changed. He emphasized the need for more simplicity, to "chuck out the chintz" or as he put it, just as graphically, to clear the "farrago of rubbish" and to replace it with objects that are "natural and reasonable". Interestingly he issued his first attack on excessive ornament in 1884, at a public hygiene conference. Although some would argue that this anticipated the end of ornament and the birth of functionalism, others show that this aesthetics, this link between nature and built form in housing, and this link between aesthetics and health, has persisted.

At the turn of the century some philanthropic industrialists, for example Leverhulme, Cadbury and Rowntree, invested in the design of new "healthy" environments for their workers, both as a vehicle for moral reform and because they realised that a healthy workforce produced more goods. In the low density housing that resulted, both the aesthetics of Britain in the Middle Ages and the relationship of nature to built form, were central.

In the early 20th century two differing views of aesthetics, well-being and health emerged in the Garden City Movement and in modernism. There are clear links between the earlier philanthropic schemes and the development of Ebenezer Howard's Garden City ideas. At the same time, the other quite separate thread of thinking was also beginning to influence our housing form, as the modernist ideas of Corbusier and CIAM spread to Britain.

Fishman (1977) argues that Howard and Corbusier shared their negative perceptions of the 19th century urban context, and a utopian approach to social change through the design of the built environment. They saw the industrial city as "a cancer", unhealthy and out of control, and they shared an enthusiasm for the new technologies and their possibilities. They each proposed a radical new urban design, coupled with radical social change. The contrast between the details of their physical and social proposals though, is considerable.

Howard's Garden City ideas came to be exemplified in built form through the designs of architects such as Raymond Unwin. The Garden City was based on what Howard saw as the combination of the best aspects of the town and the country. It was based on low density, low rise design, self-sufficiency, and social cooperation. The incorporation of nature in the built form was seen as essential to well-being and health and is illustrated in the famous poster advertising Welwyn Garden City. Although initially built as private investments, the Garden Cities of Letchworth and Welwyn were later incorporated into the post-war, state-funded British New Town Programme. This was extensive and 32 New Towns have been built.

The vernacular and Garden City aesthetics dominated the design of the early-1950s New Towns. The low rise housing was made of brick, with front and back gardens, set in tree-lined streets, with neighbourhood parks, and the towns were located in green field sites with surrounding countryside.

In contrast, Corbusier and others proposed a universal architecture that was based on the city. This was "modern", both in the sense of not referring to any particular past and in its use of the new technologies and materials. It was to eschew ornament and yet aesthetics was seen to be important for everyone, rich and poor, and it was still felt that elements of nature related to human well-being and health.

Their urban design proposals included high density, high rise, built form with the centralised and bureaucratically controlled city seen as the place where both cooperation and individualism find their best expression. Corbusier foresaw "vertical communities without politics" with "streets in the air". New concrete technology and industrialised building methods would enable the large-scale developments envisaged.

For housing, Modernism proposed a different manifestation of the link between aesthetics, health and well-being. Design involved the careful manipulation of sunshine, light, air and space in housing to improve the health and well-being of its residents. Housing was to be raised above the landscape to give everyone beneficial views and the open space below would be freed for play and recreation.

Corbusier proposed a "house tool" that would combine comfort and beauty with efficiency "a machine for habitation" in which ornament was rejected on hygienic as well as aesthetic grounds. "Light" and "white" came to be seen as "healthy" whereas dark and dust, and objects that could harbour it, were seen as dangerous and "unhealthy".

Corbusier's ideas, and in particular his Unité d'Habitation housing scheme in Marseille, inspired British architects and influenced both the design and the large-scale implementation of the post war state housing programme. The housing schemes of Alton West in Roehampton on the edge of London, and at Parkhill in Sheffield, with its "streets in the air", exemplify the influence of modern movement thinking on British post-war housing.

In a wider context, there was a shift in anti-urban attitudes as city environments improved generally. With the new technologies of heating and glazing, all housing interiors began to change from being cold and dark, to lighter warmer spaces where the natural world could be brought inside through plants and conservatories. The garden, particularly in the rapidly growing suburbs, was no longer seen as "a vista" but lawns could be mowed and outside activities became part of family life (e.g. Oliver et al. 1981).

Looking back with the benefit of hindsight, one can see both the considerable progress and the problems resulting from these two utopian approaches. Some of the problems arise from limitations in the approaches, others from the ways in which they were implemented. Both visions are perhaps overoptimistically determinist in seeing a new built form leading to social change. But the ideas were often not fully realised in built form anyway. They were taken out of context (deliberately in some cases) and implemented in adapted and watered down versions. There are lessons, both good and bad, to be learned from both "experiments".

The particular problems for Modernism in Britain arising from an imposed switch to high-rise living in a cultural context of living on the ground, have been well documented. These problems were exacerbated by putting families in high rise housing, which had neither been intended by policy, nor anticipated by the designers, and this then combined with a number of other problems of finance, construction techniques, poor quality materials and inflexible management, left a predominately negative legacy in the public's perception.

The case study by Boudon (1972) of the alterations made by the residents to Corbusier's workers' housing in Pessac is illuminating. He shows how they made both internal and external changes to the structure and aesthetics of the houses. But perceptions and policies change over time, and I have heard recently that the scheme is now being changed back to Corbusier's original design and being protected as architectural heritage!

The lessons from the British New Towns have been less widely publicised, although research was established to feed lessons forward into later designs within the Programme itself. When the early expectations of the benefits of the new physical environment were seen to be naive, a "social development" structure was put in place to help residents to make the social, as well as the physical, transition into this new context of their lives.

Designers criticised the early New Towns on aesthetic grounds for not being truly urban, but "suburban", and for their lack of variety. Later, 1970s New Towns, such as Milton Keynes, which were conceived as new cities not just towns, sought design variety by bringing in a number of different architects. Research by Jeff Bishop (1986) into residents' perceptions of Milton Keynes shows, however, that they feel they are not living in a "city" at all, but in a series of "villages" and, importantly, that they are happy with this!

In a thoughtful review Robert Maxwell (1975) traces the aesthetic and social heritage behind two contrasting housing schemes in Milton Keynes by two very different designers, Chris Cross and Ralph Erskine. It shows, amongst other things, that the two schemes link to the two differing threads, from Corbusier and Ebenezer Howard, that I have been outlining.

In his conclusion Maxwell says that too much is expected of the built form of housing - that no one housing scheme can be ideal. He advocates that architects design with the courage of their convictions, and then people can choose the housing that suits them from the different alternatives available. There are particular difficulties with this "market" approach in Britain, where a large proportion of our housing stock has been state owned, and people have been allocated to housing with little or no choice. In a careful analysis Scoffham (1984) shows that, with hindsight, on a number of criteria, for many British residents, "The building of images, whether of Corbusier or Ebenezer Howard, does not create satisfactory housing."

There have been many shifts in approach since Modernism and the Garden City, and the late 20th century situation is much more varied. Other approaches include green or ecological approaches, Postmodernism and Deconstructivism.

In the green approaches in Britain one can see links back to Morris and Howard in, for some, a growing disenchantment with technology and a growing interest in and understanding of ecology. John Farmer (1996) traces the origins of todays green sensibility back through sometimes neglected aspects of architectural history. He argues that it has always been there, just that at certain times other positions and aesthetics have dominated. He also argues that this is a contextual approach and will lead to its own aesthetics.

In the debates within architecture for and against Modernism and for and against Postmodernism and Deconstructivism, aesthetics has been central. With Postmodernism, colour and ornament returned but in another manifestation. Designers used external aesthetics to once more acknowledge links with the past, but in their particular interpretation of the general public's interpretation! This is a seemingly contextual and humane approach to design, but Menzies (1979) argues that it is neither contextual nor humane; it is, in his terms, "rejection through half acceptance".

Public debate about architecture in Britain is very fragmented. Interventions by HRH The Prince of Wales for example, although carrying some public sympathy, ironically seem to have increased divisions within the architectural profession and between the profession and the public. Two recent examples serve to illustrate both that the public cares about architecture and aesthetics, and yet that their views vary from design professionals. There was dismay at the unveiling of Daniel Libeskind's proposed deconstructivist extension to the very ornate, Victorian building of the Victoria and Albert Museum in London and, secondly, the proposal by English Heritage to "list" as part of our national heritage many post-war, high-rise concrete housing schemes, including both Alton West and Parkhill, was *"greeted with incredulity by the press"* (Building Design 1996). As Groat points out, there is current evidence of both a designer-user gap and of a designer-researcher gap:

"...as many architectural commentators (eg Safdie 1981, McLeod 1989) have observed, the more recent manifestations of post-modernism and deconstructivism have evidenced a purposeful antipathy not only to the epistemological assumptions of empirical research but also to the substantive concerns raised by non-architects - including both clients and environmental psychologists."

(L. Groat, 1995 p. 22)

Social and psychological research shows that the built environment is not solely a "container" for peoples lives but differentially perceived by them as the "context" of their lives. Rod Lawrence (1987) makes a strong case for a "contextual" approach to housing design and to housing research, which could benefit all sides, designers, users and researchers.

Social/psychological observations
From the wide range of social and psychological research into peoples' relationships with the built environment, I wish to comment on some aspects which have aesthetic implications, and which can have an important bearing on residents' physical and psychological health: nature, expressing identity and place attachment, human comfort and individual control.

The relationships between people and nature are being extensively studied. Uzzell's (1989) comprehensive review shows that many different approaches are now being employed and that our attachment to nature is important to our health and well-being.

Questions remain, however. It is not clear whether people have a different relationship with the built environment and the natural environment. And which natural aesthetics do we become attached to? Morris promoted the medieval English aesthetic at a time when most people in Britain were captivated by "exotic" landscapes. Spirn (1984) shows how American perceptions of nature in the city have been shaped by the English aesthetics of the country house estate. She argues that, as these planned landscapes are not self-regenerating, planting becomes "an expensive aesthetics" which modern cities now cannot afford. She then shows how to harness the vital social and physical benefits of plants in the urban setting, with indigenous and "wild", self-regenerating plants.

One of the tasks of our Green Audit Research Project at Kingston in investigating "green design" in Europe, is to consider through case studies of "good practice" certain social, cultural and contextual aspects of green design. How do attitudes of designers, clients and users change? How and when does this affect behaviour? Which parts of the design decision-making process are different?

When one considers the relationships between people and place, both developmental and environmental psychologists acknowledge that the early spatial exploration by the child is an important part of cognitive development. Researchers such as Clare Cooper Marcus (1974) and Proshansky (1983) also argue that the identification of place is an important part of the child's identification of self. David Canter's (1977) visual metaphor for the nature of places in his book *The Psychology of Place* shows an important recognition of the interaction between activities, conceptions and physical attributes in the individual's identification of place. Research shows the importance to individuals of both this early identification of place and of the subsequent identification with place, or place attachment (e.g. Gold & Burgess 1982, Lee 1982).

With regard to place attachment, Canter (1995) has recently observed in introducing Linda Groat's collection of papers on the meaning of places, that:

> "There is a great deal of productive debate about the cognitive and affective processes that give rise to this significance (of places), but it is clear that the significance of places can include both deep emotional attachment and more abstract aesthetic enjoyment. We are still some way off any general theory that links the emotional and the aesthetic importance of places and also incorporates a detailed account of the role of objective physical parameters in these experiences, but the present volume does show that the path to this objective is being cleared."
>
> Canter in Groat 1995 (p. vii).

Other aspects of human well-being include the individual's control of, and comfort in, the environment. Social and psychological research shows that people personalise their environments as a mechanism through which to exhibit some control over their environment; as a way of expressing their self-identity and as a mediator of social interactions (e.g. Rapoport 1968) (Fig. 1).

One outcome of this personalisation is aesthetic variety both inside and outside housing. In typically repetitive British terraced housing external features which are personalised include: front door colours and details, window frame colours and other window details, curtain designs and ornaments in the window, carriage lamps, and flower boxes, baskets and pots.

In state housing, particularly in high-rise concrete schemes, there are fewer possibilities for external personalisation and fewer are permitted. The schemes lack individual variety except for the curtaining and many residents do not perceive or appreciate the architectural differences in detailing which may have been employed. Some local authorities are now giving residents a choice of colours for their front doors, but many still have a policy of one colour per floor and so on. Following the recent change in government

Fig. 1. The private sphere of home (B. Cold).

policy under Mrs Thatcher to allow the sale of some state houses to their tenants, one can now walk through a state scheme and easily identify which properties have been sold, as their owners usually quickly change the front door and the windows!

Where residents have some control over their housing they can also make personal adjustments to achieve comfort. Research shows that there are large individual differences in perceptions of comfort and that one design will not be ideal for everyone. Other research shows that if people have some personal involvement in an environment then they perceive it more favourably (e.g. Brower 1988).

It can be seen that involving people in the design and/or management of their own housing environments has social and psychological advantages for the residents and implications for aesthetics, well-being and health (e.g. Becker 1977, Wener 1988, Lee 1996).

Educational observations
Finally I would like to share some observations as a teacher of architectural students. It seems to me that environmental psychology and other research overwhelmingly shows that the relationships between people and their physical settings are complex, dynamic and contextual.

In discussing aspects of aesthetics, well-being and health with students, I hope to suggest to them:

- that their perceptions of the built environment and its problems and solutions, may not be shared by others
- that perceptions are contextual
- that their ideas of aesthetically pleasing settings may not necessarily be shared
- that they cannot design the ideal environment, as their own perceptions and aspirations, and those for whom they are designing, will change over time
- that although what people consider aesthetically pleasing may change, people nevertheless seem to need to have something(s) they define as beautiful - that aesthetics does matter
- that there may be a special or different relationship between people and the natural environment.

I also hope to suggest to them that, as an approach to design, to bridge the designer-user gap (Zeisel 1981) they should consider:

- designing with people rather than for them, if possible
- conducting and/or learning from systematic studies of environments-in-

use, to both feed forward and to feedback to design
- leaving their designs open-ended to allow the users to express their identity, to allow some individual control and to enable fine tuning for well-being and comfort
- incorporating and/or learning from environmental psychology research as a way to see how environments have evolved over time to suit particular needs, and to understand what shapes and improves design decision making.

We must recognise that these issues present a challenge to designers, particularly those working within the conservative framework of architectural practice in Britain. Both designers and researchers should show an awareness of the gaps and strive to bridge them.

* Chintz - "Cotton cloth fast printed with particoloured pattern and usually glazed" (from the Hindi word meaning "spotted or variegated") from the Concise Oxford Dictionary.

References

Becker, F. (1977). *Housing Messages*. Dowden Hutchinson and Ross. USA.

Bishop, J. (1986). Milton Keynes: the best of both worlds? Public & professional views of a new city. *School for Advanced Urban Studies Occasional Paper No 24*, University of Bristol, UK.

Boudon, P. (1972). *Lived-in Architecture: Le Corbusier's Pessac Revisited*. Lund Humphries, London.

Brower, S. (1988). *Design in Familiar Places: What Makes Environments Look Good*. Praeger, USA.

Building Design (1996). Article September 6th 1996 p. 1 and p. 5.

Canter, D. (1977). *The Psychology Of Place*. Architectural Press, UK.

Canter, D. (1995). Preface to L. Groat (ed) *Giving Places Meaning: Readings in Environmental Psychology*. Academic Press, UK.

Cooper Marcus, C. (1974). The house as symbol of the self. In J. Lang (et al.) (eds) *Designing for Human Behavior: Architecture and the Behavioral Sciences*. Dowden Hutchinson & Ross, USA pp. 130-146.

Farmer, J. (1996). *Green Shift: Towards a Green Sensibility in Architecture*. WWF and Butterworths, UK.

Fishman, R. (1977). *Urban Utopias in the Twentieth Century.* MIT Press, USA.

Frank, A. (1995). *The Diary of Anne Frank.* Macmillan Childrens Books. London, UK.

Gold, J. & Burgess, J. (eds) (1982). *Valued Environments.* Allen and Unwin, UK.

Groat, L. (1995). Introduction: place, aesthetic evaluation and home. In L. Groat (ed) *Giving Places Meaning: Readings in Environmental Psychology.* Academic Press, UK, pp. 1-26.

Lawrence, R. (1987). *Housing, Dwellings and Homes: Design Theory, Research and Practice.* Wiley, UK.

Lee, S. A. (1982). The value of the local area. In J. Gold & J. Burgess (eds) *Valued Environments.* Allen and Unwin, UK, pp. 161-171.

Lee, S. A. (1996). Developments since Black Road and Byker: participative housing in Britain. In Y. Marin (ed) *European Urban Space Colloquium Proceedings.* Annales LittÈraires. BesanÁon, France, pp. 203-240.

McLeod, M. (1989). Architecture and politics in the Reagan era: from postmodernism to deconstructivism. *Assemblage* 8 February, pp. 23-59.

Maxwell, R. (1975). Two housing schemes at Milton Keynes. *Architects Journal* 10th December, pp. 1247 - 1260.

Menzies, M. (1979). Rejection by half-acceptance: The fate of man in environmental design. *Architectural Psychology Newsletter,* Vol. 9, No. 3, pp.22-26.

Oliver, P. (et al.) (1981). *Dunroaming: The Suburban Semi and Its Enemies.* Barrie & Jenkins, London.

Proshansky, H. (et al.) (1983). Place identity: physical world and socialisation of the self. *Journal of Environmental Psychology,* Vol. 3, pp. 57-83.

Rapoport, A. (1968). The personal element in housing: an argument for open-ended design. *Royal Institute of British Architects (RIBA) Journal,* July.

Rees, R. (1993). *Interior Landscapes: Gardens and the Domestic Environment.* Johns Hopkins University Press, USA.

Safdie, M. (1981). Private jokes in public places. *Atlantic Monthly,* December, pp. 14-32.

Scoffham, E. R. (1984). *The Shape of British Housing.* George Godwin, UK.

Spirn, A. Whiston (1984). *The Granite Garden: Urban Nature and Human Design.* Basic Books, New York, USA.

Uzzell, D. (1989). People, nature and landscape: an environmental psychological perspective. *Monograph for the Landscape Research Group,* UK.

Wener, R. (1988). Doing it Right: examples of successful application of environment behavior research. *Journal of Architectural and Planning Research.* Vol. 5, No. 4, pp. 284-303.

Williams, R. (1973). *The Country and the City.* Oxford University Press, UK.

Zeisel, J. (1981). *Inquiry by Design: Tools for Environment-behavior Research.* Brooks Cole, California, USA.

Reflections on Concepts of Aesthetics, Health and Well-being

Byron Mikellides

How has environmental research influenced architecture?

"Let him be educated, skilful with the pencil, instructed in geometry, know much theory, have followed the philosophers with attention, understand music, have some knowledge of medicine, know the opinions of the jurists, and be acquainted with astronomy and the theory of the heavens."
Vitruvius, Book I on the Education of the Architect

Architectural psychology, environmental psychology, man/woman-environment studies, human factors of design or the ontoperivantic aspects of psychostructural environics, call it what you may, has been concerned explicitly or implicitly over the past 25 years with the concepts of aesthetics, health and well-being. These preoccupations have also strong undertones of the Vitruvian concepts of "commodity", "firmness" and "delight". The main difference, however, between these concepts now as opposed to Vitruvius' times is that the education of the architect has changed direction from theology, astronomy and music to an appeal to the social and behavioural sciences including psychology, sociology, neurophysiology and anthropology. Is the architect better off now and how much do we know and practice the new knowledge? These are questions the reader of this volume compiled by Professor Birgit Cold for the Norwegian Research Council, should be able to find the answer to.

The aim of this essay is to provide the reader with a "confession paper", as Bigit Cold puts it, based on the knowledge and experience of teaching Architectural Psychology to architecture students since the subject was born in 1969 at the House of Black Dell in Dalandhui, Scotland and the first conference proceedings were published by the RIBA and edited by David Canter.

There are at least three questions which need to be addressed:

1. Have research, conferences, books and journals contributed to an increase in our knowledge on the subject?
2. Has this knowledge been communicated to designers of the built environment as witnessed through the practice of architecture?
3. Has there been a change in attitudes after putting this research knowledge into the educational curriculum and after it has been facilitated by professional groups and institutions such as local authorities and professional

bodies, both at the national level (e.g. the RIBA) and the international level (e.g. EEC Directive)?

In 1969 there were very few books from mainstream psychology or sociology which designers found inspiring or relevant to the practice of their profession. Richard Gregory's *Eye and Brain*, first published in 1966, was one such book from experimental psychology, as was Michael Argyle's *The Psychology of Interpersonal Behaviour* published in 1967, which considered psychological needs and motivation in social psychology. Ervin Goffman's book *Behaviour in Public Places*, published in 1963 was another major contribution from Sociology. *The Hidden Dimension*, by anthropologist Edward Hall, published in 1966, was another such book discussing ethological issues, proxemics and cross-cultural differences in space requirements. Nico Tinburgen, John Calhoun, Robert Ardrey and Konrad Lorenz were the predecessors of Oscar Newman and Alice Coleman in the '70s, '80s and '90s, discussing the modern equivalents of territoriality and personal space within the new concepts of defensible space, surveillance and vandal-proof architecture.

Roger Barker's pioneering work in ecological psychology and his book *The Stream of Behaviour*, published in 1963, Kevin Lynch's *The Image of the City*, from 1960, and Terence Lee's work on mental mapping applications were significant landmarks of what was to follow. In the field of experimental aesthetics, Daniel Berlyne's book *Aesthetics and Psychobiology*, as well as Rikard Küller's *Semantic Model for Describing Perceived Environments* came after the first conference in 1971.

A body of specialised knowledge began to evolve in the 1970s and new publications included Proshansky, Ittelson and Rivlin's book on *Environmental Psychology*, David Canter's *Psychology for Architects*, James Gibson's *Ecological Approach to Visual Perception*, Neil Prak's *Perception of the Visual Environment*, Charles Moore's *Body Memory and Architecture*, and Byron Mikellides' *Architecture for People*.

Schools of architecture introduced the subject in various guises, ranging from human aspects of design to courses in architectural psychology or as part of history and theory. Terence Lee and David Canter moved from St Andrews and Strathclyde to the University of Surrey to offer the first MSc

TABLE 1. ARCHITECTURAL PSYCHOLOGY (AP) CONFERENCES (IAPS) 1969 – 1996

PLACE	DATE	PUBLISHER	THEME
Dalandhui, Scotland	1969	ed Canter	Architectural Psychology
Kingston, London	1970	ed Honikman	Architectural Psychology
Lund, Sweden	1973	ed Küller	Architectural Psychology
Surrey, England	1973	eds Lee & Canter	AP and Built Environment
Sheffield, England	1975	ed Smith	Education and Participation
Strasbourg, France	1976	ed Korosec Serfaty	Space Appropriation
Louvain La Neuve, Belgium	1979	ed Simon	Conflicting Experiences of Space
Surrey, England	1979	eds Lee, Canter, Stringer	Environmental Psychology
Barcelona, Spain	1982	ed Pol	Man – Environment Qualitative Aspects
Berlin, Germany	1984	ed Krampen	Environment and Human Action
Haifa, Israel	1986	ed Churchman	Environments in Transition
Delft, Holland	1988	ed Prak	Looking Back to the Future
Ankara, Turkey	1990	eds Pamiv, Imamoglu, Teymur	Culture, Space, History
Halkidiki, Greece	1992	eds Mazis, Karaletson, Tsoukala	Socio-Environmental Metamorphoses
Manchester, England	1994	ed Symes	The Urban Experience
Stockholm, Sweden	1996	ed Vestbro	Changing Ways of Life, Values and Design Practices

Fig. 1. Table 1 - Architectural Psycology Conferences (IAPS) 1969 - 1996.

course in environmental psychology outside the context of a school of Architecture. In Lund, Sweden we saw the first Department of Theoretical and Applied Aesthetics formed, which hosted the third international conference on the subject. In fact, the development of the subject can be seen in the 16 conferences on architecture psychology, where the scope was widened in 1988 to IAPS - an organisation developed to promote research and communication of these concerns about people and environments in theory and practice. Future historians will be able to assess objectively the contribution of this subject during the last 25 years within the various relevant social sciences, as well as its impact on the design professions. At this early stage, one can only undertake a "content analysis" of its development reflected in the papers presented and published at the various conferences, as well as the title themes of these events. The location and theme of these conferences, where appropriate, are given in Table 1 (Fig. 1) and the atmosphere of two of these gatherings is illustrated vividly by the best-known architectural cartoonist, Louis Hellman (Fig. 2). It should be noted that no conference picked the theme of experimental or architectural aesthetics as its main concern, although some papers have been published on the subject in the various conferences.

In addition to the books and conference proceedings, there have been many papers in the psychological and the architectural journals with specific themes of these diverse subjects. The *Journal of Environmental Psychology* was published at the University of Surrey and the *Architectural Psychology Newsletters*, published by Sue-Ann Lee at Kingston, have kept researchers in touch with each other over the years. The *Journal of Architecture and Planning Review*, published in the USA, had also contributed with Raymond Lifchez's special issue entitled *Designing with People in Mind*, followed by his book *Rethinking Architecture*, which highlighted his concern about accessible architecture to disabled groups.

The verdict on the first question raised at the beginning of this essay is that a considerable amount of new knowledge and research has been accumulated over the years in different guises dealing with matters of aesthetics, health and well-being. How this knowledge has been communicated to designers practising their profession and to students of architecture aspiring to influence our future living environments is the second question which needs to be addressed.

When we look at the real world of architecture, the vast majority of this research has gone unnoticed. Some architects are sceptical about its value in

Fig. 2. Courtship in the House of Blackdell - Dalandhui, 1969, by Louis Hellman.

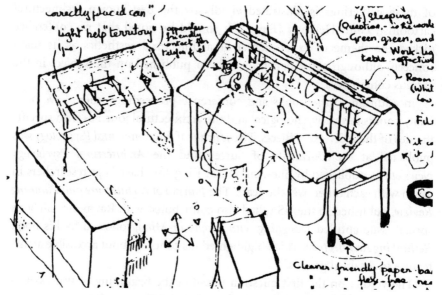

Fig. 3. An Office Landscape by Ralph Erskine (a detail),
published in Architecture for People (1980).

design and, as a consequence, design awards are given primarily for imagination and originality at the expense of the users' health and well-being. Niels Prak's book *Architects, the Noted and the Ignored* provides us with a useful analysis of the self-image and self-esteem of the profession and records the different value systems of the professional as opposed to the user. However, a growing number of established and up-and-coming architects are offering a glimpse of hope for the future when both originality and aesthetics, as well as understanding and catering for people's needs, are brought together. In these cases, the architects put the health and well-being of their clients at the top of their list.

Ralph Erskine is one such architect. Just to take one example we can look at his work in the Pågens bakery in Malmo, Sweden, he has considered the occupants' psychological needs such as the balance between "contact" and "privacy" as well as "identity" and "personalisation" while remaining very much aware of the occupants' differences in terms of personality and values, as well as the need to change the open-plan Office Landscape for various activities, whether co-operative or competitive. One could see this genuine concern about the users in the sketch he made for *Architecture for People* edited in 1980 (Fig. 3). One can also notice from the handwritten notes on the sketch that he is deeply aware of the research of Robert Sommer (Fig. 4 and Fig. 5) and Edward Hall on proxemics, personal space, social distance and territoriality, as well as the social psychological literature on human needs. His comment at the bottom of the page that *"neither buildings nor furniture solve social or psychological problems, but hopefully they can help"*, shows that he has grasped the concept of "architectural determinism" just right (i.e. he does not make extra-

Seating Arrangement	Condition 1 (conversing)	Condition 2 (conversing)	Condition 3 (co-acting)	Condition 4 (competing)
	63%	83%	13%	12%
	17%	7%	36%	25%
	20%	10%	51%	63%
TOTAL	100%	100%	100%	100%

Fig. 4. Seating preferences at round tables for different activities. This typical finding adapted from Robert Sommer's research in the 1960s shows distinct preferences for adjacent chairs for people who wanted to converse or work together. In a competitive situation participants preferred to sit directly across from each other (to stimulate visual competition).

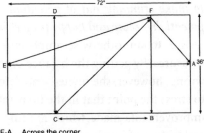

F-A   Across the corner
C-B   Side by side
C-D   Across the table
E-A   From one end to the other
E-F   Diagonally the length of the table
C-F   Diagonally across the table

Fig. 5. Relationship between seating positions and conversations. Another study by Robert Sommer and Humphrey Osgood investigated in depth the relationship between conversation and seating arrangements in the context of a hospital cafeteria. People sitting in the F - A orientation (across the corner) conversed twice as much as the C - B orientation (side by side), which in turn was three times as frequent as those in the C - D orientation (across the table). No conversations were observed in the other orientations.

vagant claims nor does he reject the role of the creative and caring architect in improving and facilitating more humane environments).

This is where I believe Alice Coleman has got it wrong. While following and replicating the work of Oscar Newman on defensible space and surveillance, she has stressed far too much design improvement as the sole factor for health and well-being. Refurbishment, management, security and landscape improvements could be just as important, however, depending on each problematic estate in its own location, whether high-rise or not. Even Oscar Newman commented that *"'Utopia on Trial' does not pay sufficient attention to social factors interacting with the physical as causes of housing disfunction"*. As for her comment that Utopian designs *"have tipped the balance sufficiently to make criminals out of potentially law-abiding citizens and victims out of potentially secure and happy people"* it is emotive language which does not do justice to an otherwise important piece of research using unobtrusive measures. By getting the balance of the concept of architectural determinism wrong, however, she invited criticism discrediting the research. She also fails to stress the point that in the final analysis it is not so much the actual design improvements made which are important but the exercise of participation and feeling of involvement of residents in the design process which contributes to the residents' well-being.

There are other architects who should be mentioned in this context who have contributed through their architecture and writing to designing with people in mind through their own idiosyncratic approaches to making healthier and happier places for people to live in.

Christoph Schulten's sensitive participation projects in Aachen and Bavaria; Walter Segal's projects in Lewisham and Stutgart University self-build housing for students; Phil Bixby's work with unemployed groups in the north of England; Herman Hertzberger's attempt to get people involved with their surroundings, each other and themselves; Lucien Kroll's motto *"no inhabitant participation, no plans"* and the late Charles Moore's dictum that *"buildings, if they are to succeed, must be able to receive a great deal of human energy and store it, and even repay it with interest"* are all genuine, non cosmetic attempts to consider, interpret and translate in their own way the concepts of aesthetics, health and well-being at their drawing boards.

However well briefed, well prepared and motivated the architect may be there will usually be problems and conflicts which cannot easily be solved. A case in point is the exemplary "Hartcliffe" project at Bristol carried out in 1969. In this pioneering experiment the architects, clients and psychologists worked together on the proposed move of an industrial and commercial complex (Wills Tobacco Co) from the centre of Bristol to the Hartcliffe suburb. The aim of the experiment was to collect the people's reactions to the proposed move, their anxieties and feelings, as well as to consider their views on amenities and working conditions. Another objective of the study, according to Brian Wells, was *"not only to promote efficiency but to promote happiness and add something to the quality of people's working lives".* The pilot study, the interviewing, the structural questionnaires and the objective analysis of data used the latest scientific techniques, yet there were problems in, for example, translating the company's desire for a single, communal dining facility (to bring together all grades of factory and all office workers) as employees wanted the hierarchy of dining facilities that they were used to. Architects, clients and psychologists had to meet again, re-educate themselves and consider how changing values in society are tempered with the users' practical wishes.

There is another problem which arises, even in the best intended experiments. There is no feedback on how successful these experiments are. How can we learn without this information? Fortunately, in the above experiment, a second-year architectural student, Jonathan Loxton, went back, as part of his Environmental Psychology course, to Hartcliffe 16 years after it was built; he found that the "caring company" was not just an image but that the users were genuinely happy about working at the Wills factory, with an interesting caveat. They would have liked to have been briefed more about the visual aesthetics of the exterior of the factory which, although it won design awards, they thought looked like a "rusty biscuit tin". Maybe another experiment to investigate the gap in taste between the professional and the user is in order.

However encouraging this example may be of architects designing with people in mind, and even though there have been a few experiments here and there, by far the best of way of communicating the new body of knowledge is through education. Architectural students may see and study some of these successful architectural experiments but, while a few may be inspired and attempt to emulate their masters, the opportunity of critically evaluating the validity and reliability of their work in formal teaching and studio projects is so unique that to ignore it is to perpetuate the naive view that architecture is only an art at the expense of articulating form which reflects human life and emotion.

I believe that by far the main contribution of psychology in architectural education is made in the first three years of the course and that once the groundwork has been laid down it does not matter what formal course in psychology or human factors the student pursues afterwards. The fact is that by this time all the students of architecture have been instilled with a "psychological eye" and are better equipped to search for those aspects they have not considered in their designs before. The criterion of success is not to be found in the practical rules of thumb that are acquired, but in the general frame-work and awareness of the nature of science in relation to our aesthetic and social needs. A few of the students will pursue some of these ideas and objective methods of evaluation further; others will concentrate on a more theoretical interest somewhere along the man/woman-environment continuum, and a tiny majority will apply for a higher degree in environmental psychol-ogy at Surrey. But by far the greatest majority of architects will not do that but will, instead, practise their profession. It is this group of architects that we are most interested in. I held this belief in 1968 when I started teaching the subject. Over the past 29 years we have produced more that 2,500 graduates in architecture who have studied architectural psychology, not as an option but as an integral part of their three-year course in architec-tural studies. Students like the subject now no less or more than they did then, and they see its relevance to architectural education in Term 1, Year 1 (see Appendix 1). Architectural psychology has not been just a fashionable subject like many other trendy theories, philosophies or subjects, such as semiology, phenomenology, deconstruction, ergonomics, simulation and nowadays chaos and catastrophe theory and quantum physics, not to mention virtual reality, whilst ignoring down-to-earth reality. Architecture should not only cater to selfish hooligan interventions but also, and to a larger degree, to pragmatic and habitable and healthy buildings which may not win design awards but can provide the inhabitants with pleasure and joy.

Unfortunately, despite this positive contribution that psychology could have in architectural education, there is little evidence that it is taught, let alone integrated within the architectural curriculum. Amber Beare (1993) carried out the only survey I have found of the 36 schools of architecture in the UK with a 60% return rate. Beare found that only parts of the subject are covered - human factors, colour theory and space perception being the most popular topics. The most popular book in the curriculum is Oscar Newman's *Defensible Space*. The only other survey of its kind is a cross-cultural comparison between Sweden and England on colour research in architectural education by Jan Janssens (Lund) and Byron Mikellides (Oxford). A total of 448 students in five Swedish and British universities took part in testing the students' knowledge on colour psychology, colour systems, myths and beliefs about colour. Despite the respondents' positive attitudes towards colour research, their actual knowledge based on the coverage of the subject in lectures and studios was very poor in both countries. We think these results are typical and represent the situation in other schools of architecture in both countries.

The architect who has had no training in psychology or human aspects of design as part of his/her education will either completely dismiss research in architectural psychology as being of no practical usefulness whatsoever (because he/she fails to understand it), or may view it with unrealistic enthusiasm, awe, or even see it as panacea for the complex problems of modern society. This is aptly illustrated by the Government's eagerness to apply Alice Coleman's ideas on solving crime and vandalism overnight as an easy, short-term solution. The emphasis should *not* be on psychology *after* the architect has qualified in terms of research projects, post-graduate courses or higher degrees, but on it being of his/her development of other concepts of architecture should also develop concepts of psychological nature too. The old proverb "prevention is better than cure" applies here as well. Perhaps we should move some of the emphasis away from architectural psychology towards a psychological architecture.

While the concepts of health and well-being may include the psychological needs of identity, control, security, experience and pleasantness, the concept of aesthetics entails different philosophical, psychological and practical considerations. However difficult, it can be tackled immediately in the first year of architectural education in a sensible and sensitive way by looking

Fig. 6. Westonbirt (B. Cold).

at beautiful elements and structures in nature and the built environment. This is what we do in a project in Year 1. By appealing to nature which has been in the design business for one hundred million years, as well as experiencing nature during the changing of the autumn colours at Westonbirt Arboretum (Fig. 6) and then driving to the beautiful city of Bath (Fig. 7), students begin to understand the concepts of rhyme - both synchronic and diachronic - as well as rhythm, balance and harmony.

They also see how these concepts have been used since antiquity; here we go back to the Vitruvius quotation at the beginning of the essay: the training in geometry and philosophy, the golden section and theories of proportion, astronomy and especially music where rhyme and contrast are an integral part of a musical composition. Perhaps we go back to basics. Students also see the relevance of poetry and Gerald Manley Hopkins' "platonic dialogue", Andy Goldsworthy, Victor Vasarely and the methods of structuralism. They may also study Küller's model of aesthetic experience relating the concepts of complexity and unity to physiological arousal. Architectural examples proposed by Professor Peter F. Smith in *Architecture and the Principle of Harmony* and the outstanding work of evolutionary biologist Nicholas

Fig. 7. Bath (B. Cold).

Humphrey are the backbone of this project. The reader of this essay can see in Appendix I the full brief for this project as carried out over the past 20 years by first-year students. During this period it has been consistently considered by students as one of the best projects they have in Year 1 and, even more encouragingly, students use the concepts learned throughout their five years at school. These are the people who will be practising aesthetics in the future and this project is a good start.

It is one thing to know about psychological needs and even to be able to recite from memory Henry Murray's list of twenty* and another thing to isolate the relevant ones for a defined problem within a particular social or cultural context. (*These needs in alphabetical order are: Abasement, Achievement, Autonomy, Counteraction, Defedance, Deference, Dominance, Exhibition, Harm-Avoidance, Nurturance, Order, Play, Rejection, Sentience, Sex, Saccorance and Understanding). *Knowing* about human needs is an important first step, *understanding* these needs a vital second, but evoking and expressing them through their *translation* in built form is a culminant third. It is at this stage that the creativity and aesthetic sensitivity that is demanded of the architect becomes the critical factor. At this point, the archi-

Fig. 8. Revitalizing Hope in Diversity - Lund 1974, by Louis Hellman.

tect may need to be inspired by nature and art, or go out to learn from experience what natural structures people find beautiful, as well as from architectural precedent and Post Occupancy Evaluation studies. Then he or she may return to the drawing board and try to emulate these structures in design not by naively mimicking natural objects but by being inspired by the 'relations between the artificial elements exhibiting the felicitous rhymes of natural beauty'. It is at this stage too that we might all breathe a sigh of relief, as there is obviously no single solution: there is no prescribed answer to a design problem, and a building cannot be based on an unvarying systematic approach alone, without art. It is in this marriage of interests, and in this understanding, that the architect's truly creative role resides.

There is no better time than now to consider how the research concepts of aesthetics, health and well-being can be communicated to the design professions. By far the best way is through education, especially now that the EEC Directive, Article 3 (see Appendix II), prescribes that architects should be trained and educated, in addition to design and technical expertise in aesthetics and the human sciences. In fact, six out of the eleven requirements touch on those aspects. Nor is it a coincidence that the RIBA strategic study carried out this year in the UK by the previous President, Frank Duffy, and to be published next year sees that the top priority for change as perceived by staff in schools of architecture is "a greater focus on design from human/social needs" (Fig. 8). Students also consider it as an important priority. This anthology of ideas and research on aesthetic health and well-being prepared for the Norwegian Research Council by Birgit Cold is a timely and gentle reminder.

APPENDIX I - PSYCHOLOGY OF AESTHETICS PROJECT BRIEF (YEAR 1)

Aesthetic principles often unformulated, continually affect the way we lead our lives. In your recent design, you have made decisions on colour, shape and their arrangement in space. Why these decisions? Why have you selected the music, sights smells and other feelings around you?

The word aesthetics comes from the Greek word "aestheticos" which means things perceptible to the senses, as opposed to "noitos" which means thinkable. The word has been misapplied in German by Baumgartem as meaning "criticism of taste". The operational definition of aesthetics in this project is the perception of the beautiful by our senses. For the purpose of this project avoid political, economic, sociological and semiological interpretations of Aesthetics. You will hear about these from your studio tutors in the years to come.

In psychology, we will look at the function of man's appreciation of beauty and the extent to which it is important for his biological survival based on the original work of Nicholas Humphrey and Peter F. Smith. The general aim of the project is to pursue the advice of the Scottish philosopher Thomas Reid: *"By a careful examination of the objects to which Nature hath given this amiable quality of Beauty"*, we may perhaps discover some real excellence in the object or at least some valuable purpose that is served by the effect which produces it.

The theoretical position we will take is not based on the cynicism of critics of aesthetics, such as Clive Bell, stating that *"any system of aesthetics which pretends to be based on some objective truth is palpably ridiculous as not to be worth discussing"*, but on William Empsom who wrote: *"critics are of two sorts: those who merely relieve themselves against the flower of beauty and those less continent who afterwards scratch it up."* (Ian Davis once commented on his introductory talk to first year students at Oxford " ... *after you look at a building for five hours you may perhaps discover why you liked it* . . ." .)

The problem of looking at common principles behind apparent diversity is not easy. Humphrey suggested that the breakthrough in the field of aesthetics came through applying methods of structuralism: *"the essence of beauty is in the relations formed between the perceived elements. But it is one thing to point to the importance of relations, another to say what relations are important and yet another to say why."* This is what you will attempt to do in this project. A start to our expedition may be found in the work of the poet Gerard Manley Hopkins. Read his "platonic dialogue" between a tutor and his student walking in the gardens of New College, Oxford in 1865 (Reference 1). Go to New College and experience it all first hand. *"Then the beauty of the oak and the chestnut-fan and the sky is a mixture of likeness and difference . . . And if we did not feel the likeness we should not feel them so beautiful." "In fact it seems to me that rhyme is the epitome of our principle. All beauty may by a metaphor be called rhyme, may it not?"* Taking rhyme as an example of beauty *"why do we like the relation which rhyme epitomises? What is the biological advantage of seeking out rhyming elements in the environment?"*

The answer according to prominent zoologists such as Nicholas Humphrey is this: . . . *"Considered as a biological phenomenon, aesthetic preferences stem from a predisposition among animals and men to seek out experiences through which they may learn to classify the objects in the world about them. Beautiful structures in nature or in art are those which facilitate the task of classification by presenting evidence of the taxonomic relations between things in a way which is informative and easy to grasp."*

Classification is the core of learning: Consider the work of Aristotle and Plato. Children have a thirst to know "what things are". Animals will work to be exposed to new sensory stimuli. "Stimulus novelty" is the most universal reinforcer of behaviour known - a challenge to incorporate new material into their model of the world.

Animals are not interested in thoroughly familiar things nor in total chaos. (Consider the balance between complexity and unity and its relationship to stimulation - R. Küller, 1980.)

Complexity
_____

Unity
_____

Understimulation ---------- Adequate ---------- Overstimulation

Psychologists called rhyme "stimulus discrepancy"; men who have been exposed for some time to a particular sensory stimulus respond with pleasure to minor variations from that stimulus (McClelland, 1953). Human babies made familiar with a particular abstract visual pattern take pleasure in seeing new patterns which are minor transformations of the original (Kagan 1970).

Consider the beauty of a flower: Flowers have a universal appeal to men and women of all cultures, all classes, all ages. Look at the static form of a simple flower such as a daisy. The petals, stamen and leaves are three sets of contrasting elements. Each petal in turn differs in detail from the other members of its class yet shares their distinctive shape and colour and the same is true for the stamen and the leaves. The features that serve to unite each set serve at the same time to separate one set from another. But more than this, while the flowers of one species rhyme with each other, the rhyme is given added sharpness by contrasting rhymes of different species. This static rhyme we may call synchronic rhyme.

Consider also a flower in its kinetic form - the living flower in its continual state of growth, changing its form from day to day; the transformations which occur as the flower buds, blossoms and decays give rise to a temporal rhyme we may call diachronic rhyme.

But we can also find rhyme and variation of a theme in inanimate objects, mountain peaks, pebbles on the beach, clouds, raindrops, in Debbie Macy's slides, in Birgit Cold's pictograms, in spiders' webs, in the paintings of your chosen artist. For example in modern abstract art some of Vasarely's paintings can be considered as a "visual poem" built up on the basis of rhyme and contrast between the visual elements. Andy Goldsworthy writes *every so often I need to teach the structures in which I work, loose control, and explore the unknown and random ... It is easy to make a mess. The task is to touch on new orders in chaos from somewhere deep within, so that form becomes more than merely a container for disorder*" (Nov. 1991). In music – the purest expression of structural relations – rhyme is a form of thematic variation, a simple melody repeated in a series of variations. As in a poem contrast is needed to highlight the unity of the rhyming elements. Rhyme and variation of a theme are not only found in visual and auditory stimuli but in olfactory, tactile stimulation. Consider also the aesthetic appreciation of the visually handicapped.

Let's go out and look at nature (Westonbirt Arboretum, New Forest, Shotover - 15 minutes' walk from this university - even "Mesopotamia" the university park in the centre of Oxford) and search for both SYNCHRONIC and DIACHRONIC rhyme. Then return to the urban landscape and try to find rhyme in structures you consider beautiful whether Oxford, Bath or Chester.

At a simple level look at those buildings or details which mimic nature, but you can go beyond this; you do not need to concentrate on the naive naturalism which would have each element mimic a natural object. We do not want cities tarted up to look like alpine meadows. (e.g. Herb Green's Chicken House in Oklahoma, or the plastic cows designed and located in Milton Keynes). "We want cities in which relations between the artificial elements exhibit the well chosen rhymes of natural beauty". Search for both SYNCHRONIC and DIACHRONIC rhyme in the natural and urban environment. Learn from nature and enjoy the project.

Definitions

Synchronic: syn-chronic : at the same time
(occurring at the same time, simultaneously)
Diachronic: dia-chronic : across time
(comparisons we make through time)
Taxonomy: (arrangement) classification especially in relation to its general laws or principles

Basic Reading: Three articles in *Architecture for People*, Studio Vista 1980:
N. Humphrey, *Natural Aesthetics*, pp. 59-73
P. F. Smith, *Urban Aesthetics*, pp. 74-86
R. Küller, *Architecture & Emotions*, pp. 87-100

Additional References
1. Gerald Manley Hopkins   *The Penguin Poets*
2. Peter F. Smith   *Rhyme with Reason:* Article in Information Centre
3. Peter F. Smith   *Architecture & the Principle of Harmony,* 1987 RIBA

4. Karl Blossfelt	*Art Forms in Nature*
5. ITV Film	Westonbirt Arboretum, 1996
6. J. White	*Autumn Colour at Westonbirt*, Forestry Commission
7. J. Stewart	*Rhyme the Essence of Beauty* (6th Year Thesis), 1981
	The Work of Aalvar Aalto
8. Andy Goldsworthy	Andy Goldsworthy, Viking, 1987
9. James Gleick & Eliot Porter	CHAOS and *Nature's chaos*, Cardinal, 1987 & 1991
10. Ralf Weber	*On the Aesthetics of Architecture*, Ethnoscapes. Avebury, 1995
11. Birgit Cold	Sketches and Pictograms, 1994

Assessment of the aesthetics project

You are to prepare a small presentation in the form of a visual presentation of a static display resulting from your observations and understanding of the psychology of aesthetics field trips and other experiences. You are to consider the idea of Synchronic Rhyme and Diachronic Rhyme as described in the brief and the basic required reading. Examples should be drawn from contrasting situations in the environment and certainly should include material from both the man made world (buildings) and nature (gardens, parks, woodland). You may use a medium of your choice including photographs, laser colour prints, drawings and diagrams.

Presentation

Choose a theme which acts as a good vehicle for your ideas. Design a presentation in the form of a static display consisting of images and words in the form of text, on two A1 cardboard. The display should be self-explanatory and not require a verbal explanation to be appreciated.

APPENDIX II EEC DIRECTIVE (ONLY ARTICLE 3)

Article 3

Education and training leading to diplomas, certificates and other evidence of formal qualifications referred to in Article 2 shall be provided through courses of studies at university level concerned principally with architecture. Such studies shall be balanced between the theoretical and practical aspects of architectural training and shall ensure the acquisition of:

1. an ability to create architectural designs that satisfy both aesthetic and technical requirements;
2. an adequate knowledge of the history and theories of architecture and the related arts, technologies and *human science*;
3. a knowledge of the fine arts as an influence on the quality of architectural design;
4. an adequate knowledge of urban design, planning and the skills involved in the planning process;
5. *an understanding of the relationship between people and buildings, and between buildings and their environment, and of the need to relate buildings and the spaces between them to human needs and scale;*
6. *an understanding of the profession of architecture and the role of the architect in society, in particular in preparing briefs that take account of social factors;*
7. *an understanding of the methods of investigation and preparation of the brief for a design project;*
8. an understanding of the structural design, constructional and engineering problems associated with building design;
9. an adequate knowledge of physical problems and technologies and of the function of buildings so as to provide them with internal conditions of **comfort** and protection against the climate;
10. the necessary design skills to meet building **users' requirements** within the constraints imposed by cost factors and building regulations;
11. an adequate knowledge of the industries, organisations, regulations and procedures involved in translating design concepts into buildings and integrating plans into overall planning.

Aesthetics in the Built Environment and its Influence on the User

Kaj Noschis

*Can beauty be a mediator between us
and "the unknown"?*

Introduction

As a psychologist who has been teaching for many years in a very design-studio oriented school of architecture my preoccupation has increasingly become to find a way of discussing the user's experience of built space in terms architects can acknowledge. Most of my architect colleagues feel that there is no special need for lectures on the user or dweller as an essential ingredient of an architectural project. On the one hand, architects are themselves users and, on the other hand, they prefer to rely on past experiences, whether of functions, materials, construction procedures or forms as experienced by human beings. The curriculum for the architecture studies is a synthesis of this past knowledge with discussions of a variety of examples and views. Thus, so the argument goes, users are implicitly always in the centre of the project as past experiences are analysed in terms of what users and designers have learned from them. With this knowledge the architect can concentrate on planning and designing shapes, construction details and colours in accordance with the cultural and contextual setting that will give the future building its unique quality, this being the essence of architecture, its beauty. The beauty of the buildings is then recognized and admired first of all by other architects and eventually also by the general public. Beauty's relations to the well-being of the users is never stated explicitly, it is implied that beautiful buildings are better for the users as well. This is how students are taught in our school, so those who eventually come to my lectures first of all have to be convinced that there is more to be known about the user that might be relevant for the designer. As aesthetics is quite at the core of the studio-teaching, to capture the students' interest. I discuss specifically the psychological model of man that is referred to when we look at architecture as beautiful design. In this paper I would like to take a look at aspects of this model.

Framing the aesthetic experience

What is the beauty of architecture - defined in the above terms as the unique quality of a built space - for the immediate user of a built space? In light of my own research I have come to consider this beauty with respect to time to be momentary and with respect to content to act as mediator between man and the unknown. Most of the time people "just go about doing their things" without caring about what their environment looks like. Yet this does not mean that the aesthetic quality of the built environment is not important to people. Those moments when they are aware of the environment's characteristics might be existentially very important. These might be called *moments of connection*, phenomena which I will expand upon here. Let us consider that an architectural work acts as a mediator between man and the unknown around him, and that this might psychologically offer a key for understanding the aesthetic dimension of architecture for the user. One, of course, could counter that modern man is no longer surrounded by an unknown world. Our ancestors may have been afraid, but today we do not have the same fear of the elements because not only do we have explanations for them, we also have tools for keeping these hazards at bay. All the same, we have no more control over the onslaught of natural forces, whether floods, storms or hurricanes, than we have over an outbreak of disease, an accident or sudden death. And when such events do occur, we are always left to seek our own answers to the questions: Why me? Why him or why now?

To some extent we can rectify and remedy ills beforehand, and knowing that we can do so is a source of relief, but still we have to live with uncertainty about what the future holds. If bearing this in mind we think about, say, our home, apartment, or summer retreat, it is not a place that simply provides shelter from the cold and the wet; it also affords us psychological protection. Thus, still today, the home protects man against the unknown. The word *shelter* refers to that familiar symbol, the shell, something that comes between us and the rest of the world.

Mediator objects

Something like the above is what I have in mind when I talk of *the mediator*. The mediator calms fears, makes helplessness more bearable, gives security, provides a link with the unknown. At a more elementary level we could say that the mediator acts as a filter between us and the outer world. Here we have the opportunity to look more closely at this phenomenon of the mediator. We are all successors of Freud, or, if the thought of being included with his lot does not appeal, of the Romantics. At any rate we should ask whether all the unknown, mysterious forces that we fear from time to time are outside - outside ourselves, that is - or whether they are also within us. Could there be something so unknown and so mysterious within us? I think that we, especially as progeny of Freud and the Romantics, should take this possibility into account. Each one of us has an unknown inner self that tends to cause much the same trouble as external forces. I believe that architecture might also be viewed as a mediator here, as a filter between us and the mysterious forces concealed within us, at those *moments* when this is needed.

I shall give three examples of what it means to be a mediator. Let us examine the object in general from this angle, from the definition according to which object is a tool or instrument to be used against the unknown forces hidden in nature or within ourselves. This perspective emphasizes the psychological significance of the object.

My first example is an amulet, worn either around the neck or on the wrist, or just carried around in one's pocket to ward off evil spirits or powers. To us this appears to be the behaviour of primitive peoples, but then many of us also wear or carry amulets: bracelets providing relief from rheumatism, lucky coins found lying on the ground, and many more.

My second example, which also explains the first, concerns the customs of the ancient Finns. Uno Harva[1] has described that when they found a sharp black stone, the ancient Finns took it home and told everyone that this was what Ukko (the old Finnish god of thunder, and chief god) made thunder with; that the God's wedge had fallen from the skies. They buried the stone under the threshold, where it provided the house with protection, particularly against fires caused by lightning. In this case, the object protects us against natural hazards; it is an instrument that controls forces over which man has no power, and that thus present a permanent threat to the continuation of life. I said that this example offers an explanation for the amulet, for there are also tales about amulets comparable to that of the wedge. The power of the object lies in the fact that it is somehow exceptional, for example, a particularly beautiful stone, or that it was found in a place so unexpected that it defies normal explanation; hence the magic power of the object.

The third example differs from the others in that it introduces the craftsman; the *enfant terrible* of modern architecture. We are familiar with this example through the writing of Mircea Eliade.[2] What we are talking about is a wedge cast and engraved by a master mason in India and then hammered into the ground in a spot indicated by an astrologist "to ensure that it lands on the snake's head" to prevent it from getting away. The wedge is also the cornerstone of the house, and once it is in place the house can be built. This ritual or, rather, these gestures that initiate the building of a house also show clearly how the house constitutes victory over chaos, how chaos has been subdued. No longer can the snake move. Order has been built on disorder. The house represents victory over the rude forces that are now outside (under) the house, and hence it is a shelter from them. Eliade emphasizes that this wedge hammered into the ground also sets the house on the "axis mundi". Once again we get the same picture, this time of the house lying between the forces above and below it; it becomes a shell between them and the occupants.

At this point I should like to say a few words about the craftsman. It is clear that, just as an Indian mason casts and engraves a wedge, so some ancient Finn could have engraved something on the "hammer of Ukko"[3] that he had found, or enhanced an amulet by carving or polishing it. But what is the point of such an act? The intention must have been to emphasize and augment the value of the object, perhaps its qualities as well. Thus the dialogue with the object has continued, a dialogue in which man, particularly the refiner of the object, may have grown in the eyes of others; they admire the skill of the craftsman while their emotional attitude to the object develops from identification with the dialogue that the craftsman has held with the object and the result of which is thus there for all to see. Perhaps we could take this as the psychological interpretation of what Marx refers to as the value of labour in the days before industrialization (although this has a rather outmoded ring to it).

The role of an object is crucial in our emotional development as well. The work of psychoanalyst Donald Winnicott[4] makes a strong case for this. In Winnicott's theory, the "transitional object" is a key concept; an object with transitional, i.e. mediative capabilities. By this he means an object that on the emotional level makes it possible for the child to (safely) be separated from its mother; a teddy bear or a blanket that the child clings to and to which he can transfer his sense of security and love, earlier devoted exclusively to his mother or nanny. This frees the child from dependency on the mother, emotions are transferred to other objects, and the child can be content with a teddy bear rather than its mother, if such a gross generalization is permitted. The objects in our examples - the amulet, the stone hammer and the wedge - can also be approached from this angle; they can be seen as "security markers" in coming face to face with the unknown. Transitional objects, therefore, open a broader dialogue with the unknown.

Another example of an emotional relationship such as this is the churinga stone, the object of many ethnological studies. Australian aborigines calm themselves in frightening situations by rubbing this small stone that they always carry with them. This offers an emotional explanation for the amulet.

Therefore, objects are mediators in our relationship with both the external and the internal world. By handling objects we become familiar with the outside world, we get a grip on it and learn its logic, after which it is no longer as unknown to us. On the other hand, by projecting our emotions onto external objects, we also realize that we can soothe the restlessness within ourselves. I suggest, therefore, that such analysis and deductions be focused on the craftsman and his relationship to his work. Here I am attempting to give a psychological view on what is traditionally valued aesthetically. If we examine details like door hinges in farm buildings, forged by smiths in various forms (such as arrows, goats' horns, hearts), one is clearly justified in seeing a kind of dialogue with matter in them, aimed primarily at expressing the role of the object as mediator. The symbolism is meant for others to see and to keep evil forces at bay.

This example also shows how the meaning of craftsmanship extends to other people as well. Mediation is not only felt by the craftsman alone; other people also recognize the result. I imagine that people experience an object as mediator differently, and that different people recognize the dialogue with the object in different situations and with different objects. However, I believe that the dialogue with objects is relatively permanent in the history of mankind. As adults we can still find it as a need in us, and it thus gives us a viewpoint from which to examine our relationship with all "objets d'art".

Ornamentation

The purpose of the above examples was to illustrate the role of the object as a tool, an instrument, a mediator in the dialogue with the unknown. Sometimes the concepts of this dialogue are individual - and this may be discerned in my examples - but at other times they are common to a whole group or community as well. When that is the case the craftsman is an interpreter in a special position. Before I return to the craftsman as the enfant terrible of the modern movement I would like to say something about the house as a transitional object. I have already mentioned the house as a shelter, a shell, or as a point on the "axis mundi". Ornamentation is also an integral part of house building. I mentioned door hinges, but the building of the whole house should be seen in the same way. Ornamentation as a component of architecture is a clear sign of the dialogue between man and the unknown, and the tangible signs give other people in that situation the opportunity to recognize their own wonder. But how are we to link the craftsman with architecture? This question, which has been topical ever since the breakthrough of industrial production, has received many a frenzied answer.

We know that, beginning in the '20s, all the figurative patterns that had been models for architects went out of fashion. Industrial standardized forms took their place. An object becomes lighter when it is stripped of decoration. Machines and industrialization remove all superfluous human traces from an object, above all the imprints of the craftsman. This is the achievement glorified by the modern movement - the simplicity and purity of form.

Does architecture still serve as a mediator? In my view, we can seek an answer from two angles. On the one hand, we are given man who creates order by drawing lines and who - most important - fears practically nothing. Reason triumphs over the unknown in nature. An object does not need to be a mediator in this case, since everything is subordinated to human skills. Signs of this view were present in the ideas of the Greek philosophers, but it did not really blossom until the 18th century. Pythagoras combined religion with these ideas; Descartes contemplated pure reason. On the surface, the achievements of our science enhance a mechanical view of the world, a world whose control is fully within our reach. All the mysteries of the elements are within our grasp. Nothing can stop the triumph of reason. When reason becomes God, there is nothing to fear and consequently no need for transitional objects or spaces. In other words, these mediators are just tools for expressing our superiority over nature. This trend has gained more ground this century. Our capacity for harnessing matter has grown: we can create any form and shape we wish; we can manipulate nature. Even our art proclaims this triumph.

On the other hand, there have been reactions to the triumphal progress of reason. The Romantic movement was the strongest opponent of such glorification of reason. Both the mystery of the meaning of life and, above all, the forces within us that are by no means mechanical are promoted and contemplated; poetry and art are seen as the best vehicle for this. The mediatory role of an object is thus assured. This ideology is also alive today, as I have attempted to show. What, then, is the relationship of modern architecture to this view?

Acknowledging our heritage

Modern architecture, expressed as the product of a logical evolution in which the prime human need is efficient action, remains hermetically inaccessible to many people. People still feel the need for the craftsmans' works. We know that for many (if not most) people this is where beauty lies. But how do we answer their needs in an industrialized age? It would be nostalgic to answer that the only possibility is to return to crafts, or that some decoration must quickly be added to external form. I think the architects who acknowledge the craftsman as their ancestor find the answer; they see themselves as the heirs of the craftsman in shaping matter in dialogue with themselves and the unknown elements in nature.

Thus, the person who lives with his fears, but who also experiences peace through beauty, recognizes this heritage. This is also a more explicit view about how beauty influences well-being - in this case psychological health. And I think there are many people who believe this. Architecture that glorifies reason is not enough for them: it amputates part of man. An architect who acknowledges a craft heritage does not necessarily use decoration. I mentioned Pythagoras' religious attitude to geometry. Pure, clear-cut forms can be interpreted thus, even today. Man does not proclaim his superiority in such a case. His opponents are nature and its forces. The point is not to conquer them, but to express human thought and feelings so that other people recognize them as part of the dialogue with the unknow. The point is not the use of decoration, though the contemporary debate centres largely on this. The point is our attitude: either we declare our superiority or we express the search in which we admit that both nature and man contain things unknown to us. This is a tradition in which architecture is the mediator.

So what does this psychological perspective add to the curriculum that my architect colleagues advocate - where users are investigated mainly indirectly as having influenced built forms through history ? And what does my argument specifically add about aesthetics for a design project ? It does make a point about the importance of "the model of man" that we have in mind when we design. In fact this model is necessarily there, so it might be good to have it explicitly based on current knowledge and concepts. Psychological knowledge that we have today allows us to view human beings from several perspectives in terms of an interplay between conscious and unconscious, rational and irrational forces. This can help us in formulating a view - as I have tried to argue - to architecture in terms of beauty. It might also help in understanding why the extreme forms of Modern architecture may be rejected as "cold shoeboxes" and might not at all sustain people psychologically. Not all beauty praised by architects is capable of acting as mediator for human beings. Its influence might then not be positive anymore for the user as it might directly influence his or her well-being. This could become a criteria for questioning beauty. At this point some students at my lectures leave, but some others remain for the rest of the course.

*

This text is close to reflections that I use in my introductory seminar on environmental psychology for students in architecture. I first referred to my examples in a lecture and paper subsequently published in ACANTHUS, 1990, entitled "Man recognizing his imprint".

Notes

1 Harva, U. (1948). *Suomalaisten muinaisusko* (Ancient Finnish religion). Porvoo, p. 74 f.
2 Eliade, M. (1964). *Traité d'histoire des religions*, Paris.
3 Cf. Harva, *op.cit.*
4 Winnicott, D. (1958). *Collected Papers*, Tavistock Publications, London.

The Mind of the Environment

Juhani Pallasmaa

What are the essential aspects of the quality of architecture?

"Like the Almighty, we also make everything in our own image, because we lack a more reliable model; the objects we make reveal more about us than confessions of faith", writes Joseph Brodsky analysing his impressions of Venice in his book *Watermarks.* The Nobel poet brings out the inescapable connection between our mental landscape and the built environment; man builds simultaneously an image of the world and himself.

Yet, our attitude to the living environment is peculiarly ambivalent. On the one hand, we regard our environment as a neutral stage, beyond our consciousness, upon which our life is enacted. On the other hand, when we look at buildings of other cultures or even remains of a vanquished culture, we consider these material structures as authentic and conclusive images of a culture and a way of life. Thus historical and alien environments make us see the connection between life, the human mind and architecture. But we consider the misanthropic environment of our time the consequence of a negativism beyond our control, neither do we wish to recognise the origin of these negative characteristics in our collective consciousness. Although we naturally recognise respected public buildings as containing conscious symbolisations and spiritual messages, we seldom think that negativism and pessimism also have their manifestations and symbols in our environment. In Finland, Senate Square, the Olympic Stadium or Finlandia Hall in the capital are universally recognised architectonic symbols of Finnish solidarity, self-esteem and identity. But also the wounds left by gravel pits or clear felled forests, ruptured village main streets or city centres have their counterpart - or actually their origin - in our minds. The fragmentation, ugliness, insensitivity and hostility of the environment can only be the consequence of a similar state of mind. The built environment can no more acquire positive than negative features independently of the intentions and values of its builders.

The deep and surface structures of the environment

As a rule, our actions are neither accidental nor arbitrary; they contain both conscious and subconscious motives. In a work of art or a building there are also conscious aspirations to reflect stylistic surface structures alongside the deep structures resulting from subconscious motives. Thus in our works, objects and buildings, there are always two narratives. The surface structure

Fig. 1. Artistic images lead into a primary encounter with the world, beyond words and intellectual concepts. Poetry takes us back to a re-oralized world. (Sigurdur Gudmundsson, Collage, 1979. Zsa-Zsa Eyck (ed.), Sigurdur Gudmundsson, Malmö, 1992.)

and its meanings are associated with stylistic conventions, applied and historically established symbolic representations, manifestations of social institutions, as well as the conscious expressive efforts of individual planners. On the other hand, deep subconscious structures and meanings express primary existential motives, such as hopes, desires, fears and anxieties. The conscious semantic content of surface structures is of little importance from the point of view of the quality, influence and permanence of a work of art, whereas the unconscious, existential content of the work gives it a vitality independent of time (Fig. 1).

Architecture, just as much as building without any conscious artistic objective, contains under its surface meaning another layer of motives. The semantic content of the surface and deep structures of the environment may be quite contradictory. For example, a high-tech hospital, shopping mall or airport may well in reality signal a fear of life, an obsessiveness with subordination and functionalisation or total necrophilia. The passivating environments of institutions, as well as the thematized settings of amusement parks and shopping centers, conditioning emotions, deprive individuals of their spontaneous experiences and emotions, and accordingly the authenticity of experience and self.

What the ordinary environment has to say

The meaning of deep structures does not differentiate between what is more or less socially valuable. Our way to cultivate land, exploit forests or build roads, reveals the structures and values concealed in our culture in quite the same way as our much revered public buildings.

The history of towns and architecture is traditionally the history of monuments. Recently, however, research into cultural geography and environmental psychology has been concerned with what is considered the less important, ordinary living environment, because it is just this that contains such a hidden message. The cultural geographer P. F. Lewis, in his introduction to "The Interpretation of Ordinary Landscapes", expresses a view of the ultimate importance of the ordinary environment that is remarkably similar to Brodsky's: *"Our human landscape is our unwitting autobiography, reflecting our tastes, our values, our aspirations, and even our fears, in tangible, visible form. We rarely think of landscape that way, and so the cultural record we have written in the landscape is liable to be more truthful than most autobiographies because we are less self-conscious about how we describe ourselves."*

Psychoanalysis of the environment

The pioneer of environmental psychology, the American anthropologist Edward T. Hall - who has studied the unconscious and cultural bonding mechanisms in space usage in his seminal book *The Hidden Dimension* - has noted that there is an unfortunate tendency in Western culture to differentiate between material and spiritual manifestations of culture. He considers that our tendency to keep the environment and the human mind separate and independent of each other is a fundamental shortcoming in our thinking. Even in the prevailing anthropological view, man does not live separately in a physical and a spiritual world, rather these dimensions are intimately interwoven (Fig. 2).

In our normal thinking, however, we put physical and spiritual cultural

Fig. 2. We build not only to house our bodies, but also to house our soul and
its memory. Dani Karavan, Monument to Walter Benjamin, Port Bou, Spain, 1990.
(Arkhitetti 5 - 6, Helsinki, 1996)

manifestations in different categories. Our ability to observe, interpret and
understand the message of objects, buildings and landscapes has become
completely atrophied. Although our biologically determined subconscious
and bodily reactions can certainly make us feel sick, alienated, fearful or
panic-stricken in a negative environment, we are unable to see or analyse the
characteristics of such an environment and its connections to the distorted
values or disturbed mind of our culture, quite apart from being unable to
verbalise the disorders of the environment. The biological and existential
wisdom of our bodies transcends our ability for rational perception and
analysis. But even our bodily and emotional reactions represent our multivariate and synthetic knowledge. Only in recent years has the intelligence of
emotional reactions become the subject of scientific enquiry. Thus the environment repulsed by our bodies and our psyche does not require verbal and
pseudo-scientific evidence of its negativeness.

In our knowledge of the connection - one could almost say the unity - between the environment and the collective mind, objects, buildings and landscapes offer a means to recognise and analyse our collective mind and its disturbances. With good reason one can talk of the psychoanalysis of the physical environment. The American architect George Nelson forecast the fall of the Third Reich already in the mid-Thirties at a time when most people believed that Nazism had only just begun its inexorable march towards world domination. Nelson interpreted the apparently paradoxical archaic massive stone architecture of the Nazis as its builders' unconscious defence against self-destruction. Thus the unconscious message of the architecture revealed - to those who understand material culture - a will to self-destruction beneath the surface of an ideology threatening world domination.

The inhumanity and negativity of today's environment equally await their interpretation. What is the psychical reason why we can no longer create a collective public space and why are we, on the one hand, so obediently submissive to total uniformity and, on the other hand, possessed by a flagrant mania for originality? Do not these features reflect our drift into loneliness and the loss of our individuality and freedom? What does the disappearance of variety, sense of place, plasticity and touch from the street scene mean? Can it mean anything else other than a loss in self-esteem and empathy, and faith and joy in life? Do not these negative features reveal the suffocating grip of materialistic values, the disappearance of handicraft and human contact, and the cynical realities of rational thought and exploitation? Do they not express a fear of life, an obsessive need to explain and master everything? This obsessive need to control grows from uncertainty, a weak identity, the overall meaninglessness of existential experience, fear and the paradoxical rejection of freedom. Is not the fragmented, ugly landscape of our time an indication of the dimming of the whole purpose of life?

Understanding the interaction between the world and our mind, makes it equally apparent that environments containing positive structures and meanings have a favourable influence on the organisation of our mind and experience of the world. In this thinking, architecture acquires a monumentally important task: to define the horizon between understanding the world and ourselves.

Fig. 3. The contemporary technological city is a city of isolated vision. (Brasilia, 1968. Photo Juhani Pallasmaa.)

The environment as a symbol of society

Town planning and architecture have been criticised for being unable to create an architectural symbolisation for our democratic age. According to this view, guilt for the negative character of the environment has been mistakenly laid at the door of architecture. I believe this is wrong. The symbols of our society, our values and our democracy, are in our built environment, in the same way as all forms of culture have always created their own constructed version of the world (Fig. 3). Rather than being nostalgic and hankering after the sublime symbols of some New Hellas in our lifestyle, we have to start assessing the essential nature of our society on the basis of our negatively regarded environment and the picture we have built of ourselves. Is it not a fact that no convincing and worthwhile plan for the most important site in the capital of Finland, the area spreading out in front of Parliament Building, has been produced, even after decades of effort, which is more an indication that our society itself lacks a core to be embodied as an architectural symbol rather than a lack of imagination among the architectural profession? Symbols of a society cannot just be invented; an artist can only give form to formless intentions shaping a culture. The only products of individual creativity that survive time are those that echo the collective mind of a society. The entire validity, or feasibility, of symbolic representation in the age of speed, images and consumption can be questioned.

In the collection of his notes entitled *Culture and Value*, Ludvig Wittgenstein, one of the most important philosophers of our century wrote: *"Architecture immortalises and glorifies something. Hence there can be no architecture where there is nothing to glorify."* When we know how seriously Wittgenstein took his architectural hobby, and how close a friend he was of the notable Viennese architect Adolf Loose, his words are worth consideration. His idea implies that any substance evident in architecture arises fundamentally from outside its own field. Wittgenstein's idea confirms the assumption that the spiritual vacuum we encounter in the normal architecture of today is a reflection of a void in our collective soul. Our age lacks ideals, utopias and hope, those mental dimensions which gave to early modern architecture a firm belief in the future.

Tradition, the individual and convention

Architecture, like any other human activity, expresses clearly the essential nature of its cultural context. The deep structures of a culture influence all mental and material forms of manifestations of a certain age. In an essay entitled "The Emperor's Old Clothes" Marshall McLuhan, a media philosopher in the 1960s, writes: *"Only small children and artists are sensuously apt to perceive the new environment. Small children and artists are anti-social beings who are as little impressed by the established mores as they are conditioned by the new."* Art and architecture are generally regarded as expressions of personal freedom, but they probably reflect just as much the limitations and conventions of their own age. Genuine art arises at the intersection of tradition and innovation, of convention and individuality, of discipline and freedom. Significant art does not approach the future by creating rootless fantasies; it resides in the continuum of the age and culture, and rekindles tradition. Genuine art is always a dialogue with earlier art, retrospectively reflecting its own meanings and interpretations. T.S. Eliot wrote in his essay

Tradition and the Individual Talent (1919) that a poet writes with the entire literary history in his bones and marrow, and converses with foregone poets. The obsessive idea that art should be something new, unique, entirely individual, supported by commercial interests, has entirely distorted the Western conception of the essential nature and message of art.

Eliot wisely observes that tradition cannot be owned or inherited, each generation has to recreate it. Eliot's *Wasteland*, one of the greatest modern poetic works, is an excellent example of how a creative mind, conscious of tradition, combines ingredients of quite different origins; in the creative fusion origins and boundaries of images lose their bonds. Wasteland, like all great art, is a rich archaeological excavation of images. Historical images of timeless myths mingle in the poem with the everyday life of Eliot's London. The poem merges references from the Bible to Ovid, from Virgil to Dante, from Shakespeare to Wagner, from Baudelaire to Hesse. The poem begins with a motto borrowed from Petronius' Satyricon and ends with repetition of the last incantation in the Upanishad.

The essential nature of tradition in creative culture is by no means self-evident and one dimensional. Assimilation and fusion of diverse influences are more important than purity. Attempts to shape the logic of tradition into a conscious programme always leads to a rough, one dimensional and sentimental interpretation. Nostalgic interpretations of our present Finnish identity are transformed into consumer society kitsch, which in fact gives a death blow to true living tradition searching for new expression.

In Paul Ricoeur's words: *"An urgent task today is to preserve the tension between tradition and utopia. The challenge is to reanimate tradition and bring utopia closer"* (Fig. 4).

The bio-cultural quality of the environment

In the background of our behaviour are many unconscious bio-cultural ways to react, likes and dislikes, with origins far back in our cultural and biological past, signs of visual centres of our fish and reptile past are even evident in the structure of our brains. Many unconscious reactions of biological origin control our behaviour and preferences in the environment. An environment considered pleasant will also be in harmony with these archaic instinctive

Fig. 4. The historical town is a kinesthetic and haptic town.
(Casares, Spain. Photo Juhani Pallasmaa.)

Fig. 5. We do not only inhabit space, we also inhabit time. Architecture domesticates both
space and time for dwelling. (Ruined wall in southern Spain. Photo Juhani Pallasmaa.)

reactions. In the book *The Wright Space: Pattern and Meaning in Frank Lloyd Wright's Houses*, Grant Hildebrandt clarifies the bio-psychological factors that explain the popularity of Wright's houses. This master architect seems to have understood intuitively the archaic reactions hidden in the human mind and instincts. A strong bio-cultural and archaic background can also be felt in Alvar Aalto's architecture.

While modern architecture produces a new and ever more technological and urbanised environment horizon, it must recognise the gatherer, hunter and farmer hidden in each one of us. Architecture's main purpose is to act as a mediator between aspects of our biological origin and our present technological culture, and good architecture includes archaic as well as new elements. A designer who understands the historical basis of architecture, recognises intuitively architecture's subconscious background, without which even the most exceptional designer can only create passing fashionable coulisses.

The fear of time and death

Architecture and towns domesticate space for humans to inhabit and comprehend. Perhaps even more important is that our built environment also tames time and makes it more comprehensible to us. Pondering the essence of architecture the American philosopher Karsten Harries says: *"Architecture is not only about domesticating space, it is also a deep defence against the terror of time. The language of beauty is essentially the language of timeless reality"* (Fig. 5).

A central theme in art and architecture is the unconscious fear of death, or the fear of the insignificance of life. In an undated draft for a lecture in the mid-Twenties, the young rebel Alvar Aalto wrote: *"Form is nothing else but a concentrated wish for everlasting life on earth"*. The French philosopher Gaston Bachelard, who studied architecture's mytho-poetic essence in his highly influential book *The Poetics of Space*, writes on the other hand: *"A house constitutes a body of images that give mankind proofs or illusions of stability. ... it is an instrument with which to confront the cosmos."*

Towns, buildings and works of art ensure the continuity of the world we experience. With their aid we recognise ourselves and our belonging to a certain cultural continuum. In his book *The Shadow of the Conquest of*

Nature, the American therapist Gotthard Booth writes: "*Man gets natural satisfaction in life when he organically participates in the lifeforms that have a longer duration than the individual himself*". It is evident that participation in the process of tradition offers us such a supra-individual lifeform.

The difficulty of experiencing the dimension of time in a new urban environment is, perhaps, the characteristic that produces the greatest feeling of rootlessness and estrangement in the environment. On the whole our civilisation has a negative attitude towards the arc of time, aging and dying. The old and the sick are pushed out of society's sight and mind. Our problematic attitude towards time shows also in buildings where wear and tear are regarded as negative signs of deterioration, not as patina and stratum that enrich the experience of time, as in the environments of traditional societies.

The psychological and phenomenological aspects of the environment

Environmental psychology studies the interactive relationships of the environment and the human mind and seeks the causalities of environmental characteristics and the contents of the mind. However, in existentialist and phenomenological thinking, the world and the mind are not separate, but interwoven and continuously defining each other. "*You cannot divorce man and space. Space is neither an external object nor an internal experience. We don't have man and space besides each other*", observed Martin Heidegger. The French poet Noel Arnaud gave final expression to the togetherness of man and space: "*I am the space in which I am*."

However, even the collective identity of societies and nations is tied to the features of space and environment. In actual fact, the collective identity grows just from this intertwining of the individual mind and the shared world. Individuals participate in maintaining the mythical images and symbols created with the aid of the collective imagination, and these images both mould individual identities and direct the behaviour of nations.

The mind is expressed in the world and the world in the mind. Man's existence in the world is realised just through the encounter of world and mind. Encountering the world lies at the root of all art. "*How would the painter or poet express anything other than his encounter with the world*," as Maurice Merleau-Ponty writes in his book *Signs*. He ties the mind, the body

Fig. 6. Healthy architecture evokes an embodied experience of the world; I exist in the world, and the world exists through me. (Stepping stones in a Japanese garden, Kyoto. Photo Juhani Pallasmaa.)

and the world into a singular existential complex: *"Our own body is in the world as the heart is in the organism: it keeps the visible spectacle constantly alive, it breathes life into it and sustains it inwardly, and with it forms a system."* As in the other branches of the arts, architecture articulates man's existential experience. Architecture defines our cultural and individual identity, as well as our relationship to the continuum of historicity and time (Fig. 6).

The existential space

Man does not live in an objective world of material and fact. Characteristic of our mode of existence is our imaginative ability in projecting a world of possibilities. We live in the worlds of the mind in which the experienced, remembered and imagined are entwined. The past, present and future are interwoven into a single plastic mental state and tense. The reality of the mind is thus free of the absoluteness of physical space and time. This lived and experienced space could be called an existential space to distinguish it from physical and geometrical space. The lived space is organised and visualised in a way that diverges from the Euclidian rules of space. The basis for organising the existential space are the meanings, images, associations and values reflected by the experiencer.

The existential, lived space is also the actual subject of architectural planning. However, the planning and building of the environment takes place within the insensitive and distant world of geometry, and the experiential quality of the environment remains dependent on the insight and empathy of the builders. The planned object or environment is transferred from the planner's world of experience and imagination - via material and Euclidian reality - to the user's existential world of experience. This transmission that occurs at the level of imaginary and existential knowledge should play a major part in the training of planners. *"The ability to fantasise space and form is not the most important aspect of an architect's talent, but the ability to imagine the human condition,"* as Professor Aulis Blomstedt so wisely taught his students at the Helsinki University of Technology in the 1960s. Unfortunately, the main attention in the training of planners and in architectural criticism continues to be focussed on the formal and visual organisation of the object being planned. The phenomenological, the lived and interpretive attitude, is, however, gaining a foothold.

In planning the spatial and material structures for living and being, the architect irrevocably shapes the contents of our mind, because our built world is the inevitable framework and horizon of our experience and consequently of our mental contents. The environment and architecture are mental horizons, or - expressed as a Heidegger concept - preunderstanding, a part of the constitution of the human mind. The environment thus either enables or excludes specific contents of the mind and so it is either mentally positive or negative, supportive or activative, rejective or pacifying.

In this respect, the tasks of the architect and the therapist become very close to each other; whereas the therapist deals with a person's external condition and tries to make his experiences and interpretations of his own life condition more favourable, the architect, working in the same dimension, endeavours to make the spatial-material experiential horizon of life more positive.

Fig. 7. Alvar Aalto: Tuberculosis Sanatorium, Paimio, 1929-33.The building radiates optimism and promise; it is not only a symbol of healing, it entices us to project our images of hope onto itself. (Photo Museum of Finnish Architecture.)

The curing environment

One of the most important architectural works of our century is Alvar Aalto's Paimio Sanatorium from the early 1930s. The building is a masterpiece of functionalist design and modern aesthetics, but it is also an architectonic metaphor of healing and hope (Fig. 7). Whilst designing the sanatorium, Aalto fell ill and had to spend some time in a hospital where he could examine the surroundings from a patient's point of view. He took careful note of the irritation caused by even the most trivial things, such as the sound of water splashing into the washbasin, but also to the simple fact that a patient spends most of his time staring at the ward ceiling, thus its shape and colouring assumed a particular importance. Aalto understood that a patient's experiential perspective differed radically from that of the nursing and administrative staff or visitors; this is one perspective of "the horisontal mah", as Aalto called his hospitalized client.

On the basis of his hospital experience, Aalto concluded that the subject of the design should always be "man at his weakest". In thinking of man at his weakest the designer should consider even the most insignificant details of

Fig. 8. The task of architecture is to mediate between us and the world, to house us in space and to place us into the continuum of culture. (Alvar Aalto, Villa Mairea, Noormarkku, 1938-39; detail of the sauna terrace. Photo Juhani Pallasmaa.)

the building in order to help in orientation, movement and the use of spaces, as well as in creating a feeling of security, comfort, meaning and familiarity. Of particular importance, the sensible organisation of the environment, the unconscious meanings and messages of spaces, scale, and the sensory and stimulative content, are natural to the therapeutic environment of the mentally disturbed. Hospitals organised like factories turn the patient into the object of impersonal mechanical treatment devoid of any individuality. This happens inevitably if the starting point in planning is to rationalise treatment. It is typical of our culture with its adulation of strength and performance that more attention is paid to the characteristics of the work environment than to the characteristics of the curing environment from the point of view of the patient and his cure.

It is obvious that the caring environment should offer the patient a safe place from which he can observe his world and self. The curing environment offers a rich stimuli, an experience of stratified time, as well as experiences of nature and its cycles, *"so that ... the world appears as it is"*, as Pentti Saarikoski says in his anthology of poems "Tanssilattia vuorella" (Dance floor on the mountain). Above all, the curing environment should offer experiences of life and hope. In other words, there is no difference between a curing environment and a positive living environment in general. *"Architecture must facilitate man's homecoming,"* as the Dutch architect Aldo van Eyck has so lyrically said. This need of homecoming equally concerns the environments of healthy as much as of sick people (Fig. 8).

A hilly terrain
demands an asymmetrical
architecture
intermediate floors many doorways
different sized windows
so that from inside the house
the world appears as
it is
pines and fields and spruce forests
other houses
and houses built at a different time.

Poem by Pentti Saarikoski. (Translation: Michael Wynne-Ellis.)

References
Bachelard, Gaston (1969). *The Poetics of Space*. Deacon Press, Boston.
Booth, Gotthard (1974). *The Shadow of the Conquest of Nature*. The Edwin Hellen Press, New York and Toronto.
Brodsky, Josef (1994). *Veden peili* (Watermarks). Tammi, Helsinki.
Eliot, T. S. (1964). *Selected Essays*. Harcourt, Brace & World, New York.
Hall, Edward T. (1964). *The Hidden Dimension*. Anchor Books, New York. 1990.
Harries, Karsten (1982). *Building and the Terror of Time*, in *Perspecta, The Yale Architectural Journal 19*, New Haven.

Hildebrandt, Grant (1991). *The Wright Space: Pattern and Meaning in Frank Lloyd Wright's Houses.* University of Washington Press, Seattle.

Kearney, Richard (1991). *The Poetics Imagining from Husserl to Lyotard,* Harper Collins Academy, London.

Kearney, Richard (1994). *Modern Movements in European Philosophy.* Manchester University Press, Manchester and New York.

Kepes, Gyorgy (1966). (ed), *The Man-Made Object: Vision and Values.* George Braziller, New York.

Meining, D. W. (1979). (ed), *The Interpretation of Ordinary Landscapes: Geographical Essays.* Oxford University Press, New York.

Merleau-Ponty, Maurice (1992). *The Phenomenology of Perception.* Routledge Press, London.

Saarikoski, Pentti (1977). *Tanssilattia vuorella.* Otava, Helsinki.

Schildt, Göran (1984). *Alvar Aalto: The Early Years.* Rizzoli, New York.

Wittgenstein, Ludwig (1980). *Culture and Value.* G. H. von Wright and Heikki Nyman, (eds) Oxford University Press, Oxford.

Aesthetics, Order and Discipline

Jens Schjerup Hansen

*Is the perception of beauty still dominated by controlled order
and the bourgeois concept of what is "nice and tidy"?*

The concepts of aesthetics and order refer to the very same dimension of our cultural universe - to what we find beautiful and delightful. However, the aestetical is more beautiful than the orderly, and the un-aesthetical is worse than the disorderly. Thus, we might say that aesthetics and order refer to different levels of beauty, and also that order is a subset of our aesthetics, or that aesthetics is a level of unique order.

In everyday usage the concept of order clearly refers to sets of social values and conventions. Orderliness is something acquired in childhood, or should we fail to do so, something our social environment will keep reminding us of forever after. "Order" has the social function of enabling us to orient ourselves in a given physical or social context.

The concept of aesthetics is not applied in a similar way, in terms of social conventions. Actually, when it comes to architecture and the design of our surroundings, the concept is often associated with cases where the achievements of an architect or artist go beyond social conventions. My belief is that aesthetics and order have the same, culturally based relation, and also that our aesthetics, i.e. whatever we find beautiful and delightful, basically amounts to culturally conditioned order.

One fundamental point made by the French philosopher Merleau-Ponty concerning our culturally defined consciousness is that we are in the cultural landscape before we are aware of the fact. This proposition was part of his departure from the subjective cognitive philosophy of Descartes, later to become synonymous with his maxim: "*I think, therefore I am!*" At the same time, however, his statement pinpoints the conditions of creative work, e.g. art and architecture. We "form" art, we "form" architecture, we "form" our environment and our cultural landscape; but all along we are being "formed" by our cultural landscape and our architecture as well. We are in our own cultural landscape, before we become aware of it, and our cultural legacy is all-important to whatever innovations we are able to create. In other words: our aesthetics and norms of beauty are something we carry with us, as much as they are creations of our own. They form the mental order, by which we organize our environment into a physical order. This is the context in which I wish to place the concept of aesthetics.

With the Danish allotment garden as the physical setting I propose to discuss two issues. First, what happens when we upset our mental order - our paradigm. And second, what is typical of our physical order and our aesthetics.

On upsetting mental order

In the early 1980s I was doing a research project on the new value basis and the new concept of nature apparently evolving in the wake of the environmental movement. During my work I kept a keen eye on the allotment garden movement, believing that something new might be under way in this "green" movement. Above all, I was eager to see when a an ecological discussion on cultivation methods would find its way to the allotment garden people. I was to wait for quite a while; but finally, in 1984, an article appeared in the allotment garden paper, written by an adviser to the Corporation of Allotment Garden Societies. The article compared the yields of two allotment gardens, one ecologically, and the other conventionally cultivated. The conclusion was that in terms of yield no significant differences could be identified. However, the article had the following, highly remarkable closing statement, *"It would seem redundant to explain why ecological gardening - along the stated lines - is unpalatable to allotment garden people. Nevertheless, there is no harm in stressing one specific aspect. The stench of dung, fly pest, weed seeds across the hedge - indeed, the mere notion of having a dungheap next door is quite unaesthetical."*

Today garden composting has come into widespread use, and in retrospect, the horticultural adviser's vehement statement seems incomprehensible and peculiar. Obviously, as I see it, more was at stake than two different types of cultivation. The horticultural advisers' conventional scientific understanding of horticulture was challenged, meaning that the "paradigm" - his nature concept and ideas of good garden practice - had been challenged. He was actually standing up for his own paradigm regarding mental order and meaning in nature, and with the most powerful invocation: Not only is the new paradigm gross disorder - it is un-aesthetical, which is about as bad as it gets.

One of the things we find most hard to bear is having our notions of order put in doubt. This goes for our relations to nature and for other aspects of life as well. When our mental order is disrupted, or lost, we lose our sense of direction; we are bewildered - which is about the worst we can think of. I can still recall the violent feelings in a TV newscast showing angry farmers who - at the pitch of the environmental debate between townsmen and farmers - had shown up at a minor Jutland slaughterhouse to force the local veterinarian to eat his words. The culprit had vented his criticism not at the farmers, but at contemporary Danish stall husbandry, based on the injuries he was able to identify in animals on delivery to the slaughterhouse. We have a rich history of condemning any offenders to our world picture and to "canonical order", whether they claim the Earth to be round, or the firmament to be infinite.

The ruling physical order

As I see it, our overall principles on physical order are embodied and can be observed in Danish allotment gardens. Some may find this statement presumptuous, arguing that allotment gardens are not representative of general order; they would much rather have an order and aesthetics of their own. Their argument would be that more than any other Danish garden type, the Danish allotment garden stands out with its clearcut and definite form idiom. These small, well-kept, lush gardens behind their trimmed hedges - with their fanciful arbours surrounded by luxuriant vegetable beds and flower borders, with fruit trees, trellises and the Danish flag - are the epitome of domestic comfort - sanctuaries of "the man in the street" (Fig. 1). No one doubts their very special quality - indeed, some would consider these gardens to have a specifically popular identity and aesthetics. But do they have an aesthetics of their own which makes them stand out from other garden types? No - quite the contrary. Actually, Danish allotment gardens are those most narrowly conforming to the overall principle of order that has reigned since the Renaissance and to our day.

An "aha" experience

A few years ago I was in Tuscany studying Renaissance gardens. I visited a number of famous villa gardens around Florence and followed their evolution history since the Renaissance, in which central perspective symmetry and a strict geometrical form idiom gradually developed into an aesthetics and a form idiom that helped to keep the spatial surroundings in check - as seen in a number of stunning garden compositions.

Fig. 1.The baker's allotment garden - the epitome of the Danish allotment garden.
(Photo ISM 1995.)

To exemplify the point I would like to mention the garden of Villa della Petraia, from where, when stepping out of the prince's door, you will cast your eyes upon not only a strictly organized paradisaic garden, but also the proprietor's extensive estate. Your eyes feasting upon the vista across the valley to the city, and further on to the hillside behind the city - a truly magnificent view (Fig. 2). However, from the prince's position, you are not merely looking upon a beautiful garden; you are also observing a controlled space, in which all things have their proper place, and where the prince, at a glance, can assure himself that everything is in place and in the best of order. For the prince himself is standing right in the control centre of his own controlled space - a handsome order.

On my way back I had an "aha" experience when, near Munich, I ran into a number of small, meticulously kept allotment gardens. They were arranged in rows, with neatly trimmed hedges and strict footpaths, neat little houses,

Fig. 2. The newly established garden at Villa della Petraia. Lunette by Giusto Utens 1599.

surrounded by decorative gardens, one next to the other, row by row. A thought immediately crossed my mind: *"I've seen this once before! This is the controlled space of the Renaissance, pure and simple."*

The new spatial concept of the Renaissance

Amongst the most far-reaching achievements of the Renaissance was the invention of linear perspective, constructed by the architect Filippo Brunelleschi. Linear (or central) perspective is a gnomonic projection on a plane in which lines of projection from the represented object converge in a centre. The linear perspective yields a precise, geometrically defined reconstruction of reality, in which the depicted persons and objects are rendered mathematically consistent, according to their relative dimensions and positions in space. This representation of a motif in a picture space is perceived - by our own culture group - as a correct rendering, in terms of dimensions and spatial depth.

Brunelleschi's form of perspective representation was so convincing that not only did it lead to a radical re-structuring of fine arts traditions; it also changed the design of the human environment, such as towns and buildings. The representation method was virtually liberated from the canvas and superimposed on the physical environment, thus fixing the points of observation from which a given space should be contemplated and experienced. From then on people began to organize their surroundings so as to appear as a perspectively organized space, thus making perspective the basis of an entirely new perception of space - perspective space.

Gradually the new spatial concept superseded the former concept of picture space that had reigned in the medieval period - in which foreground and background more or less merged into each other in a picture plane with a dominantly vertical character, practically without depth, and in which space was viewed as a projection on a vertical picture plane, made graphic by optical axiality.

Perspective spatial perception offered the viewer a distance and an overview in relation to space which was new and radically different from the spatial perception of the medieval and antique periods, in which the spectator was subordinated and overpowered by the picture space. Linear perspective enabled Renaissance man to place himself right at the centre of his understanding of the world, from where all things can be observed. The individual is made the hub of the Universe, and the world is seen in perspective order.

The new order of Renaissance

The advent of linear perspective, along with increasingly sophisticated disciplines in mathematics and geometry, enabled Renaissance man to introduce a new order and coherence within a building, between building and city, and between the city and the surrounding landscape. The following will summarize how Renaissance spatial order principles came to shape our environment - buildings, gardens, landscapes, fortifications and town plans - according to a strict, visually controlled order.

The building

The Italian villa, as developed in the 14th and 15th centuries, came to play a significant part in Renaissance construction and horticulture. In the early 1400s Leon Battista Alberti, architect, collected and recorded contemporary ideals and experience in an architectural treatise, also dealing with the major property types of the free citizen: the palace and the villa. All architecture was based on mathematics and geometry, and according to Alberti's definition, "beauty" amounts to a rational integration of proportions in all building parts. This implies that each part is absolutely fixed as to size and form, and that nothing can be added or deducted without ruining the overall scheme. Being a humanist Alberti propounds two more theses on how to structure the architecture of a palace or a villa: Firstly, man measures everything by himself; so solutions should be based on human dimensions, which should be reflected in the proportions of a building. Secondly, the building should be laid out in a simple and transparent manner.

The first-time visitor to a palace or a villa should experience that he is meeting his host as his peer. In the event that such a guest (an unprepared individual) is to present and orient himself in an unfamiliar social context, where he is left to rely on his own vision, then the building should be *"actually accessible, functionally self-evident, and clear and unambiguous in its implicit meaning. Its very exterior should be of such clarity that the mere sight will make him feel welcomed and at ease"* - says Lise Bek, art historian. Therefore the building should be laid out symmetrically around its central axes. Window distribution on the facades should reflect the underlying room divisions; access to the building should be axial, and by following the main axis through the house, the guest should be able to establish, at any time, his own whereabouts in the building, and the location of individual rooms. Thus, the central axis is made the very nerve centre of the architectural structure.

Finally the treatise has ideas on the location of the villa, which (as something new) include and attach particular significance to the landscape. According to the treatise the villa should take on a dominant position relative to its environs; it should have a magnificent view of the city, the owner's estate, a sea or a wide expanse of plain, of familiar hills and mountains, and in the foreground, the most delightful garden.

The garden
The villa garden is a fenced space. The garden is laid out to form an architectural unity with the villa, and based on the same proportioning and structuring principles. The visual axis is emphasized by a central axis, the furnishings

being geometrically designed borders and shrubbery, and trees and shrubs trimmed to form.

The garden of Villa della Petraia outside Florence, mentioned above, is an exemplary Renaissance garden layout. The garden was established in the late 16th century, as part of a radical re-build of a medieval manor house. A contemporary lunette by Giusto Utens shows the garden as a perfectly symmetrical layout relative to the central axis of the villa. Garden design is based on two geometrical forms, during the Renaissance held to be the most perfect: the circle and the square. The upper terrace has two orchards on either side of the villa, their rows of fruit trees forming four squares. On the next terrace, extended between two pavilions, is a number of square beds with herbs and flowers, and a large, rectangular fish pond. On the lowest slanting terrace we find two large squares, each inscribed with two circular bowery walks and planted with fruit trees. The entire garden is framed with a heavy wall.

The Renaissance garden was a garden of overview, and it was a sine qua non that its order lent itself to visual perception. However, the proportional relations and the geometry of the gardens could be fully appreciated only from the windows of the prince's residential floor. Garden sections that were not open to a direct overview had to be otherwise visualised in engravings and pictures, such as Giusto Utens' lunettes. In early Renaissance the garden's axes rarely extended beyond its boundaries. Axes were not used as a structural element connecting the garden with the surrounding landscape. The garden axis merely served to guide the observer's eye towards the vista, thus mediating the transition from the villa to the surrounding landscape.

With the development of Renaissance into Baroque, motif perspective acquired added interest, and in the words of the urban historian Benevolo, we should understand the large-scale axial layouts of the period as a fascination with fixed infinity (Fig. 3). Axial layouts, superimposed on both towns and landscapes, continued to develop into larger and increasingly complex geometrical structures - with the Versailles as the culminating point, its longitudinal axis measuring eight kilometres. However, in layouts of such magnitude, the controlled space defied visual acquisition. It was no longer possible to take in the entire space at a glance. The dimensions and complexity of

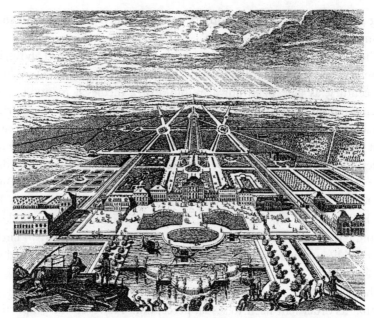

Fig. 3. Fixed infinity. Nymphenburg at Munich. Engraving by J.G. Sarron.

these arrangements were such that they could only be embraced and communicated in a plan.

Fortification and urban plan
In the Renaissance, as in our day, the military complex had a key role in contemporary development. State-of-the-art martial technology replaced the stone cannonballs of the artillery with iron cannonballs, which in turn provoked a complete reorganization of urban defence systems and brought changes to the exterior form of the towns and to their internal organization as well. The tall ring wall with defensive towers that used to encircle the town - thus giving it an outer, more or less regular shape - was found unable to cope with such modern technology and had to be given up. Instead a new regular-shaped fortification system was erected, consisting of ramparts, walls and bastions, which lent a geometrically strict exterior and internal form to the town. The severe regularity was underlined by sharply chiselled bastions

subdividing the outer space of the town into precise shooting fields. The new and costly defence systems placed narrow limits on how the town proper could be built up and developed. The historian Helge Gamrath points to two exemplary types of Renaissance towns - the radial town and the grid-iron or chess-board layout - as embodying the new concept of order. Both were inspired by antique ideals. However, as realized by the urban planning praxis of the Renaissance - around the central town axes - they were of a far more acute geometrical and symmetrical precision.

A rather more significant aspect was the development and sophistication of calculation and plotting systems for the highly complex bastion layouts. Concurrently such calculation systems were being applied for a number of other Renaissance spaces, simply because fortification engineers and architects were also those in charge of most civilian physical planning. Therefore military experience and praxis indirectly came to play a significant role in establishing controlled space.

Renaissance in Scandinavia

A parallel process was evolving in Scandinavia, though with a delay of nearly a century, as in to Northern Italy. The first Renaissance garden was introduced in 1562 by Dorothea, King Christian III's Queen, as a small-scale pleasure garden at Koldinghus Castle. However, it was only when Christian IV, her grandson, started his large-scale urban development works that (in the words of the architect Vilhelm Lorenzen) *"Renaissance concepts of order were really let loose in the Kingdom of Denmark"*. During his rule Christian IV carried out no less than 19 major urban construction projects, from Rørås in the north to Glückstadt in the south. Ten of these were completely new towns - mostly fortified towns in the border regions of the kingdom - the rest being large scale re-alignment works in existing towns, with the new fortification of Copenhagen as the most comprehensive project. Moreover, a considerable number of plans never came to be implemented.

After the vigorous efforts of Christian IV, which as we know comprised much more than military construction works, the following centuries saw a dissemination of Renaissance order principles. They first gained ground in the urban and garden spaces of the aristocracy, later to be adopted by the wealthy bourgeoisie. Following the parcelling out of farmland in the late 18th century, and the adoption of rational forest management in compliance with the forest directive, large parts of the landscape were subjected to the principles of controlled order. As a detail, even the miniature landscapes of the cemeteries were parcelled out, to finally create order amongst the dead.

However, the Renaissance concept of controlled order was not allowed to reign undisputed. In the second half of the 18th century new ideals on the inherent order of nature, as embodied by the English landscape garden, gained ground throughout Europe. Now geometrical forms - the constructive element of controlled order - were superseded by a variety of scenic motifs. However, the basic layout of controlled space remained largely unchanged. The spatial structure of English landscape gardens continued to rely entirely on perspective.

Furthermore, the disobedience of the bourgeoisie was largely limited to their garden spaces. Beyond the garden fence, in the rural areas - in the farmland - parcelling out continued, following the agrarian reforms; new linear structures in the rural landscape were set off by kilometres of new stone walls and hedgerows, sharp-cut wood fringes and ruler-straight drainage ditches.

The layout of urban space according to the principles of controlled order continued, e.g. with boulevards modelled on Haussman's Paris. In the attractive suburban areas sites were parcelled out for bourgeois single-family houses, and all the while the allotment gardens of the workers were sprouting up in more humble locations on the urban fringe.

The emergence of allotment gardens

Opinions differ as to the origins of Danish allotment gardens. Some studies include the Fredericia rampart gardens. However, I consider the Aalborg gardens of the late 19th century to be the first. Only with these gardens did the organizational structure emerge on which the allotment garden movement was based. The first Danish allotment gardens were started in 1884, by Jørgen Berthelsen, an Aalborg haulage contractor. Berthelsen was the chairman of Arbejderforeningen af 1865 (The Workers' Association of 1865). To begin with he tried to persuade the association to realize his great idea: Establishing workers' mini-gardens. However, when this failed, he rented a

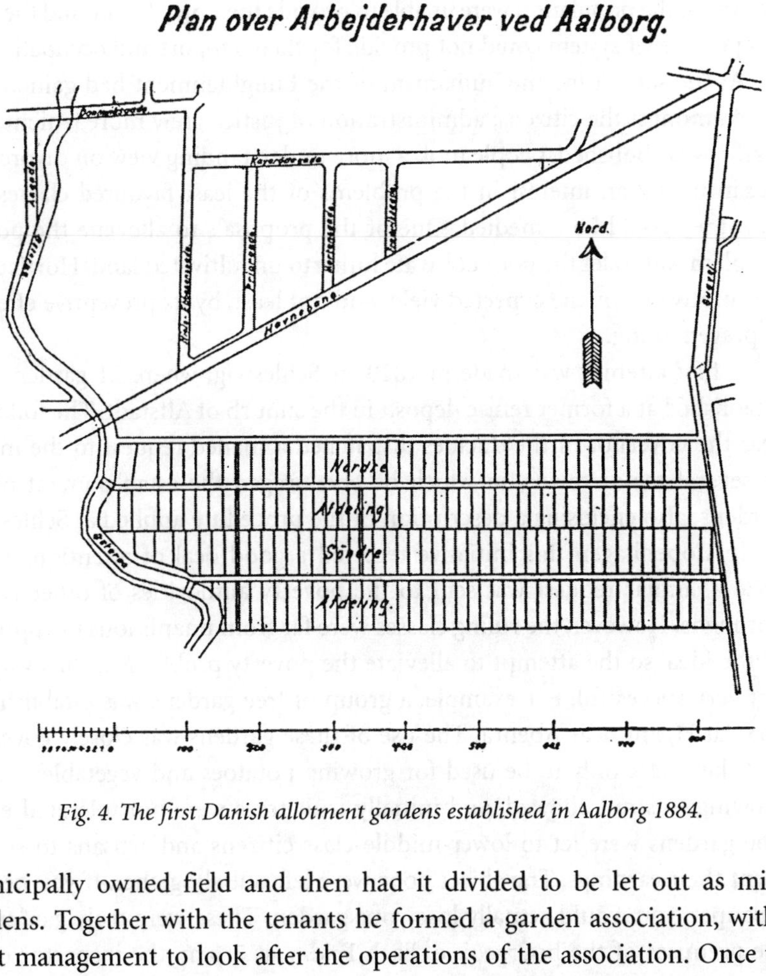

Plan over Arbejderhaver ved Aalborg.

Fig. 4. The first Danish allotment gardens established in Aalborg 1884.

municipally owned field and then had it divided to be let out as mini-gardens. Together with the tenants he formed a garden association, with a joint management to look after the operations of the association. Once the concept had found its final form, allotment garden associations began to pop up like daisies in a field. By the turn of the century there were more than 10,000 gardens all over the country (Fig. 4).

However, the predecessors of the Aalborg gardens were the free gardens, or "Armengärten", established in the early 1800s in the major towns of several Northgerman duchies. Their background was the urgent poverty problems, aggravated by the Napoleonic Wars and the following state bankruptcy. Large groups of the population were unable to provide their own bread, and the existing poor relief system could not provide for their support and occupation.

At the same time the humanism of the Enlightenment had gained foothold amongst the citizens: administration of justice grew more lenient, slave traffic was abolished, people took a more understanding view on divorce and began taking an interest in the problems of the least favoured classes, and how they could be remedied. One of the proposals to alleviate the poverty problem was to let the poor cultivate hitherto uncultivated land. Horticulture was motivated by the expected yield, and not least, by its preventive effect on depraved idling.

A first attempt was made in 1820, at Schleswig, where 21 gardens were established at a former refuse deposit in the suburb of Altstadt. The following year the governor of the duchies dispatched a mailed request to the mayors of several major towns, in which he encouraged the establishment of free gardens, also enclosing a description of the procedure applied at Schleswig.

In Copenhagen this initiative received a good deal of attention, and in 1826 a similar request was sent to the poverty authorities of other Danish boroughs. However, the ruling classes were far from unanimous in approving of the idea, so the attempt to alleviate the poverty problems in this way was not very successful. For example, a group of free gardens was established in 1833 at Hjelm near Åbenrå. The use of these gardens was closely governed, and they were only to be used for growing potatoes and vegetables. Grain-growing was not allowed, and initially fruit trees were not tolerated either. The gardens were let to lower-middle-class citizens and artisans to supplement their earnings. The abject poor were left out altogether. If you became a pauper, you would actually lose your garden. These were truly gardens on the premises of the bourgeoisie: Each Friday at 7 p.m. the inspector of the municipal authoritities would appear to ensure that all was in good order.

The free gardens did not last long, and by the mid-1800s most of the free gardens had been closed down. However, what had failed as a state initiative proved very successful with the joint management of the allotment garden people themselves. People got together at their workplaces and in urban neighbourhoods and rented nearby fields or municipal building sites with no current construction plans. The fields were divided into gardens and cultivation was started. The garden associations were thriving. The allotment garden movement perpetuated the original objective of the free gardens: to secure a much needed extra source of food for the poorest people, and to secure a healthy life away from the perils of the city, such as idleness and drinking.

During the first few decades of its existence the movement had an incredible dynamics. The members promoted the movement by arranging exhibitions, setting up demonstration gardens and model allotments, and garden associations shot up all over the country. In 1908, the majority of the garden associations joined a corporation of allotment garden societies. The number of allotment gardens increased steadily, peaking at well over 100,000 gardens in the late 1940s; since then the figure has decreased to some 60,000 today.

Initially the gardens were cultivated with the explicit aim of supplying vegetables for the family, above all cabbage and potatoes. Later the choice of vegetables grew more varied, and luxury commodities such as strawberries found their way to the beds. Right from the beginning people used to leave a bit of space for flowers, e.g. a rose bed fringed with lavenders. Up to the 1950s the self-sufficiency concept prevailed. Later, food-prices gradually dropped so much that growing vegetables was no longer economically worthwhile. Instead flowers and ornamental plants gained a foothold. But still, most gardens have preserved a small space for growing the first new potatoes of the year. In the most recent decades the gardens have changed character. They have become leisure gardens, with a lawn, flowerbeds and marigold edgings, and last but not least, evergreens such as pines, firs, junipers etc., copied from the gardens of detached houses.

The form idiom of the allotment garden - and how to acquire it

Obviously, to the informed observer, the structure and design of allotment gardens have a definite and pervading form idiom. However, what defines and characterizes the allotment gardens of the movement is anything but a unique and original aesthetics - what we see is really Renaissance norms of controlled order, and bourgeois conceptions as to what is "nice and tidy".

When the free gardens were first established, the "penniless" had no say - indeed, we hardly know who they were. It was entirely in the hands of the bourgeois to decide who would be given gardens, where to locate them, how to design them, and how they could be used. When workers and humble folk entered the scene and began to set up allotment gardens on their own, they continued to submit unconditionally to bourgeois style and taste. What mattered to them was getting the chance to cultivate a spot of land - not making their mark as individuals. In Berthelsen's small garden development in Aalborg, with its severe footpaths and regular pattern of parcels, a clear physical order was created, which with minor variations has remained the basic pattern of allotment gardens ever since.

The very fact that these gardens have a strict physical framework provides a regimenting and subordinating effect; any individual break or deviation from the overall order of the garden structure will reveal itself right away. From the outset, in an effort to comply with demands on tidiness and order from others, the allotment garden movement invested much energy into disciplining its membership, so they were taught how to lay out and grow their gardens true to approved principles, and to maintain order and discipline on their own. Model gardens were laid out, horticultural advisers were hired, expositions and competitions held, and each year the best gardens were awarded a prize. The executive committee made regular garden rounds to oversee that members kept their gardens according to the precepts, and to reprimand eventual slackers.

The movement itself emphasizes their regimentation and strict social control with its own members as a distinctive feature. *"In the recent thirty or forty years there has been a systematic clean-up of those individuals who are disinclined to toe the line; furthermore there is a far more rigid 'membership control' in our association than what is seen in other social circles ... ,"* said A. Dalskov, a prime mover in the corporation of allotment garden societies during the interwar period.

Their pronounced conformity in relation to established aesthical norms and conventions should be considered under two headings: First, as part of the legacy of a working-class background, with its need to display "clean fingernails" to the citizenry. Second, as linked up with the precarious basic conditions of the movement, often as short-term tenants on municipal or private land with current development plans - a circumstance that would make non-conforming members appear as a threat to the entire existence of

Fig. 5. Parade at the Nazi rally in Nuremberg in the beginning of the 1930s. From Benevolo.

an allotment garden association. Part of the insecurity regarding the future existence of allotment gardens only cleared up in the mid-seventies when - following the amendment to the Danish planning acts - they were finally "recognized". Municipalities were directed to set aside land for allotment gardens in their municipal plans, and wherever possible to preserve those already existing. Notwithstanding, the allotment garden has remained the garden form most narrowly conforming to society's fundamental concepts of order in a perspectively appropriated, geometrically designed, controlled space.

Summary and conclusions
With perspective and geometry the Renaissance era formulated a concept of order regarding physical structures which has remained a tenacious legacy of our culture ever since. A legacy by which we have introduced order in our physical environment as well as our minds. An all-embracing order has filtered into the remotest parts where Western culture has left its imprints, encompassing everything, from the spaces of the mighty to the sanctuaries of the disenfranchised. Only in nooks and niches do we still find, as reminiscences, other forms of cultural order.

As a comprehensive illustration of controlled order I have selected a photograph from the Nazi party rally in the early 1930s; the picture amply illustrates the beauty as well as the regimentation implicit in the controlled order of the Renaissance (Fig. 5). In most people the picture of ostentatious Nazi power still evokes disgust and repugnance, however, once we overcome our aversion, we realize that the picture is an exemplary illustration of architectural elements derived from Renaissance aesthetics. The picture space is arranged in a strict perspective axiality, based on simple forms in monumental dimensions.

Its design alludes to the classic Renaissance garden and its classic vista of garden and landscape, as prescribed by Alberti's architectural treatise. In the foreground is the neat garden, laid out in a strict square pattern, which at the same time provides an optical measuring unit for the progression of the central axis towards infinity. At middle-distance the huge falanx of disciplined party-members, is arranged as large geometrical units. And in the background, like a range of hills delimiting the space and measuring its width, the large platform with Nazi symbols as its familiar emblems.

An image of classic beauty, and an image of power and suppression. Today, the detached observer will not fail to find its air of dominance and control striking. But someone placed within the framework of controlled order, and sharing its value basis, would hardly perceive the regimentation, dominance and control aspects of order. Even the last Nazi member, in the back row, at the edge of the outermost unit, would hardly concede that the Nuremberg parade was about submission and dominance; no more than the allotment garden owner would concede that in his allotment garden - behind the protective green hedges, under the waving Danish flag, surrounded by roses, marigolds and new potatoes - he is submitted to regimentation by controlled space.

A distinctive feature of the controlled order of Renaissance is that it embraces beauty as well as discipline. However, only its beauty aspect is visible; discipline and domination are not experienced as long as you partake in and share the value basis of this order. In the course of time the order and legitimacy of controlled space have often been disputed. The bourgeoisie tried to replace the strict geometrical forms with the organic elements of the landscape garden. Impressionists tried to break up linear perspective by moving close to their motifs, cubists by insisting on perspective pluralism, and functionalists by choosing scientifically reasoned human needs as their starting point. There were many who wished to create a new aesthetics, and to replace one controlled order with another. But despite their efforts and energy, true changes in the robust cultural conventions that govern the design of the human environment are surprisingly few and far between.

Thus, both our mental and our physical order are tenacious ideological structures, carried along for generations, indeed (as for the ruling physical order) for centuries. We are thoroughly permeated with a controlled order, generated by our fascination with perspective space, and in order to enable us to orientate in space without needing to face the unexpected.

It is also a rigid order, and it is an open question how it can be harmonized with other ideals of a modern society, including a growing focus on the values of individual freedom: Will it be possible for us to continue living in and with this order, or are there any indications of changed priorities?

In my view there is some evidence that changes in our value basis are under way, in terms of how we organize and design our surroundings. My observation is that the most eloquent indication is the broad and persistent criticism and debate on the way our physical environment has been designed since the early sixties. In the growth phases of a welfare society we were basically, in most areas of life, content with the principles governing the social production created; whether general living conditions, such as working conditions, education system, healthcare system, old-age care; or actual products, such as housing, foodstuffs, cars, television and so on. Only in one field has persistent scepticism and criticism prevailed during the entire period: in relation to the production landscape of the welfare society, i.e. the design of our physical environment, broadly speaking. More than anything the house building of the sixties and the seventies has come under fire, because of the physical design of the buildings as well as recreational spaces. However, the general urban restructuring - ranging from urban renewal to industrial/commercial and road construction - has been subject to persistent criticism. In a similar way, the industrialized "farmscapes" were exposed to severe criticism, both from ecological and aesthetical viewpoints.

A possible interpretation of this criticism and its scope could be that we are going through an emotional break with controlled order - that the present criticism of our house building, construction and physical environment springs from changed value premises. I base my interpretation on the fact that the criticized production landscape conforms, in every respect, to the premises of controlled order. This makes it more than likely that the foundation of our criticism has changed, meaning that our demands regarding the design of our environment are based on new premises.

A similar interpretation could apply for the environmental debate of the past two decades which, beside pollution and resource issues, also holds visions for a different man-nature relationship. One which is closer and more sensuous, thus also implying a break with controlled order. Such a broad interpretation foreshadows an upheaval in our mental order; an upheaval, however, that has only just begun to penetrate in the design of our actual, physical environment by which we will still be socialized into controlled order and - for better or worse - for years to come.

I Live in a Beautiful House, on a Beautiful Street in Beautiful Montreal: Notes on Well-being and the Experience of Place Aesthetics

Perla Serfaty-Garcon

Are early, multisensory experiences of places significant for a person's ideals and self-image?

I have traveled to and lived in many countries, where I have enjoyed many nights and days in unfamiliar rooms and streets, enthusiastically "taken in" by a wide array of landscapes, and admired old and new neighborhoods. I have loved and acted upon many places away from home, transformed and maintained them with great determination and pains. Yet, the word "beauty" still evokes for me essentially the many facets of a Mediterranean landscape, garden and house, as well as what I spontaneously recognize as the characteristics of Mediterranean human beauty.

I have had this knowledge about this deeper me as long as I can recall, while many other facets of my own self have long been hidden to me, or remain obscure and hardly sketched in my conscience. I thus conduct my life with a clear awareness of the meaning to me of the word "beautiful", while, on the other hand, I continue my struggle to better know many aspects of my own self.

Yet, my walk along the meandering path to self-understanding and my sense of beauty are one. For what I call "Mediterranean beauty" is the anchor of my search, its foundation, and the limpid conviction from which I spring to more discoveries, sometimes in grace and many times in distress. It is the stable element in the flow of my life, the reference that gives measure to my pace.

I do not, however, experience this reference as a secure fixture. As stable as it may seem at first glance, my silent walk towards my own self often brings me to unstable grounds where "Mediterranean beauty" is much less a solid certitude than a multifaceted experience, a home base from which I appraise the places I inhabit or visit, where I confront obstacles, and to which I return.

Light
Mediterranean beauty is light, fresh, unsullied summer light at dawn, the serene and brief moment of silence and pause between sleep and being awake on the roof of my childhood house.

It is the active early morning light, during the only hours when work seems legitimate. It is the still noon light and the pounding afternoon light you love but retreat and protect yourself from, the light of the secluded hours behind closed windows. This light means pause, a retreat into oneself, and loving distance from the world, secure in the knowledge that it is indeed

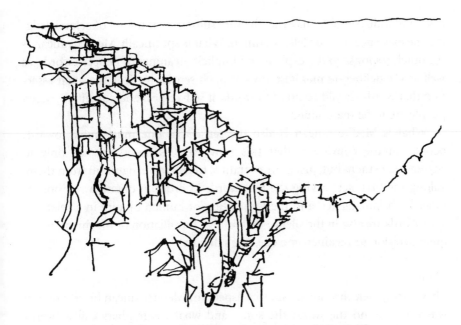

Fig. 1. "Mediterranean beauty". Manarola, Italy (B. Cold).

waiting outside beyond the walls. It is the light of the siesta and farniente, and, indeed, the true light of intimacy.

Thus Mediterranean beauty is in essence a rhythm, a movement that allows the withdrawal into homes and oneself before bringing people together, that requires them to take their leave, only to soon insist that they reassemble later, at the fall of the day (Fig. 1).

Words

To a foreign ear, I am told, talk among Mediterranean people sounds at times like quarreling, and at times like·a song with too many peaks. Fast talk, dizzying talk, changing facial expressions, lively hands' talking, all Mediterranean, I have heard.

Everywhere in the world, talk is in the gaze and the smile, in the body posture and the movements of the hands, in active words as much as in silence. To me, Mediterranean beauty is the acute awareness that talk is the basic and indispensable material, the very substance of the act of acknowledging the existence of your fellow human. What is specifically Mediterranean is the quick response to the explicit and implicit meanings of people's words, as well as the deliberate manifestation of one's sensitivity. It is the open assertion that words should respond to words, if self-respect and equality between people are to be maintained.

What is Mediterranean is also the sense that one must move towards people, in the conviction that this movement is necessary, not only to acknowledge them but, just as importantly, to receive recognition from them. Taking the first step, saying the first words in order to obtain a response is indeed a balancing act, and the foundation of human dignity in a relationship.Words are also in the silence that follows humiliation or the threat, in the quiet decision to regain, some day, one's dignity.

Place

I have always felt that some essential aspects of Mediterranean beauty bloom wherever around the world the sun - and what geographers call a "warm climate"- make people close windows early in the morning to keep the cool fresh air in like a precious possession, and to open them at night, dragging chairs on doorsteps, parading late into the night on crowded streets, before spending most of the night under the stars, submerged in the songs of cicadas.

I am fully aware that this kind of beauty that translates into the daily dance of people in and out of the houses and in the streets not only comes from the sun but is grounded in the Mediterranean sea. However, my intuition is that I would also experience some of its aspects and variations, for example, in South American villages, country homes and city neighborhoods, as well as in some southern cities in the United States.

Indeed, while in the Caribbean islands, in Mexico or Arizona, even in Kansas, I complained only indifferently about the blinding sun, the unforgiving heat, the slow pace of things, the nonchalance of people or the half-finished repairs to houses and hotels. For, in my heart of hearts, all these things happen in a warm place, under a hot sun, which are redeeming qualities in my eyes, not only because they make beauty what it essentially is, but also because they make such places at once foreign and familiar to me.

Because of this rich paradox I accepted and sometimes even welcomed with excitement what in fact hindered my daily activities but evoked familiar human patterns of behavior so far away from home.

Orange trees in California, oleanders in Israel, palm trees in Venezuela ... such encounters at once take me back to my long lost southern home in a city at the edge of the desert and give to each newly discovered place a richer texture, a more complex identity. In such cases and when it comes to the experience of my well-being, the knowledge that these trees have been imported for agricultural or ornamental purposes is of little relevance to me. They give a specific accent to the strange or exotic landscape, stir in me a secret and brief emotion, reassure me that Mediterranean beauty has its own scattered presence in the world.

Water is one of Canada's impressive riches and beauties. Yet, to this day, I cannot approve of the fact that Montrealers do not have to pay for the water running from their taps. Fresh water remains to me a precious resource in the house, as well as a rare part of the southern landscape. Lakes and rivers are fragile and sometimes merely seasonal, as in the case of the water that briefly rushes through wadis and disappears quickly in the soil. The powerful and vital images of the sea in Mediterranean countries does not clash with the deeply ingrained attitude of restrained use and appreciation of fresh water. Swimming in a Canadian lake or Norwegian fjord still gives me, after years of absence from southern countries, a sense of splendid luxury, the way Mediterranean fruit groves create a sense of plenitude. Indeed, the bounty of fruit is everywhere the result of adequate use of fresh water, but most particularly in Mediterranean countries where both remain, to some degree, miracles.

Yet, my keen awareness of the aesthetic qualities of Mediterranean places makes me a skeptical and partial visitor to many arid places around the world where some of these qualities are attained and even exceeded at great cost. At the core of this personal contradiction is my love of gardens. I approach arid places with the familiar knowledge and past intimate experiences of Mediterranean countries, where a shaded garden is a privilege and a prized possession, the essence of poetic longings and expressions of peace and intimacy, as well as the very translation of the oasis. It is from this experience that, for example, large expanses of lush parks and gardens, lawns, and flower beds around institutional or corporate buildings in Arizona or California, and even homes, sometimes lend an air of dubious beauty to me. On the other hand, the evocation of the Israeli pioneers' legendary motto "make the desert bloom", I hold dear and admire in its applications, in spite of reservations I draw from my readings, in particular from Israeli literature. This "logical" contradiction is summed up by the fact that while I appreciate the beauty of vast lands rendered hospitable and fruitful, as for example in Arizona, and feel comfortable in its hotels and campuses surrounded by beautifully tended grounds, I am moved and exhilarated by a fuller sense of beauty at the sight of the Negev, comparatively tiny dates groves or the streets and lanes of its kibbutzim. This more intense experience – and the well-being that comes with it – is due in part to my sense that in the Negev the desert itself is still palpable, each oasis is narrowly self-contained, and the fragility of the place is still there to a degree.

North

I am happy in Norway. I have several good friends in Norway, and one great and close one there whom I visited during winter as well as summer. I have fond memories of winter weeks spent in Finland. I have frequently traveled to Denmark, each time with renewed pleasure and excitement. I have lived one memorable year in Sweden with my family, and I hold towards that country what may be considered an illegitimate sense of familiarity. I do not understand or speak any of the Scandinavian languages, but I can tell when Danish as opposed to Swedish or Norwegian is spoken, and this tiny link to those languages also gives me what is, doubtlessly again, an unjustified sense of familiarity.

Yet, yet … legitimate or not, justified or not, I cherish this feeling because it stems from my discovery of an entirely different beauty which remains, in my opinion, blissfully half proclaimed in the world, in the same way a truly great poem is said in the simplest manner.

After the brief, fragile and precious dawns of the Mediterranean summer, its torrid mid-days and its black nights, the unexpected experience of the north's summer, its warm, flowing, much less rhythmic days and long white nights came as an exhilarating widening of my world. Hot summer days on

Fig. 2. Håholmen, an island not far from Trondheim, Norway (B. Cold).

one of the islands of Stockholm's archipelago did not absolutely require that I retire inside before mid-morning, and although the days were wonderfully warm on the islands off Trondheim, the water of the fjord was ice-cold. White on white, cold on hot, a continuous flow of time moving slowly towards the end of summer make the soothing beauty of the North (Fig. 2).

Luminous winters and falls, Canada's beauty is much more than that, but the consoling, calm and generous luminosity of its winter and fall days are at the core of my well-being in this country, as they counterbalance the length of the cold season. More than the objective coldness of the weather, to me, the long succession of short days and long nights is the real burden, for they require from me a full array of very small, sometimes hardly conscious daily efforts to appreciate my lot here and simply be happy. These efforts are obviously the backbone of my adaptation to this country, but they also are much more than that since they take me beyond nostalgia into the active absorption of Canada's beauty. Thus, even if my comfortable life in Canada has its edge of fantasies of sun-soaked Mediterranean cities, olive groves and parched countryside, it is sustained, even succored, by aesthetic qualities that are not evocative of them, but are place-specific and the source of dynamic experiences of a wide range of daily fleeting joys.

Home

My house is beautiful, not because it fulfills any elevated aesthetic code, has rich objects or unique furniture but because I inhabit it with a sense of happiness. Every dweller could obviously write this same sentence about his or her home, the legitimacy of such an assertion lying simply in the process of appropriation.

My appropriation of my home, and therefore my private sense of my wellbeing, is a subtle negotiation between my search for a renewed experience of Mediterranean beauty even in Montreal, and my acceptance of given, placespecific circumstances. House hunting in Montreal was a disappointing search for a while until I entered a sun flooded house whose living room looked on a mature grape vine. I am now aware that the instant decision to live precisely in this house and to overlook several of its objective defects is rooted in my sense of returning to the possession of the grape covered arbour in my father's garden, and therefore, in a symbolic way, to my southern childhood home. Anyone with an objective approach to the architectural qualities of these two houses would be at a loss to find any similarities between them. I do not find any either. But both homes have plenty of light and sun and an arbour that provides me with a sense of beauty and well-being. And, as I distribute around me the bounty of grapes at the end of each summer, I recall the acknowledgement of one's neighbor and the warmth and expressiveness that to me are the mark of southern human relationships, and it becomes clear to me that it is from the Mediterranean sources of my well-being that I can say that I live in a beautiful home, on a beautiful street in beautiful Montreal.

Environmental Aesthetics and Well-being: Implications for a Digital World

Daniel Stokols

Is digital communication a "dead end" for developing and experiencing real-life aesthetics?

Does the aesthetic enrichment of human environments enhance individuals' health and community well-being? The links between environmental aesthetics and health have received limited empirical attention, but several theoretical perspectives suggest that the relationships are strongly positive. At an empirical level, several studies have examined the links between individuals' perception of built and natural environments, and their emotional and physiological well-being. A large number of these investigations have focused on people's preferences for natural environments and have demonstrated the "restorative" capacity of these settings to reduce attentional fatigue and psychological stress.[1] Another line of research has examined the material and symbolic qualities of built, as well as natural, environments that evoke positive emotional reactions and feelings of restoration among persons exposed to them.[2] These two lines of research converge to suggest that

(1) people routinely develop strong preferences for built as well as natural environments; and

(2) individuals' exposure to their favorite or most preferred settings is generally associated with enhanced emotional and physiological well-being.[3]

The empirical studies of environmental preference and well-being, noted above, have focused primarily on individuals' cognitive and emotional states, rather than on aggregate indices of community health and civic participation. However, several urban design theorists suggest that the presence of aesthetically enriched objects and places within the broader community, such as public spaces that have historic and symbolic significance, art museums, concert halls, and repertory theaters that provide social settings for experiencing beautiful art works, dramatic and musical performances, has a positive influence on community cohesion and well-being.[4] The enhancement of community health, resulting from exposure to aesthetic and symbolically meaningful public environments, might be manifested through a stronger sense of collective identity and attachment to place, greater participation in civic organizations and public settings, higher levels of civility in interpersonal transactions, and reduced levels of violence in the population.

Whereas little scientific attention has been paid to the links between environmental aesthetics and community well-being, there are reasons to expect that these relationships will attract greater research interest in the coming years as digital information technologies become more pervasive in society. The present discussion considers the potential impact of the internet and World Wide Web on people's aesthetic values and experiences. The term internet denotes the vast array of electronic connections that link millions of computers and their users throughout the world. The internet supports several different forms of computer-mediated communication (CMC) including electronic mail, e-mail listservers (groups of e-mail users organized around certain topics), electronic bulletin boards and newsgroups, and sites on the World Wide Web that range from non-interactive to interactive displays of textual, graphical, and auditory information and media.[5]

The major premise of this discussion is that society's growing reliance on the internet and World Wide Web may undermine the cultivation of aesthetic qualities within the large-scale sociophysical environment and, thereby, reduce the positive influence of environmental aesthetics on personal and community well-being. Before tracing the links between telecommunications technology, environmental aesthetics and well-being, it is important to differentiate between the following key terms: aesthetic quality, media, values and experiences. The *aesthetic quality* of an environment is the extent to which a particular geographic area is characterized by aesthetically enriched stimuli, objects and or places. The beauty of an environment can be enhanced through a variety of *aesthetic media*, including music, dance, repertory, cinema, architecture, sculpture, photography, artistic sketches and paintings. *Aesthetic values* refer to an individual's or group's commitment of energy, time, and resources toward the cultivation of aesthetic quality in the sociophysical environment and in society as a whole. *Aesthetic experience* refers to an individual's perception and appreciation of the beautiful qualities of an environment.

The terms aesthetic quality, media, values and experiences provide a basis for examining the potential impact of telecommunications technology on environmental aesthetics, and the influence of aesthetic environments on personal and community well-being. An essential starting point for considering these relationships is the phenomenal growth of the internet and World Wide Web during the 1990s. A recent survey of Web usage found that the number of recorded sites on the World Wide Web grew from 10,022 to 650,000 between December, 1993 and January, 1997 - a 65-fold increase.[6] In the US alone, the number of households using the internet grew from 3.1 million in 1994 to an estimated 28 million by 1998.[7]

The internet and World Wide Web, like the revolutionary technologies of the automobile, television and the jet engine that preceded them, have the potential to fundamentally alter the ways in which people live and work.[8] For instance, the increasing prevalence of desk-top computing in society and greater access to the internet and World Wide Web have made telecommuting and home-based work much more feasible for large segments of the population. At the same time, the development of instantaneous communications via the internet, incorporating multiple media such as text, graphics, video and audio, have given computer users much greater access to geographically distant people and places. In the realm of aesthetics, it is now possible to take "virtual" (computer-simulated) tours of the world's great art galleries and museums, and to "download" digital recordings of classical and contemporary music from a multitude of musical archives located on the Web.[9]

The translation of aesthetic media into digital form has given millions of computer users greater access to diverse art forms on the internet and World Wide Web. Digital technologies have made possible the high-fidelity recording and dissemination of music, photography and graphic arts for those in society who enjoy convenient access to the internet. Moreover, several sites on the World Wide Web serve an important educational function by providing detailed information about the evolution and distinguishing features of various art forms, thereby promoting artistic appreciation and stronger aesthetic values among the participants in these virtual settings. Thus, there are compelling reasons to believe that digital communications technologies have enriched the quality of people's residential and work environments by expanding their opportunities to learn about and experience a variety of aesthetic media. In view of these positive developments, is it reasonable to suggest that the internet and World Wide Web could have an *undermining* influence on environmental aesthetics and, in turn, on personal and community well-being?

In addressing this question, it is important to distinguish between an individual's experience of aesthetic media as they are digitally transmitted and displayed on their personal computer, in the context of their residential, work, school or other settings; and a group's shared experience of aesthetic media and events as they occur in public or semi-public places. Whereas the internet can expand computer users' access to aesthetic media through digital technologies, it also has the potential to reduce the frequency of social events in which community members share aesthetic experiences "face-to-face" with fellow citizens in public settings. This potentially limiting influence of the internet on socially-shared aesthetic experiences can occur in at least three ways.

First, to the extent that computer users spend increasing amounts of their time on the internet - e.g. during leisure or work hours - they have less time available for participating in community environments and events that reinforce shared aesthetic values and experiences. For instance, they may spend less time visiting art galleries, concert halls, repertory theaters, or participating in civic organizations that promote artistic appreciation and the aesthetic enrichment of public environments. In a related vein, some researchers have suggested that the solitary nature of individuals' participation in the internet as they sit alone in front of their computers may constrain their participation in public places and events, eventually leading to an erosion of "social capital" - those "features of social organization such as networks, norms, and social trust that facilitate coordination and cooperation for mutual benefit".[10]

Second, the experience of computer-based aesthetic media often occurs during relatively short intervals and in conjunction with other computing activities such as word processing, sending and receiving electronic mail, and visiting multiple web sites to obtain news updates, weather reports, or other information. Computer-based experiences of aesthetic media are channeled through a video display terminal and interspersed with a variety of non-aesthetic stimuli and information. These non-aesthetic stimuli can disrupt the individual's experience of aesthetic media while using a desktop computer. By contrast, direct experience with an aesthetically-enriched environment typically requires the individual to be immersed in a three-dimensional place that surrounds him or her, and may be characterized by an aesthetic gestalt or "ambiance".[11] The ambiance of a real, or "non-virtual", place encompasses not only the visual features of the setting, but also its acoustic, olfactory, tactile, kinesthetic, and non-verbal behavioral qualities that enable people to experience aesthetic objects and stimuli within a broader, more coherent sociospatial context. Direct contact with aesthetically-enriched environments in "real time", is thus likely to be more engaging and compelling than the experience of aesthetic media while using a desk-top computer.

Third, although digital technologies have enlarged the opportunities available to computer users for learning about art and experiencing a variety of aesthetic media through the internet, these opportunities are disproportionately unavailable to less affluent groups in the community – particularly those who do not own computers or possess the requisite knowledge and training to use them. The potentially undermining impact of the internet on environmental aesthetics and well-being may be especially pronounced among these disadvantaged groups.

The preceding discussion suggests that the rapid growth and expanded use of the internet and World Wide Web could adversely affect the relationships between environmental aesthetics and human well-being. From the vantage point of individuals, the restorative capacity of aesthetic media to reduce psychological stress, mentioned earlier, may be offset by their experiences of stimulation overload resulting from a surfeit of electronically-transmitted information and communications.[12] Moreover, the greater number and rapidity of electronic transactions may be so distracting and overloading that individuals find themselves unable to focus on and appreciate the aesthetic qualities of their environments.[13]

At the community level, the negative impact of people's solitary use of computers on their participation in public places and civic life could weaken their sense of collective identity and cohesion. These developments might also undermine the cultivation of aesthetic values by reducing citizens' commitment of energy, time and resources toward the improvement of aesthetic quality in the sociophysical environment and in society as a whole. As noted earlier, the weakening of aesthetic values in society may have the greatest negative impact on low-income groups in the community, whose neighborhood environments are most degraded and in need of aesthetic enrichment.

The plausible links between environmental aesthetics, individual and community well-being, noted above, remain speculative in the absence of confirmatory scientific evidence. Given that such evidence is presently lacking, some useful directions for future research include:

(1) the development of time-budget measures to evaluate the relative frequency of individuals' computer-based experiences of aesthetic media, and their first-hand experiences of aesthetically-enriched objects, places, and events;
(2) systematic comparisons of internet users and non-users with respect to the frequency and duration of their participation in aesthetically-enriched public places and events that foster artistic appreciation among community members;
(3) assessments of the strength and depth of aesthetic values in a community; and
(4) empirical studies to test the hypothesized links between the frequency and duration of individuals' aesthetic experiences - including those that are computer-mediated or, alternatively, involve direct encounters with aesthetic objects, places, and events; and indicators of personal and community well-being, such as self-reports of stress, information over-load, and community-level measures of citizens' collective identity, sense of place and social cohesion.

The lack of scientific evidence for the causal links between environmental aesthetics and community well-being raises an important strategic question: Should community members and decision makers avoid taking steps to reverse the potentially negative effects of digital communications technologies on environmental aesthetics and well-being, in the absence of confirmatory scientific data? A reasonable answer to this question is that there are sufficient theoretical, if not empirical, grounds to warrant the initiation of community programs aimed at improving the aesthetic quality of public environments and fostering aesthetic values and appreciation in society. Examples of these programs include the commitment of greater public resources to the support of art museums, concert halls and repertory theaters;

the enactment of public policies to preserve the historic significance of community environments; and neighborhood "gentrification" and beautification programs designed to enhance the aesthetic quality of urban areas.[14] The societal stakes are too high, and the potential toll on civic participation and community health too great, to warrant the delay of these programs while waiting for confirmatory empirical evidence to become available.

Notes

1 Kaplan, S. (1995). The restorative benefits of nature: Towards an integrative framework. *Journal of Environmental Psychology*. 15, 169-182; Kaplan, R., & Kaplan, S. (1989). *The Experience of Nature: A Psychological Perspective*. Cambridge University Press, New York. Ulrich, R. 1983, Aesthetic and affective response to natural environment. In I. Altman & J. F. Wohlwill (eds), *Behavior and the Natural Environment*, 85-125; Plenum Press, New York. Ulrich, R. S., Simons, R. F., Losito, B. D., Fiorito, E., Miles, M. A., & Zelson, M. (1991). Stress recovery during exposure to natural and urban environment. *Journal of Environmental Psychology*, 11, 201-230.

2 Korpela, K. M. (1992). Adolescents' favourite places and environmental self-regulation. *Journal of Environmental Psychology*, 12, 249-258; Korpela, K. & Hartig, T. (1996) Restorative qualities of favorite places. *Journal of Environmental Psychology*. 16, 221-233; Nasar, J. L. (ed) (1988). *Environmental Aesthetics. Theory, Research and Applications*. Cambridge University Press, New York.

3 Hartig, T. & Stokols, D. (1994). Toward an ecology of stress and restoration. Man and nature: Working Paper 54-1994. Humanities Research Center, Odense University, Odense, Denmark; Parsons, R. (1991). The potential influences of environmental perception on human health. *Journal of Environmental Psychology*, 11, 1-23; Swan, J. A. (ed) (1991). *The Power of Place: Sacred Ground in Natural and Human Environments*. Wheaton, Ill: Quest Books.

4 Alexander, C., Ishikawa, S., Silverstein, M., Jacobson, M., Fiksdahl-King, I. & Angel, S. (1977). *A Pattern Language*. Oxford University Press, New York 610-613; 889-892; Carr, S., Francis, M. Rivlin, L., & Stone, A. (1992). *Public Space*. Cambridge University Press, New York. Katz, P. (in press).

New urbanism. In W. van Vliet (ed), *Encyclopedia of Housing*. Sage Publications, Thousand Oaks, California. Lang, J. (1988). Symbolic aesthetics in architecture: Toward a research agenda. In J. L. Nasar (ed), *Environmental Aesthetics. Theory, Research and Applications*. Cambridge University Press, New York. 11-26. Nasar, J. L. (1994). Urban design aesthetics. The evaluative qualities of building exteriors. *Environment and Behavior*, 26, 377-401; Nasar, J. L. (1998). *The evaluative image of the city*. Sage Publications, Thousand Oaks, California.

5   Negroponte, N. (1995). *Being Digital*. Vintage Books, New York. Rheingold, H. (1993). *The Virtual Ommunity: Homesteading on the Electronic Frontier*. Reading. Addison-Wesley Publishing Co, Minnesota. Schuler, D. (1996). *New Community Networks: Wired for Change*. Reading. Addison-Wesley Publishing Co, Minnesota.

6   Gray, M. (1996). Internet statistics: Growth and usage of the Web and the internet. http://www.mit.edu/people/mkgray/net/.

7   Emerging Technologies Research Group (1997). U.S. Internet Household Forecast. Http://etrg.findsvp.com/timeline/forecast.html.

8   Stokols, D. (in press). Human development in the age of the internet: Conceptual and methodological horizons. In S.L. Friedman and T.D. Wachs (eds), *Assessment of the Environment across the Lifespan*. American Psychological Association, Washington, DC.

9   Mitchell, W. J. (1995). *The City of Bits: Space, Place, and the Infobahn*. Cambridge, MIT Press, Minnesota.

10 Putnam, P. D. (1995), p. 67. Bowling alone: America's declining social capital. *Journal of Democracy, 6*, 65-78; cf., Blanchard, A., & Horan, T. (1997). Can we surf together if we're bowling alone? An examination into virtual community's impact on social capital. Paper presented at the American Sociological Association Symposium on the Internet and Social Change.

11 Ittelson, W. H. (1973). *Environment and Cognition*. Seminar Press, New York.

12 Davidson, J. (1996). Handling information overload. Chapel Hill, Breathing Space Institute, North Carolina. http://www.brespace.com/artspub-overload.html; Glass, D. C., & Singer, J.

E. (1972). *Urban stress*. Academic Press, New York.

13 *op cit.*, Kaplan & Kaplan, (1989).

14 Gale, E. (in press). Historic preservation. In W. van Vliet (ed), *Encyclopedia of Housing*. Sage Publications, Thousand Oaks, California. Smith, N. (in press). Gentrification. In W. van Vliet (ed), *Encyclopedia of Housing*. Sage Publications, Thousand Oaks, California. Taylor, R. B. (1988). *Human Territorial Functioning*. Cambridge University Press, New York.

Reasonable Persons and Their Aesthetic Preferences

Einar Strumse

Are there certain environmental attributes that enhance the perceived quality of the environment for most people?

I have never been enthralled by the idea that the quality of the physical environment should be of only minor importance to people, implying that people easily can learn to thrive anywhere, even in settings such as windowless offices or surroundings void of nature or natural elements. On the contrary, personal experience tells me that certain qualities in my physical surroundings, such as air quality, the absence of noise, the presence of nature, an open view from my window and aesthetically pleasing indoor and outdoor design, are crucial to my well-being. I do believe in being serious about the quality of our everyday surroundings, something we too often fail to be. It often seems as if the only way to convince employers, designers and environmental decision makers to take these aspects of life seriously, is to provide scientific documentation of the rather obvious fact that environmental aesthetics does matter.

My own environmental preferences definitely tend towards the rural setting, a consequence of my childhood as well as much of my adulthood spent in such surroundings. Thus, the objection that my conclusions about environmental aesthetics might be too prejudiced by such personal experiences to be taken seriously would undoubtedly be true if my intention had been to argue on the basis of these experiences alone. There is no need for this, as there is ample evidence from studies within the field of environmental psychology to supplement the more intuitive conclusions about aesthetical preferences.

In the following I will discuss some of the effects of natural and built elements on aesthetical experience from the perspective of cognitive environmental psychology. It is important to note that I am looking at that part of the aesthetical experience that can be labelled visual environmental preference, defined as how much a person likes a particular landscape scene. I will focus on some benefits of taking lay people's aesthetical (i.e. visual) preferences into account in environmental design, and suggest a possible procedure for how this can be done. A few additional remarks may help to clarify some of the assumptions underlying this essay.

Let us assume that most people would tend to prefer, visually at least, some categories of natural surroundings over many human-made ones. On common sense grounds, I think this can be defended for at least the following reasons: Knowing that human evolution, with the exception of the last few thousand years, has taken place in natural settings, it seems likely that the human perceptual apparatus over the generations gradually has come to respond positively towards those characteristics of natural settings that facilitate survival. Thus, it would be useful to develop a visual preference for settings that promise relief from uncomfortable states such as thirst and hunger, and that seem to nurture feelings of security, control and so on, in other words, environments where one will be able to function effectively. Many natural environments certainly satisfy these demands, such as those including water, vegetation and some degree of openness. These settings would probably more often than not also be aesthetically pleasing, although it would be misguided to believe that natural settings always are preferred. For example, there is little reason to believe that this would be so in the case of inaccessible, overgrown natural areas.

On the other hand, some human-influenced settings, particularly those in which most or all natural elements have been removed or are clearly dominated by built structures, would, unless well designed, most likely not be visually preferred by many. It would, however, be terribly wrong to assume that all human-influenced environments are disliked. Consider the fact that historical buildings and traditional settlements are such popular tourist attractions, suggesting that certain blends of natural and built features may result in highly attractive environments. It seems important to identify the precise nature of these blends, both because the human-made aspects of our surroundings are inevitable and increasingly omnipresent, and because they exert a non-negligable influence on the quality of aesthetical experience and human well-being. For this reason, it becomes strongly desirable that human environmental modifications serve to enhance the perceived quality of the environment. For a variety of reasons, this seems far too often not to be the case, although there is an increasing willingness to heighten the aesthetical value of some settings, such as older downtown areas.

Seen from a psychological perspective, one such reason appears to be that environmental design often is dictated more by fashion and pragmatic factors, such as cost of implementing a certain design solution, than by knowledge about human environmental perception and well-being. However, it should come as no surprise that design and planning flawed by insufficient or inappropriate knowledge does not result in successful outcomes. Indeed, a significant body of evidence suggests that negative outcomes in landscape planning and management in many cases can be traced back to a lack of knowledge about people s landscape preferences, and to the fact that designers and other decision makers' environmental preferences often differ sharply from those of the public.

Far from everybody accepts the position stated above that people - more or less intuitively - would tend to prefer visually nature-dominated or nature-compatible surroundings. On the contrary, many writers hold that visual environmental preference is nothing but a function of familiarity, of getting used to certain surroundings, and that people born in cities feel perfectly at ease there, having no particular need for more nature in their surroundings. Likewise, rural people would thrive in rural surroundings exactly because they are used to them. Not being necessarily false, I think this position is far from telling the whole story. How do we, for example, account for the fact that so many urban residents escape from their presumed favourite setting every weekend to recreate in some wilderness or rural area, or why is eco-tourism increasingly popular among urban populations? Although a need for variation may account for some aspects of the phenomena, one is left with a suspicion that heavily human-influenced and built areas fail to satisfy important human needs. In the cities, the existence of a large number of parks and recreation areas indicates a general awareness of the need for natural surroundings, even if this is not founded on behavioural or social-science knowledge.

Before looking at the records of visual preference research, I would like to underscore that there is concurring support for the arguments above: In particular, a theoretical framework recently proposed by Steven C. Bourassa in his article "A paradigm for landscape aesthetics" appears to present an alternative to the dispute between those who hold that nature is intuitively preferred and those who hold that learning is the most important factor to consider when explaining visual preferences.

Bourassa suggests in his conceptual framework that aesthetical activity, just like any other human behaviour, has both biological (innate, intuitive) and cultural (or learned) components. Building upon the Russian psychologist Vygotsky's developmental approach to human experience and behaviour, he puts forth a theory of aesthetical experience, suggesting three different modes of aesthetical behaviour, the biological (phylogenesis), the cultural (sociogenesis) and the personal (ontogenesis), and that all of these have to be taken into account, as they represent three distinct domains that should not be confounded. Moreover, none of the three modes or approaches can explain the whole range of aesthetic behaviour. Pertaining specifically to landscape aesthetics, Bourassa speculates that

(a) natural landscapes could be assumed to be experienced primarily through the biological mode, i.e. through evolved psychological mechanisms;
(b) the experience of more human-influenced or urban landscapes would probably be dominated by the cultural mode, i.e. heavily influenced by learning and group membership; and that
(c) landscapes that have no particular meaning to any cultural group will be subject to entirely individual preferences.

These hypotheses require more research before any conclusions can be reached. However, we confind research that supports the existence of two perceptual modes: First, various parts of the brain appear to be specialized on, respectively, innate and learned behaviours, and the visual and other sensory systems are directly connected to these different parts. Moreover, results from psychological experiments indicate the development of preferences for stimuli in the absence of cognitive knowledge about them, and that affective judgment can take place in the absence of recall. Thus, these findings suggest that responses to landscapes can be seen as partly independent of conscious processes, and that the existence of separate innate and learned responses to landscape is a real possibility. Bourassa's theoretical framework for landscape aesthetics is also supported by existing research on visual landscape preferences. In the following, I wish to highlight a few insights from environmental psychology concerning

- how the interplay between natural and built elements in outdoor environments affects visual environmental preference,
- the need to integrate input from the general public into environmental design, and
- a procedure by which this information can be obtained.

The aesthetics of the natural and the built

The assumption that people often prefer the natural over the human-made environment is supported by a series of psychological studies of landscape preferences, suggesting both that the degree of naturalness is an important, if not fundamental dimension by which settings are differentiated, and that people tend to prefer natural scenes over partly natural or built scenes. However, a number of studies suggest that built elements can be highly preferred when they are in harmony with, or do not dominate, the natural elements in the setting. On the basis of thorough analyses of the results of these studies, the environmental psychologists Rachel and Stephen Kaplan, in their important book *The Experience of Nature*, formulated their prefer-ence model, highlighting a set of more formal, relatively content-independent criteria for a scene to be preferred: In the model, two cognitive domains are assumed to be of crucial importance to human information-processing; understanding/exploration and the degree of inference needed to process visual information (see Table 1). First, the direct processing of information must be possible. For this to occur, the scene in question must be easy to understand both immediately and more indirectly, thus it needs to possess a certain Coherence, as well as a degree of Legibility. Second, if we agree that exploration is a pervasive human motive, preferred environments should also possess qualities such as Complexity and Mystery (the latter defined as a promise to learn more if one could enter into the landscape) encouraging this. There is as yet insufficient agreement on how many of these dimensions we need to assess a scene adequately, and it appears that the way we combine the dimensions in judging one scene is not always the way we combine them to judge other scenes.

Table 1. Kaplan & Kaplan's Preference Model

	Understanding	Exploration
Direct (two dimensions)	Coherence	Complexity
Inferred (three-dimensions)	Legibility	Mystery

As a more detailed example of how the balance between natural and built elements may influence visual preference, I will present some findings from my own visual preference study of traditional and modern agrarian landscapes in western Norway. Previously, little has been known about lay people's visual perceptions of such landscapes in Norway and how they differ, for example, from those of landscape experts. One important application of such knowledge would be to estimate acceptable levels and forms of human impact in agrarian settings.

Conforming with common sense assumptions stated above, the most preferred settings were those where human influence did not dominate the natural elements present in them, whereas landscapes containing dominating human influence received low preferences. There are two particularly obvious interpretations of these findings. First, low preferences appear to be explained by an intrusive style of human influence, such as modern farm buildings, bridges and road constructions seen in some modern style agrarian landscape scenes, where the natural elements are pushed aside (Fig. 1), whereas high preferences in most cases were associated with a traditional style of human influence, such as stone walls and stone bridges, which could be characterized as being more in harmony with the natural elements in the scenes (Fig. 2). One might speculate that the latter scenes suggested to the observer a more caring relation to nature, or even that they symbolize, to some observers at least, a critical view of contemporary society.

Second, at the level of formal aesthetical factors (such as coherence, legibility, complexity and mystery) the preferences for old traditional farm

Fig. 1. Landscapes containing dominating human influence received low preferences (Photo L. Hauge, Sogndal).

buildings seemed to be explained by their high degree of perceived age, which appeared to be positively related to preference in scenes containing human influence, but not always when vegetation was depicted. Furthermore, old farm environments were also rich in Mystery, i.e., indications that related information could be learned immediately around the corner, thus making the observer want to explore the setting further.

One practical implication of these findings is that public preferences for agrarian landscapes probably would increase if agricultural practice strived to minimize visually negative environmental impacts. Also, the characteristics of traditional agrarian landscapes deserve special attention from agricultural authorities, as the introduction of such characteristics in modern agrarian landscapes would often likely increase their aesthetical value.

The study revealed a far from perfect overlap between expert-based a priori landscape categories, according to which the sample of scenes employed in the study were selected, and the empirical landscape categories derived from statistical analyses of preference ratings of these scenes. The good news here is that the identification of such differences in categorization may serve to enhance communication between experts and lay people in landscape planning and design issues.

*Fig. 2. Settings where human influence did not dominate the natural elements
present in them were highly preferred (Photo L. Hauge, Sogndal).*

Lay people's aesthetic preferences and environmental design

A framework which appears useful both for environmental decision making
in general, and for the proper use of visual preference data in landscape planning and design in particular, has been proposed by Rachel and Stephen
Kaplan in their article "The visual environment: Public participation in
design and planning". In the article, they develop their Reasonable Person
Model, which aims to make public concerns more articulate, make better use
of the talents of the environmental professional, and make the process more
satisfying for all concerned. It is based upon three principles:

- People can be reasonable (i.e. constructive, cooperative, respectful of one
  another's rights) depending upon the circumstances surrounding them.
- People actively seek to understand their world, but are often confused and
  alienated. In complicated matters, visual information appears to be particularly well-suited.
- People's needs are many and varied, and people do not always want the
  maximum amount of things.

According to this model, a satisfactory procedure for obtaining public input should include the following:

- The situation, both in terms of the presented information and reactions called for, must be compatible with human inclinations and capabilities.
- The needed information must be provided in a format facilitating effective understanding.
- The procedure should permit the expression of multiple needs, and not concentrate all needs into one unitary value of which one should be expected to desire the maximum quantity.

I will conclude by providing a brief description of this type of procedure. The most common method applied in the collection of visual preference data is the photo-questionnaire. The usefulness of photographic material has repeatedly been demonstrated in comparison with responses to on-site evaluations, showing that colour slides, colour movies and a naturalistic model were the most valid simulations. By using photographic material one also avoids the control problems involved in taking subjects into real-world settings, such as changing weather conditions, and other uncontrollable and unforeseen events. On the other hand, this type of procedure does not account for many of the other on-site qualities that beyond a doubt affect landscape perception, such as smells, sounds and variations in temperature.

In the context of, for example, public hearings, a special strength of the photo-questionnaire is its capacity to elicit information on a broad spectrum of needs. This is so because participants are not forced to choose among settings, only to rank each alternative (such as a scene representing an environmental design solution for a particular location) in terms of preference for it. If this information is obtained early in the planning process, the development of alternatives can offer a better match to public concerns than what is often the case. Moreover, the visual format has an important advantage over the verbal, because people's concerns about spatial arrangements and visual features are typically not experienced verbally. While verbal items may provide a better idea of the stereotypic response, photographs appear to tap more differentiated and site-specific reactions. Thus, visual images and preference ratings seem well-suited for tapping issues that do not readily lend themselves to discussion, as well as issues where available verbal labels would tend to stereotype a situation.

Concluding remarks

One satisfaction from conducting psychological research on environmental aesthetics has been the confirmation of the everyday experience that the visual qualities in the surroundings, human-made or natural, are far from trivial. As I have tried to make clear, there appear to be certain environmental attributes that enhance the perceived quality of the environment for most people.

As a frame of reference for the application of visual preference data to landscape planning and design, the Reasonable Person Model appears to prepare for a necessary understanding and communication between experts and the public. While experts still should be considered competent in generating design alternatives, the public should be actively drawn into the process of evaluating them. The criteria for successful public participation in environmental planning and design described in the Reasonable Person Model will be satisfied to a high degree by using visual and spatial material in participatory environmental decision making.

I have briefly described some results from a Norwegian study of aesthetic preferences for agrarian landscapes. Based on this study, two future applications of visual preference procedures in the planning and designing of Norwegian agrarian landscapes can be suggested:

(a) Related to the restoration of traditional agrarian landscapes, the procedure could be used as a way of mapping local residents perceptions of the effects of restoration, or of simulations of alternative outcomes of restoration.This would provide experts with insights into peoples subjective categorizations of landscapes and highlight environmental attributes particularly salient in people s minds. Furthermore, information on preferences for the landscapes in question would be of help in making informational and educational material on these landscapes.

(b) The picture preference procedure could be an interesting tool in the exploration of farm environments for the future, for example combining and comparing visual features of, say, traditional, modern and ecological farms. Samples of such scenes could be generated either by using photos of real world settings, simple physical models or by means of computer-manipulated photographs.

References

Bell, P. A., Baum, A., Fisher, J. D. and Greene, J. D. (1990). *Environmental Psychology*. Holt. Rinehart & Winston, Inc, Fort Worth, Texas.

Bourassa, S. C. (1990). A Paradigm for landscape aesthetics. *Environment and Behavior*, 22 (6), 787-812.

Kaplan, R. & Kaplan, S. (1983). *Cognition and Environment. Functioning in an Uncertain World.* Ulrichs Bookstore, Ann Arbor, Michigan.

Kaplan, R. & Kaplan, S.(1989). *The Experience of Nature. A Psychological Perspective.* Cambridge University Press, Cambridge.

Kaplan, R. & Kaplan, S. (1989). The visual environment: Public participation in design and planning. *Journal of Social Issues,* 45 (1) 59-86.

Kaplan, S. (1992). Environmental Preference in a Knowledge-seeking, Knowledge-using Organism. In Barkow, J. H., Cosmides, L. & Tooby, J. (eds). *The Adapted Mind. Evolutionary Psychology and the Generation of Culture.* Oxford University Press, New York/Oxford.

Strumse, E. (1996): The psychology of aesthetics: Explaining visual preferences for agrarian landscapes in Western Norway. Thesis submitted in partial fulfillment of the requirements for the degree of Doctor Philosophae. Research Center for Health Promotion, Faculty of Psychology, University of Bergen, Norway.

Zube, E. H., Simcox, D. E. & Law, C. S. (1987). Perceptual landscape simulations: History and prospect. *Landscape Journal,* 6, 62-80.

Conversations on Aesthetics

David Uzzell

*How may aesthetic preferences of experts and the public be
dealt with in the planning process?*

Context

At the end of 1995, the Building Research Establishment (BRE) asked me to undertake research to assess the feasibility of establishing criteria for assessing the visual impact of buildings.[1] The objective of the study was not to define what a good building is, but to highlight criteria that can be used to assess a building in a manner that is not only acceptable and meaningful to developers and architects, but also to a broader audience that includes, amongst others, the public. If it was deemed feasible, an assessment method would be incorporated into a procedure called the Building Research Establishment Environmental Assessment Methodology (BREEAM).

The BREEAM procedure attempts to set construction standards as a result of assessing the local and global impact of different types of buildings (e.g. residential, retail outlets, offices, industrial) in the context of typical sustainability issues such as CO_2 emissions and energy conservation. With the emphasis to date on sustainability indicators, it is possible for buildings to score well on current assessment criteria but have a poor visual impact. Consequently, the BRE recently decided to extend BREEAM to include an assessment of the visual impact of different types of buildings in the urban and rural landscape. By incorporating visual appearance as a BREEAM criteria, the process can be considered to be a more comprehensive view of environmental quality, especially at the local level.

One of the important elements of the research was to elicit the views of design professionals and the public as to the criteria they consider central to assessing the visual impact of buildings. The discussion which follows is a representation of the conversations held during the research. The interviews were conducted with each of these groups as part of the research, and the following "conversations" represent a distilled and summarised version of these discussions. Therefore, while the words were not spoken by any one individual, the views expressed represent those of each particular group we interviewed.

The paper also incorporates three further "conversations", with Susan Sontag[2] (American essayist and author, based on her influential essay from 1964 entitled "Against Interpretation"), Prince Charles[3] (architectural critic, organic farmer and future king) and my son Jacob, six years old.

DU: Architects have long been held responsible for the quality of design in our cities, but there is a growing realisation that developers are playing, and probably always have played, a critical part in determining the visual appearance of buildings. It is sometimes said that your concern with cost control and maximising financial return per m^2 has meant that issues of aesthetics often taken a secondary role. Do you think this is so?

Developer: At the end of the day I am interested in putting up a building that meets the needs of my client. The first consideration is cost. In any case, the problem is that you will never get agreement anyway on aesthetics - it is not even appropriate to try and define the criteria to assess visual aesthetics. And even if you could define the kind of criteria you would use, you would never get agreement amongst people as to the application of these criteria. It is more appropriate to assess environmental quality than issues directly related to design features. It is so subjective. If you have to have an assessment, you must come up with an objective measure if it is to be credible.

DU: I think it was Fraser Reekie[4] who said over twenty years ago, "What is needed is an objective approach based upon design principles that meet with common agreement, and that will lead to an environment visually acceptable to the great majority." As an architect, do you agree? Is it possible to come up with an objective set of criteria with which everyone will agree?

Architect: You could ask half the architects in this room and they would say that devising a scheme for assessing the visual appearance of buildings is potentially beneficial. Another third would feel that the scheme could be beneficial provided it was implemented with extreme sensitivity and a flexible outlook. The remainder would argue that such a scheme should not be implemented as it is not possible to place simple, unambiguous values on aesthetic quality. Any scheme that attempted to do so would restrain designers and lead to increased conservatism.

Having said that, although there might be difficulties in implementing some kind of procedure for assessing design aesthetics, there are potential benefits. These include an increased visual awareness and debate amongst all professional groups and the enhanced design/planning process leading to, for example, better architecture derived from more stringent planning. It may promote more creative thinking, which can have a positive impact on design without too much extra cost. There is a downside as well though, and this probably outweighs the benefits.

DU: Such as?

Architect: It may encourage pastiche through the misuse, poor implementation or mechanistic application of a scheme. Architects would start to design in order to achieve a particular "look", perhaps a look that they thought those who were responsible for making aesthetic judgements might prefer. Furthermore, visual impact has no precise definition and the concept has a suitable vagueness that defies easy quantification. Nevertheless, I think our training and expertise puts us in a better position than most to judge aesthetic quality.

DU: If, as an architect, you believe that there are criteria essential to good design, do you think it would be possible to reach a consensus with other architects or professionals as to what those criteria might be?

Architect: The problem is different proffessional groups respond to build-ings in different ways making communication and consensus difficult. Even within the profession there is low consensus with regard to good design. Many architects will judge a building on its overall viewpoint and meaning.

DU: This reminds me of Susan Sontag's central argument in her essay, *Against Interpretation*. Sontag's thesis was that art has been subject to too much interpretation. What was it that Susan Sontag wrote? "Interpretation is the revenge of the intellect upon art. Even more, it is the revenge of the intellect upon the world. To interpret is to impoverish, to deplete the world - in order to set up a shadow world of "meanings." It is to turn *the* world into *this* world". The crux of the matter for Sontag is that because art can be about content, because it is supposed to *mean* something, it has been subject to intense interpretation. Things which just appear, which are not ostensibly meant to be anything other than what they are have not come under such widespread rigorous scrutiny.

DU: If you were to try to establish criteria for assessing good design, what would they include?

Architect: The criteria should be broadly devised and applied with flexibility; they should primarily be context based. One also has to remember that visual impact is also an affordability concept. I would like to see such a scheme part of the planning process but independent of planners.

DU: There seems to be a tension between architects and planners in matters of design - at least this is the impression given by architects. You seem to suggest that planners' views are often more closely allied to those of the public rather than those of architects. Perhaps I should ask planners whether they see themselves more as representing public opinion on matters of design. Some of your architecture colleagues suggest that planners often seem to take the side of the public in matters of design control. Indeed, you now have the means to exercise such an advocacy role. In Britain at least, the statutory mechanisms of development control provide planners with the necessary powers to temper excesses and ensure a balanced environment. Is this a fair comment?

Planner: The visual impact of buildings is subject to constraints under current building regulations and planning controls. Such controls are probably more highly developed in the UK than in many other countries. Design, or aesthetic control has applied to all parts of the United Kingdom's development process since 1947. Planning Regulations and Building Regulations, whilst distinct and legally entirely separate, are complementary to one another. Planning and Development Control is concerned with the correct use of land, the appearance of buildings and the consequences of development on surrounding areas, while Building Regulations relate to the physical structure of a building and its stability. The current system requires that any design be reviewed with reference to its external appearance, layout, surroundings, physical impact, circulation, access etc. by planning officials, the Local Authority Planning Committee and, where appropriate, members of the public. The system is "a reasoned, accountable and transparent process" that has raised the standard of design by forcing developers to be more accountable for their actions.

Both planning and building regulations impact the visual appearance of a building, though planning regulations are generally believed to exert more influence in this area. Given that within this framework the objective of planning control is to protect the public interest, it's therefore unsurprising and reassuring that of all the design professionals, planners' values are continually found to be most closely allied to those of the public. Furthermore, local authorities or municipalities are now being encouraged to promote quality design and improvements to the visual environment. This is thought to have positive social and environmental consequences. With the recently introduced Quality Initiative, and the active support of the Secretary of State, the powers of planners to reject developments on the grounds of quality is increasing. The quality concept encompasses issues related to the height, scale, massing, density, size, bulk, landscaping, design features, general architectural quality and usage of a building in terms of the existing character of the area. Planners are not able to reject a design simply because they think there is a better solution. This would be, after all, a subjective judgement. But they are able to reject it if the design is of poor quality or an inappropriate style. Planners must therefore have sufficient skills to distinguish between personal preferences and suitable solutions.

DU: You sound fairly optimistic that a framework for good design is now in place and that, in conjunction with Government initiatives, the quality of the visual environment should continue to improve. You seem to be giving the impression that you would be in favour of more powers to strengthen your ability to control and set design standards. Is this so?

Planner: I tend to agree with the architect who said that one potential pitfall of a scheme is that it may encourage pastiche and the creation of dull buildings by those whose only objective is to achieve some stamp of design approval. There is always the danger when you identify criteria, that good buildings that do not meet the criteria will not be accredited, while poor design that does meet the criteria may be accredited.

DU: Do you think it would be possible to identify criteria to guide design aesthetics?

Planner: Yes, but any measure of appropriateness should be reliable and rigorously determined. At the same time though, the criteria should be flexible and applied with discretion. As a starting point, any system which attempts to formalise design evaluation must make reference to the place-specific context of development to ensure that the process encourages environmental quality. Good design must respect the environment.

DU: Would planners be able to reach a consensus with other professional groups in determining the criteria?

Planners: Yes, I think it would be possible to reach a consensus. There are a number of examples of successful collaborations including the development of new housing estates in West Oxfordshire, the development of Birmingham's City Centre, and the preservation of the London Skyline.

DU: Surely you are not arguing that the present London skyline is living proof of successful collaboration amongst the design professions. I think Prince Charles would disagree with you there.

Prince Charles: Can you imagine the French doing this sort of thing in Paris, on the banks of the Seine around Notre Dame? Or the Venetians building tower blocks next to San Marco? When did we lose our sense of vision? How could those in control become so out of step with so many Londoners who felt powerless to resist the destruction of their City. There is no need for London to ape Manhattan. We already possessed a skyline. They had to create one. And there is no need for buildings, just because they house computers and word processors, to look like machines themselves.

DU: I'm sure that view would receive considerable support from conservationists. Conservationists, however, are often criticised for their inherent conservatism, stifling innovation and initiative in design and generally only liking what they know and knowing what they like. Do you think this is a fair criticism?

Conservationist: No I do not. I appreciate that we often come up against planners and architects, but we do have the best interests of the community and the built environment at heart. I think we have an important moderating voice which, at the end of the day, leads to a general raising of standards of architectural design. In a sense our role can be educational - we can raise expectations of all concerned, provide a framework for discussion and enhance the quality of designs.

It is simply not true to say that conservationists are conservative and resist innovation when it comes to design. Conservationists welcome novel design. However, novel design is only likely to work if it respects the environment.

Our job is to act on behalf of the community in order to encourage responsible design. If the Quality Initiative is to mean anything, and we are to get a better quality of design, especially in historic towns, then expert judges are needed to assess the merits of design proposals. These can come from within the municipalities but they could also come from other bodies such as conservation organisations. From a historic perspective there are many local authorities who do not have staff that are qualified to judge applications relating to historic buildings. Adaptations of use are probably leading to more damage than demolition. The use affects the character. When considering a change of use, especially in historic buildings, it is essential that the implications of that change are considered.

DU: Do you think identifying criteria which can be used to assess visual impact and design aesthetics is a good idea? The architects I have spoken to think it might be possible to arrive at a consensus as to the kind of criteria one would use. Do you agree?

Conservationist: Yes, the introduction of some kind of assessment system could be used as a guide and a process to influence pre-planning application discussions and the design brief. It could also be used at the outline planning permission stage as well as when considering detail design submissions.

As to the question of reaching an agreement between the various groups involved, it may be possible to derive a sufficient degree of consensus - it is at least worth trying. However, architects tend to look from the site outwards, whereas planners tend to look from the context to the building. Funding institutions and developers look at the cost. This difference in attitude tends to produce friction.

Mr. And Mrs. Public: I think most people are more concerned about what goes on inside a building rather than the outside. But having said that, the outside of a building is important isn't it? It contributes so much to the way a place looks.

DU: But the visual appearance of a building is more important than that surely. Does it not tell us something about the nature of the activities going on inside? Does it not invite us to enter? What do you think, Jacob? Do you think it is important that places look nice?

Jacob: Yes, because if a place looks nice you'll want to play there.

DU: That's an interesting point of view because it suggests that it is not just a question of assessing buildings in terms of form or function. Rather, there is an important interaction between the two - not just in the obvious sense that form may suggest function, but form can also invite use.

One cannot look at aesthetics without reference to meaning or use of place in the larger context. This leads one to ask to what extent can aesthetic judgements by architects, planners, developers, politicians and the public be specific, site-related or meaningful at the community scale,[5] or to what extent should they be abstract and universal?

Principles of good design are place-centred and expressive of time and culture. Design excellence is not easily defined by the objective, hard and fast principles that this would dictate.

Concern for visual quality should not be confined to a few limited architectural set pieces, or post-hoc landscape work - it should apply equally to the whole built environment and be an important criteria from the earliest stages in the planning and design of buildings. One cannot make an assessment of the visual impact of buildings in isolation. Any visual assessment of buildings has to take into account their environmental context and the degree to which they "fit" into the environment. This raises a number of questions, for example, what are the factors that make a building suited to its context and environmentally compatible? Of these, which are the most important factors? Which of these are under the control of the architect and which are determined by national or local building and planning regulations? Some people will measure contextual fit through the sympathetic use of materials, scale and proportion. Other people will assess it in terms of the spatial link between the building and the surrounding environment. Others again may choose functional or purely aesthetic/design features. Any assessment of the visual impact of buildings must take into account their environmental setting and how they interact with the surrounding buildings and spaces.

Then there is the issue of the multiplicity of views. How, for example, do you take account of different people's aesthetic responses? I suppose that because much of my background has been influenced by participatory theory and practice, I would also argue that any judgement about aesthetics should be inclusive rather than exclusive. That is, it ought to involve as many people as reasonably possible.

Mr. & Mrs. Public: Generally, I think people feel ill-equipped to comment on building design. Aesthetics is difficult isn't it? What I like, the next person may detest. For every person who likes modern buildings and the materials they use there will be another who does not. It's all a matter of taste.

Architect: This is one of the problems we face. On the one hand you seem to be making the case that we should be listening to the public more, but on the other hand the problem is the public have a low level of discernment making communication difficult. They tend to be very conservative and generally dislike modern styles.

Mr. & Mrs. Public: I may be able to comment more articulately on function and the degree to whether a building meets my needs, but I'm also sure I could say what particular things about a building I like or dislike. In fact, come to think of it, there are quite a few things about building design that one notices, such as the contextual siting of buildings and their relationship to nearby buildings, the legibility and functionality of buildings and their maintenance. Sometimes it's easier to comment on the things you don't like such as the occupancy density, a lack of privacy, a lack of landscaping, poor control over the environment, too obtrusive and inappropriate signage, and the inadequate maintenance of the environment.

It depends on the type of building. For example, it's appropriate for cathedrals to be large, but I don't like tower blocks when they are large, tall and square. I think that concrete flats are ugly, dilapidated and look like ghettos. I tend to like traditional buildings. It's not just a question of style, it's more than that. I think many traditional buildings are not too regular, they are well proportioned, have pleasing interiors, and use appropriate building materials like stone or brick. They also tend to have a certain amount of detailing so they are not stark.

It is only when buildings are overpowering and inappropriate that I really dislike them - modern offices are nice when they are not too big. The blending of new and old often makes for an interesting environment.

DU: You started by saying that aesthetics is difficult and that you feel ill-equipped to comment on building design. Yet as soon as you really start to talk about the subject, it is clear that you have very definite ideas about aesthetics and the visual appearance of buildings.

Mr. & Mrs. Public: One of the problems is that when you talk to architects about design, they give the impression that theirs is a special language and that unless one can truly understand what they are trying to achieve one is not qualified to comment or pass judgement. The problem with this is that, as you suggested earlier, it results in an exclusive world, not an inclusive one.

Planner: If this is the case, then it seems to me that a scheme for visual assessment would not only assist the design process by clarifying design considerations, but in so doing it would also provide a language for the discussion or negotiation of these issues thereby reinforcing the need to pay attention to visual design. It would assist the design process by reducing misunderstanding. At present, the discussion is pre-empted because the field of negotiation is limited.

DU: I think that the issue of communication between groups and the existence of a shared language that can make this possible is extremely important. I am reminded of George Bernard Shaw's comment: "*England and America are two countries divided by a common language.*" Although we often use the same words I am sure that we do not communicate particularly effectively and actually understand what the other is saying. Our discussions on occasions seem to be in parallel rather than in series.

Sontag contrasts the critical appreciation of art with that of the cinema. She made the point that cinema has been firmly grounded in mass culture and not elevated to the ranks of high culture. The consequence of this is that films or movies have been seen as ephemeral and not worthy of study or comment by people with minds. As Sontag argues with respect to films, there is a vocabulary of forms which can be analysed which relates to issues such as lighting, framing, cutting, etc. Sontag makes a plea for the generation of "*a vocabulary - a descriptive, rather than prescriptive, vocabulary - of forms.*"

Should we not be making a similar plea when it comes to architecture? Architecture too has a language of forms, but it is a language that is neither widely spoken nor understood. Architecture has invariably been seen as part of the fine arts - at least, that has been an essential part of the rhetoric put forward by many architects - and therefore a part of high culture.

Is a language needed for architecture which would permit more people to engage in a public discussion about the quality of architecture, their understanding of architecture, and their preference for different architectural forms? Maybe we are not all experts or informed in an academic sense, but most people are not totally blind to stylistic issues. If we do not even have a shared language of form that is meaningful and unintimidating, how can we expect people to communicate and contribute to a public discussion, advancement and ultimately acceptance of new urban forms? Architecture is a public art and therefore its inspection and criticism is the concern of everyone and not just architects and developers.[6] Intuitively, people are often aware of what is a good and bad building, the difficulty comes in trying to specify exactly what elements constitute aesthetic design without compromising the creativity of architect.

One objective of aesthetic judgements about the environment is to recognise the significant role that the built environment has in our lives. It is significant not only in terms of providing a visually pleasing backdrop or scenery against which we act out our lives, but is much more than this. A beautiful environment can lead to a sense of well-being, it can be uplifting and invigorating. It is perhaps noteworthy that there is considerable research interest today in the creation of restorative environments[7] - how can environments be designed and managed in such a way that they can, for example, aid the recovery rate of patients in hospitals, or reduce stress amongst the workforce? Creating a visually pleasing and aesthetic environment is an essential part of that process.

I must admit, however, to being a bit nervous about advocating this kind of position because it is so easy to slip into a deterministic mode - if we do x to the environment then we will have y effect. Olsen's study[8] of the hospital environment showed us that it can be the other way around. You probably recall, Olsen found that patients in a progressive care unit of a hospital rated their environment as more pleasant and cheerful, were more positive and felt that the hospital environment affected them in a more positive way than those patients who were in a traditional care régime ward.

But I think there is little doubt that an aesthetically pleasing environment is good for people's mental health. The problem we return to though is by whose criteria do we judge aesthetically pleasing. I have heard someone stand up at a conference and say that an old rusty pram in a river can be beautiful. People like Prince Charles have suggested that we should not be coy about raising issues of aesthetics. It may well be that we do not all agree about the nature of beauty, but the starting point surely is a discussion amongst all "consumers" as well as "producers" of our physical environment about our perceptions, preferences and priorities.

Prince Charles: We all need beauty. We can't live without it - as we've all discovered to our communal cost. We should therefore no longer be nervous about "aesthetic" questions, and no longer anxious about applying aesthetic judgements. Where we failed to exercise such judgements in the recent past we allowed buildings which are the very opposite of beautiful. But it wasn't inevitable that they should be so. We don't have to let it happen anymore. The secret, surely, is to accept that each person lays different emphases on his or her requirements ... Our fellow citizens are demanding that we do better. It is up to the developers, the architects, the planners and the politicians to respond.

DU: I think these conversations have shown that achieving agreement between people as to urban aesthetics is problematic. Different groups have different views. It's not impossible, but again, one of the clear messages that comes out of our discussion is that all of these groups have got to talk and mutually educate each other to a shared language so that we can meaningfully communicate with each other and understand the other's point of view. I am not sure that this is the case at the moment.

It's all too easy to think of ourselves as being "architects" or "planners", but the problem with this is we don't just occupy one role and have one identity. We possess multiple identities.

An interesting study was carried out many years ago on occupational communities in general and that of architects in particular.[9] Members of occupational communities use their community as a primary reference group. The values held by the individual are derived from the reference group, and other members of that reference group will be "significant others". Other architects function as a source of values or as a perspective - one perspective amongst many that could be held - but an extremely important and salient one. Furthermore, the architects will regard their fellow professionals and those in cognate disciplines as the only other people who are capable of judging their occupational output and understanding the constraints under which they work. Consequently, it is in the nature of many occupational communities - and architecture (like psychology) is no exception - to be inward looking into a professional world, rather than outward looking to a wider world. This is the point that Mr. and Mrs. Public were making earlier. Thus when architects' professional skills are challenged, their identity is threatened too. This neither makes for a profession open to outside influence or an environment that is responsive to the needs and wishes of those outside the design and decision-making process.

One way of overcoming these problems is to encourage more participation at all stages in the planning, design and decision-making process. We don't want to get too side-tracked here with a discussion on participation, but it is something worth considering.

Another approach - recognising the multiple identities that we all have - is to try and put ourselves into the shoes of different user groups and see the environment through their eyes - to co-orientate with them.[10] One only has to think of the differences in the way children and planners see the environment.[11] Kenneth Olwig[12] suggests that planners think of the environment in spatial and geometric terms and give priority to the visual qualities of perspective, vista and content. This, he argues, is not likely to produce a sensory-rich environment with a potential for manipulation and activity.

It seems as if we have come back again to the importance of environments being visually and aesthetically stimulating. I am sure Susan Sontag would want to make a comment here. What message would you like the reader to go away with, Susan?

Susan Sontag: Think of the sheer multiplication of works of art available to every one of us, super-added to the conflicting tastes and odors and sights of the urban environment that bombard our senses. Ours is culture based on excess, on overproduction; the result is a steady loss of sharpness in our sensory experience. All the conditions of modern life - its material plenitude, its sheer crowdedness - conjoin to dull our sensory faculties. And it is in the light of the condition of our senses, our capacities (rather than those of another age), that the task of the critic must be assessed.

The aim of all commentary on art now should be to make works of art - and, by analogy, our experience - more, rather than less, real to us. The function of criticism should be to show *how it is what it is*, even *that it is what it is*, rather than to show *what it means*.

What is important now is to recover our senses. We must learn to *see* more, to *hear* more, to *feel* more.

Conclusion and Outcomes

It was the conclusion of the project that appropriate visual criteria can be identified which receive a high degree of consensus amongst the design professions, conservation groups and the public. This necessarily means a reduced set of criteria from the full range of criteria that might be employed. However, on the basis of our consultation with design professionals, conservationists and members of the public (including local politicians), it was agreed that it might be preferable to adopt a process-based approach to visual assessments. By adopting a process approach it becomes valid to assess all criteria because no inherent judgement of what constitutes good design is required. The exercise is to promote the consideration of factors thought to be important in good design. This approach would require those applying for BREEAM recognition to demonstrate why they had made particular design decisions. Given the perceived need for, and the limitations of BREEAM, a two-track approach to the devel-opment of a visual impact methodology was proposed.

A credible, reliable, simple and practical assessment instrument should be constructed through further rigorous research and a more extensive consultation process. This would be incorporated into the current BREEAM procedure. This should be based on a representative sample of the full spectrum of criteria, possibly including those areas for which there was no consensual agreement amongst the various parties. It should determine whether, and how, projects have taken visual impact into account during the design and development phases. This would take the form of a checklist with additional supporting/explanatory statements. The emphasis therefore should not be on judging whether a building is "good" or "bad" in particular design terms, but rather on whether the architect or developer can justify the design decisions that they have made.

The second recommendation was that guidance should extend beyond BREEAM. Detailed guidelines should be produced to facilitate the integration of visual quality issues at all stages of the planning and development process. This would ensure that even those not volunteering for assessment will have sufficient opportunity to benefit from the procedure. This would also be a process-based approach and would draw on those criteria for which there is not necessarily a consensus, but which should be considered in any planning development. Rather than the situation which typically occurs at present whereby local politicians make decisions based on inconsistently applied and *ad hoc* criteria, the introduction of this assessment procedure would provide decision-makers (especially politicians without any formal training in planning and design) with a comprehensive and systematic *aide memoire* of criteria that they can use in judging planning applications.

Assessment Criteria
The final list of assessment criteria identified in the research project were:

Context
Appropriate use of materials, building techniques and architectural features; Congruity (not replication) with nearby structures, with ecology of meaning with area (with reference to history, cultural events, economics); Blend of regional characteristics and methods with the knowledge and techniques culled from designers' experience and knowledge so that new materials and methods are interfaced with existing places; Appropriate form for function and appropriate location; Skyline

Design Features
Scale; Height; Size; Density; Roofline; Windows; Massing; Materials; Colour; Texture; Apparent age

Spaces and relationship between buildings
General housekeeping and maintenance of parks, the building and surrounding areas; Design of side-walks, parking spaces, street furniture, bus shelters, kiosks, signage; Landscaping

Legibility
Wayfinding; Accessibility

Durability of materials (quality) and maintenance

Lighting

Natural Lighting (including seasonal and daily changes); Illumination; Reflectance; Overshadowing

Public areas

Ease and safety of access; Identity (where appropriate); Privacy (where appropriate); Public amenities

Participation

Community satisfaction is linked to social aspects of the environment (reputation, friendliness, similarity of people), its upkeep, attractiveness, safety, privacy, convenience and openness

Zone of Visual Impact
Movement

Notes

1 Acknowledgement should be made at the outset to the research undertaken on this project by Ellen Jones, who was the co-author of the Final Report, *BREEAM and the Visual Impact of Buildings*. Final Report to the Building Research Establishment, Garston, April, 1996.

2 The conversation with Susan Sontag is constructed from her essay "Against Interpretation", republished in *A Susan Sontag Reader*, Harmondsworth: Penguin, 1982.

3 The conversation with Prince Charles is constructed from his book *A Vision of Britain*, London: Doubleday, 1989.

4 Reeki, R. F. (1975). *Background to Environmental Planning*. Edward Arnold, London.

5 Scheer, B. C. and Preiser W. F. E. (1994). Design Review, *Challenging Urban Aesthetic Control*, Chapman & Hall, USA.

6 Delafons J. (1994). Democracy and Design. In B. C. Scheer and W. F. E. Preiser *Design Review, Challenging Urban Aesthetic Control*, Chapman &

Hall, USA.

7   Ulrich, R. S., Simons, R. F., Losito, B. D., and Fiorito, E. (1991). Stress recovery during exposure to natural and urban environments. *Journal of Environmental Psychology* 11(3):201-230. Hartig, T., Mang, M., and Evans, G. W. (1991). Restorative effects of natural environment experiences. *Environment and Behaviour* 23(1):3-26. Kaplan, S. (1995) The restorative benefits of nature: Toward an integrative framework. *Journal of Environmental Psychology* 15(3):169-182.

8   Olsen, R.V. (1984). The effect of the hospital environment: Patient reactions to traditional versus progressive care settings. *Journal of Architectural and Planning Research* 1(2): 1-136.

9   Salaman, G. (1984). *Community and Occupation.* Cambridge University Press, Cambridge.

10 Uzzell, D. L. (1982). Environmental Pluralism and Participation: A Co-orientational Perspective. In Gold, J. R. and Burgess, J. (eds) *Valued Environments.* Allen and Unwin, London.

11 Hart, R. (1979). *Children's Experience of Place.* Irvington, New York. Moore, R. C. (1986). *Childhood's Domain.* Croom Helm, London. Uzzell, D. L. (1976). Children's Perception and Understanding of their Environment. *Bulletin of Environmental Education,* 66, pp. 9-18. Ward, C. (1976). *The Child in the City.* Penguin, Harmondsworth. Weinstein, C. S. & Thomas G. David, T. G. (1987). *Spaces For Children: The Built Environment and Child Development.* Plenum Press, New York.

12 Olwig, K. R. (1990). Designs upon children's special places? *Children's Environments Quarterly* 7(4):47-53.

Buildings Imagined as Bodies

Ann Westerman

Is it possible to create architectural identity across cultures?

Introduction

Aesthetics and art-criticism are pursued by experts who analyse and interpret works of art for seriously committed readers. The initial premise of art-criticism is seldom the influence of the fine arts on the well-being and health of a broader public, but when we look at architecture or the broader built environment, the situation is quite different. Buildings stand in direct relation to man´s life when living and working. Architecture is to a certain degree an expression of this and thus is a matter for society. Political decisions on building regulations are focused on ensuring that citizens have access to buildings which further their safety and health. The well-being of people in terms of the aesthetic qualities of architecture is a field where the responsibility is mainly left to the builder.

In times such as these, which grow more diverse day-by-day and where cultures - not the least because of major developments in media technology - are continuously clashing with each other in an almost brutal and apparently unplanned way, the vulnerable nakedness of the human being stands out as something that needs more and more to be taken into consideration. Can the aesthetic qualities of buildings in our time affect people's well-being and health? I think that the architectural expression of the exterior of a building has great importance forthe well-being of people by strengthening their identity, enhancing confidence and being a permanent source of enjoyment. During a war, why should abandoned buildings systematically be destroyed if not in order to inflict not only material but also mental torment on the enemy. This is due to the fact that the aesthetic qualities of buildings are in a dialogue with the conventions of the society. When people say that buildings are beautiful or ugly they may mean several things. A building which is considered to be beautiful has a shape or form languagewhich in some way is known. If people say that a building is ugly, they may be expressing that it is considered to have a shape which is experienced as alien, strange or incomprehensible. This can happen to new architecture, which to begin with is considered ugly only because its shape - or why not its purpose - seems unfamiliar. Anyone who against her will has to live in surroundings which she considers to be ugly has to overcome this, while anyone who can live in surroundings which are considered to be beautiful feels strength and well-being. This explains why it is important to increase our knowledge about how people experience the aesthetic qualities of buildings and architecture.

The theory of evaluation

In order to say something on how the aesthetics in architecture may influence people, you must first be able to describe the aesthetic qualities of a building, second be able to understand man's experience and evaluation of the building, and third be able to demonstrate the connection between building, aesthetic evaluation and well-being. The complexity of this task is enormous. To make it more manageable I have concentrated my research (Westerman, 1976) on building exteriors and people's estimations of how beautiful they appear to be.

My basic assumption is that aesthetic evaluations are compounded by different kinds of independent impressions and considerations. The impressions of the senses - in this case the visual impressions - are primary. In *The Senses Considered As Perceptual Systems* (Gibson,1966), James J. Gibson has pointed out that visual perception of the outer world develops by means of the individual learning to extract information from the impressions of the senses obtained through the nervous system. The kind of information that Gibson is referring to is the invariable perception that depends on the individual's capacity to discover invariant relations and not to attach too much attention to the flow of changing impressions. The visual impressions are part of the visual field, while perception is the experience of the visual world. For example, the individual learns quickly to distinguish between such visual invariants as surfaces and facets, perceiving their inclinations from changes in the texture of the surface, the edges of a surface in the room, which specify a discontinuity in the optical textural flow, or the corner of a surface in the room where the angle is specified by a discontinuity in the flow. Gibson also believes that, at first hand, information that is required in order to "economically" - that is by as few clues as possible - identify an object, a building volume, is recorded from a complex of stimulus information. All other accessible stimulus information that is needed to specify the unique and complete identity of the object under these circumstances is disregarded. I here want to add that part of the power of aesthetic expression when dealing with architecture is to arouse the onlooker's interest to better avail herself of the accessible stimulus information. Since the amount of information coming from the senses into the nervous system is greater than we can be fully aware of, it is necessary for the individual to create for her own sake distinctive forms, shapes or representations in her mind of what is seen - besides the basic perceptions - in order to be able to retain and make use of the information she is seeking. For example, conceptions are formed as to how different objects should look. You learn to distinguish between a church and an apartment block. Associations, feelings and estimations are then added to these conceptions. Such associations, feelings and estimations may be more or less conscious for an individual.

From my research and my own experiences I will describe the complexity of the experience and evaluation of building exteriors:

1. When standing in front of or inside a building we receive a lot of impressions from our senses.
2. When it comes to visual perception, the "economical" perceptions retain the invariant form perception in surfaces, textures, edges, corners, lines and so on, and create an image of the volume of the building, its exterior or room. "Superfluous" visual impressions other than what are perceived by the "economical" visual perception are disregarded, but are still present as latent excitement. When first sighting a building, the eyes scan the visual information that is to be found in contours, volumes and details and the individual is at the same time stimulated in some way by what she sees. The visual experience is estimated as more or less positive. The visual content of the observed building can in some way be evaluated as more or less beautiful.
3. We make images of a building from previous experiences. Perhaps we have previously been in front of or inside similar buildings, or we have seen pictures of and have read about them. To the inner picture is added synesthesia, that is an accompanying sensation from other senses. Such synesthesia may have reference to warmth, intimacy, smell, taste, sound and so on.
4. We value and react emotionally to what we see and the inner picture is a

result of what is seen. In this phase sense-impressions and the degree of visual stimulation are balanced with different kinds of appraisements of the building developed from our needs and expectations. In the valuation we also find conscious or unconscious feelings concomitant with sexuality and eroticism.

Research: Procedure and results
My research questions have been:

- Do people have an understanding of how much more beautiful one building exterior is as compared with another?
- Is it possible to describe what characteristic marks in a building exterior lead it to being evaluated as more beautiful than another?
- Do men and women have the same evaluations of how beautiful a building exterior is?

The experimental method employed involved eliciting aesthetic value judgements from the test subjects. Photographed and filmed exteriors of buildings, models of exteriors and abstract three-dimensional objects resembling exteriors served as stimuli. The building exteriors employed represented a wide selection of commonly occurring residential buildings. In an investigation of aesthetic value judgements of office and university buildings (Westerman & Sahlin, 1992) using reference objects selected according to the earlier results of my investigations, the same values of estimated beauty were found.

I will present some hypotheses about what is behind the valuations men and women make of the three-dimensional qualities of building exteriors.

People's experience of what is beautiful and what is ugly
As we make our way from childhood to adulthood the concept of what is beautiful and what is ugly develops. What we like we call beautiful and what we do not like we call ugly. To a large extent our opinions have been coloured by what we have been brought up to call beautiful or ugly and in this process what we call beautiful or ugly is given a certain signification, namely in the sense that the notion of beauty stems from social evaluation of what is common, that is well-

known, while ugly stands for what is not. We assimilate that which is beautiful and we reject that which we experience as ugly or strange.

At the same time there is another aspect concerning the evaluation of the beauty of man-made objects, e.g. buildings. Visually we can experience objects as more or less beautiful. Through our perceptual system we learn to perceive, that is to interpret, what we see, and we build up a discretion of the visual field and the visual world around us. Visually there are features belonging to objects which are significant for the brain when the inner picture of the object is built up. According to the psychologist James Gibson, such features are surfaces, outlines and intersections between surfaces. By means of nuances in texture on inclined surfaces we learn to observe the inclination of a plane in a room and its size and also the form of a three-dimensional, composite object.

In my research on building exteriors I have found that the three-dimensional components of the architectural composition of a building produce a visual impact upon the observer. I also found that all variation of three-dimensionality in building exteriors can be described by five types of "plasticity" and that these types can be distinguished from each other when men and women evaluate how beautiful a building exterior is.

The five types of plasticity are defined as:
- S-plasticity = flat surfaces dominate with only slight projections or indentations occurring (Fig. 1).
- U-plasticity = flat surfaces dominate, while against these clearly protruding areas are delineated (Fig. 2 a).
- I-plasticity = flat surfaces dominate with clear indentations present (Fig. 3 a).
- U + I-plasticity = both indentations and protrusions are clearly delineated on a flat surface (Fig. 4 a).
- UI-plasticity = the protrusions and indentations alternate, eliminating the flat surface (Fig. 5 a).

Each of these types can be described further, for example, according to depth composition: variation in the degree of depth in the exterior, or in other

words, amplitude (Figs. 2 b, 3 b, 4 b, 5 b).

My results were:
- that the subjective experience of beauty is not a random phenomenon
- that buildings featuring S-plasticity are seldom regarded as beautiful
- that buildings featuring U-, I-, and UI-plasticity are regarded as beautiful and that U+I-plasticity is often adjudged the most beautiful.

In my experiments, men and women have generally had the same main preferences and to some extent different preferences about the type of plasticity in building exteriors and the degree of beauty experienced. Both men and women adjudged U + I-plasticity as the most beautiful and S-plasticity as the least beautiful. But men and women have different preferences concerning U-plasticity and I-plasticity.

Men prefer I-plasticity while women prefer U-plasticity. These facts have led me to the following assumptions when it comes to experiencing buildings.

The exposed human body
The human body is, and has always been, a momentous object, the object of paintings, reproductions, conceptions, dissection and manipulation. Today it is almost impossible to escape photographs of dying, starving, debased, amputated, disabled and dead human bodies, people in flight or terrorizing each other, or plundering and destroying each other's bodies and dwellings. If we were not aware of it earlier then we will be today: the human being is exposed, her body fragile in the world of dead material. Yet for us the human body is the pre-requisite for survival and well-being. And the most hedged about conception is the room of the womb from which our lives emanate (Fig. 6). Our thoughts on our own and the opposite sex, desire and the relieving sexual act are the zenith of strength on which we reflect. I believe that representations of the corporeal are always more or less a conscious part of our experiences and valuations, even when it comes to buildings and architecture.

Buildings can remind us of bodies
Can a building remind us of a body? How can it be that a building could

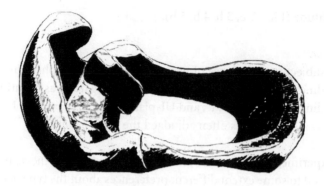

Fig. 6. Reclining Mother and Child by Henry Moore.

make us experience, for example, closeness to a body? In his book *Experiencing Architecture* Steen Eiler Rasmussen describes some boys playing football in front of a church in Italy. The ball bounces off the wall and then down the stairs in front of the church. The boys experience the church as a solid body. The shaping of porches, gateways and entrance-sections have always been an important part of the art of building and architecture. It cannot have escaped anyone's attention that this has the symbolic significance of marking the opening to the entry into the posterior room with strong associations to the opening to the woman's womb. Ruins with their obscene hollows and skeleton fragments call forth within us a horrifying fascination. Facades, riddled with bullets, holes left by explosion and other ulcers fill us with sorrow, as if it was the body of one's mother which had been affected by some inconceivable illness (Fig. 7). Caves, the openings of which sometimes are hidden with vegetation, and within which deep room formations - not infrequently mingled with damp - can be found, are the first dwelling places - the protecting womb of the progenitor. The surface of the facade is like the skin of a body. The texture of the surface gives us visual and tactile experiences that influence our evaluation of the architecture. Inside the body of the building you expect to find warmth, water and outflow, rooms and openings, that is a vital condition: a place that vouches for survival and health. Within the theory of architecture there are also references to the human body. Vitruvius writes in *The Ten Books of Architecture*: *"Symmetry is*

Fig. 7. Ruin of Borgholm Castle.

Fig. 8. Louis Sullivan: Merchant's National Bank in Iowa.

Fig. 9. Summer villa inTynningö.

a proper agreement between the members of the work itself, and the relation between the different parts and the whole general scheme, in accordance with a certain part selected as standard. Thus in the human body there is a kind of symmetrical harmony between forearm, foot, palm, finger and other small parts; and so it is with perfect buildings."

Male and female experience of the beauty of buildings - a discussion of my research findings

My thesis is that people; men, women and children, associate on an unconscious level the whole of a building or parts of buildings with different parts of the human body. Everyone has experienced the enchantment children feel from crawling into little huts or into the space under a table or squeezing into small cupboards. This is an expression of the unconscious longing of children for something that reminds them of the room of the womb from whence they came.

Men are fascinated by spaces, cavities and openings into rooms - distinctive features associated with I-plasticity - (Fig. 8) out of an unconscious need to strengthen the imagination of the penetration into women's vaginas. Correspondingly, women are attracted by protruding, salient parts of a building, such as balconies, towers and pillars - distinctive features associated with U-plasticity - (Fig. 9).

The most richly modelled architecture, containing both strongly protruding parts and indentations, cavities and spaces, and also smooth and generous surfaces and ornamental elements - distinctive features associated with U + I-plasticity - is highly valued with respect to beauty by both males and females in my experiments (Fig. 10 and Fig.11).

My conclusion is that the evaluation of the beauty of a building is a compound of several aspects. Among these, the most important is the stimulant of richness of visual information in the building. The visual stimulation is afforded by the number of surfaces and edges and the degree of depth amplitude in the visually experienced three-dimensional building. The experienced visual stimulation is also afforded by the type of plasticity, referred to as S-, I-, U-, U+I- or UI-plasticity, as a consequence of the building giving associations to the safety as well as to the stimulus which a body or a part of the

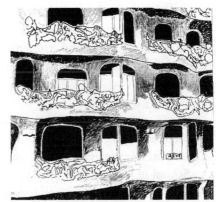

Fig. 10. Mayan Architecture, Yucatan.   *Fig.11. Casa Mila by Antoni Gaudi.*

body gives. And then there is also the experience of the building being well-adapted to its purpose and that it is carefully built, and, as was said earlier, that the building-shape is well-known in its main features. The aspect of purpose may, however, differ between experts in the architectural profession and laymen and also between people from different cultures. In this aspect differences in gender and probably in age may also play a part.

In terms of architecture men are attracted by a compact whole, solidity, cavities and smooth surfaces.

When viewing architecture women are attracted by curved shapes, protruding elements, towers and ornamentation.There are also - I think - other mental preferences: in men for dissection and construction; in women for wholeness.

Research about aesthetics in the built environment and its influence on well-being and health

It is my conviction that research in this field must include the evaluations of both men and women. Probably an analysis of children's evaluations could also be instructive. In order to feel well we need both the safety in the well-known and allurement to be able to make discoveries. Conscious and sensibly shaped architecture can give us this. In a world where people's identities as citizens in a certain culture tend to be more ill-defined or called into question, a conscious elaborated language of architecture, which is valid for all human beings, can contribute to safety and well-being. Architecture then ought to clarify men's and women's similar and different needs for architectural identity, not the least by means of contrasting effects.

Sketches by the author

References

Colomina, Beatriz (ed) (1990). *Sexuality and Space.* Princeton University School of Architecture.

Gibson, J. J. (1950). *The Perception of the Visual World.* Cambridge, Mass.

Gibson, J. J. (1966). *The Senses Considered as Perceptual Systems.* Boston.

Hesselgren, Sven (1969). *The Language of Architecture.* Kristiansstad.

Rasmussen, S. E. (1957). *Om at opleve arkitektur.* København.

Robert, Rigmor och Uvnäs Moberg, Kerstin (1994). *Hon och han födda olika.* Halmstad.

Sanders, Joel (ed) (1996). STUD. *Architectures of Masculinity.* Princeton Univ. School of Arch.

Tschumi, Bernhard (1995). *Questions of Space.* London.

Vitruvius. *The Ten Books on Architecture.*

Weimark, Torsten (1996). *Akademi och anatomi.* Stockholm.

Westerman, Ann (1976). *On Aesthetic Judgement of Building Exterior.* Stockholm.

Westerman, Ann (1980). *Estetisk värdering av storlek och upprepning i byggnads-exteriörer.* FR,R151. Stockholm.

Westerman Ann (1992). Kvindeidentitet i moderne arkitektur, Tidskriften HUG, nr 62, *Byens sjæl og form.* København.

Westerman Ann & Sahlin, Bernt (1992). Tycka om arkitektur, *Byggnads-styrelsens informationer.* Stockholm.

Presentation of the Contributors

 David Canter was born in Liverpool 1944. He received his B.A. in 1964 and his Ph.D. in 1968 from the University of Liverpool. He is currently professor of psychology at the University of Liverpool. He founded the *Journal of Environmental Psychology* in 1980 and is still its managing editor. He is also co-editor of the "Ethnoscapes Series" and was co-founder of the International Association for Person-Environment Studies (IAPS). He has published widely on people's experiences of places, and the evaluation of buildings, including explorations of people's behaviour in fires and other emergencies. This work gave rise to studies of safety in industry which he developed into very successful management consultancy. Some aspects of these interests have been developed into a new field christened "Investigative Psychology", as described in his book *Criminal Shadows* (1994). His work and other research interests are all informed by an approach to research known as "Facet Theory" (1985). His recent environmental research has focused on the experience of landscape and the appropriate context for creativity.

 Birgit Cold was born in 1936, in Denmark. She graduated as an architect at the Royal Academy of Fine Arts in Copenhagen in 1961. She has an architectural practice together with Professor T. Brantenberg and Professor E. Hiorthøy with social housing as their main field. The office has received several awards from architectural competitions. She is Professor of Architecture at the Faculty of Architecture, Planning and Fine Arts at the Norwegian University of Science and Technology, Trondheim. She lectures and publishes within the following research topics: school environment; quality in architecture; sketching; the quality of research units; environmental evaluation and aesthetics, well-being and health. She is a member of the Norwegian Academy of Technological Sciences, has been a member of the Scientific Advisory Board for the Swedish Building Research Council 1993 - 1997 and president of the Nordic Association of Architectural Research 1995 - 1998.

Kim Dovey was born in Australia in 1951. He received his M.A. degree in 1978 in Architecture at the University of Melbourne, and his Ph.D. in 1987 at the University of California, Berkeley. He is associate professor at the Faculty of Architecture, Building and Planning at the University of Melbourne. His main field of research is meaning in the built environment with a focus on social issues. He is a board member of the International Association of People-Environment Studies. He has published numerous works in both the academic and popular press, and his book is entitled *Framing Places: Mediating Power in Built Form* (Routledge, 1999).

Aase Eriksen was born in Denmark. She received her M.A. degree in social science from Rochester University, and an M.Arch. and a Ph.D. from the University of Pennsylvania. She is a member of the Academic Architects Council, MAA, and The Practicing Architects Council of Denmark, PAR. She is a practicing architect who owns firms in Denmark and USA, and has been professor in the USA and Norway. Her research has dealt with the relationship of human behavior and physical space. Her architectural firms design different types of projects including office buildings, housing and interiors, however, her main focus has been on architecture for children, such as schools, childcare centers, museums, healthcare facilities and a new concept in children's hospitals. She has published widely with books and articles.

Arnulf Kolstad was born 1942 in Norway. He received his Civ. ing. degree in 1966 in Engineering Geology and his Dr. ing. degree in 1973 at the Norwegian Institute of Technology. He also received his Dr. philos. degree in Psychiatric Epidemiology in 1984 at the University of Bergen. He is a professor in social psychology at the Norwegian University of Science and Technology and Scientific Adviser at the Norwegian Institute for Hospital Research, SINTEF. His main field of expertise and research is epidemiology, planning and evaluation of health services, socialization, political psychology and psychology of law. He has lectured and published numerous scientific works and articles for the press. His interest and approaches are inter-disciplinary.

Rikard Küller was born in Sweden in 1938. He received his Ph. lic. degree in psychology in 1972 and became a Dr. Sc. in Architecture in 1973 at the University of Lund. He is a professor of environmental psychology at the School of Architecture, Lund Institute of Technology, and director of the Environmental Psychology Unit at the University of Lund. His main research areas are light and colour in the built environment, environments for the elderly, work environments, and environmental attitudes and traffic behav-iour. Küller has published numerous scientific papers and reports including a chapter in the *Handbook of Environmental Psychology*. He was one of the founders of the International Association of People-Environment Studies and its first chairman.

Roderick Lawrence was born in 1949, in Adelaide, Australia. He received his Bachelor of Architecture degree (first class honours) in 1972 at the University of Adelaide, his Master of Letters degree in 1978 at the University of Cambridge (England), and his Doctorate of Science in 1983 at the Ecole Polytechnique Federale in Lausanne, Switzerland. He is a master of teaching and research at the Center for Human Ecology and Environmental Sciences at the University of Geneva. His field of research is quality of urban areas and housing, ecological perspectives on healthy housing, building and planning, citizen participation, empowerment and public and private responsibility in urban affairs. He has published numerous works including, *Housing, Dwellings and Homes: Design Theory, Research and Practice* (1987) and *Better Understanding Our Cities: The role of Urban Indicators* (1997). He was a member of the Scientific Advisory Board of the World Health Organization's European Center for Environment and Health from 1994 to 1998.

Sue-Ann Lee was born in 1947. She received her M.A. (Hons) degree in Social Science (majoring in psychology and geography) at the University of St. Andrews in 1969. She is the director of research for the Faculty of Design and Principal Lecturer at the School of Architecture at Kingston University. Her research interests include community approaches to design and social aspects of green design. She was a founding member of IAPS and she edited the Architectural Psychology Newsletter from 1972 until 1996. Her recent publications include "Developments since Black Road & Byker: Participative Housing in Britain" in Y. Marin (ed) *L'espace Urban Européen*, Annals Litteraires, Besancon 1996, and the introduction to B. Gauld (ed) *Green Shift Symposium Proceedings*, Kingston Univ. Press & Cat, Wales 1997. She is currently working on the 2nd edition of J. Farmer's 1996 *Green Shift: Towards a Green Sensibility in Architecture* and is also one of the editors of the journal *Environments BY DESIGN*.

Byron Mikellides was born in 1943, in Cyprus. He received his B.A. degree in psychology from London University in 1967, his diploma of education at Hertford College, University of Oxford, in 1968, and his Ph.D. at Oxford Brookes University in 1989. He is a professor in environmental, social and architectural psychology at the Oxford School of Architecture, Oxford Brookes University. A regular contributor to the Architectural Psychology Conferences, he has lectured extensively in Europe and the United States and published numerous works including *Colour for Architecture* (1976), *Architecture for People* (1980), and *Emotional and Behavioural Reaction to Colour in the Built Environment* (1989).

Kaj Noschis was born in Finland in 1950. He received his M.A. degree in 1975 in Geneva, and his Ph.D. degree in 1980 in psychology from the University of Lausanne, Switzerland. Since 1985 he has also been a practicing Jungian analyst and consultant. He has been a lecturer in environmental psychology at the Department of Architecture of the Swiss Federal Institute of

Technology Lausanne since 1983 and at the University of Jyväskylä in Finland. His field of research is the affective meaning on the environment. He is author of many publications, among these the book *Signification affective du quartier* (Paris, Meridiens-Klincksieck, 1984), and is the co-editor with H. Dunin-Woyseth of *Architecture and Teaching. Epistemological Foundations* (Comportements, Lausanne, 1998).

Juhani Pallasmaa was born in Finland in 1936. He graduated as an architect in 1966, is a member of SAFA (the Finnish Association of Architects), an Honorary Fellow of the American Institute of Architects, and was professor of Architecture at Helsinki University of Technology 1991-97. He practises architecture and design, and exhibition and graphic design at his architectural office in Helsinki. He lectures and writes extensively on the philosophy of architecture, architectural criticism, the phenomenology of art, and the relation between architecture and cinema. He has published numerous books and exhibition catalogues and has taught in various universities in Europe, North and South America and Africa. He has received the following major awards: Finnish State Architecture Award 1992; Helsinki City Culture Award 1993; Russian Federation Architecture Award 1996; Fritz Schumacher Preis (Germany) 1997. Honorary doctorates: Helsinki University of Industrial Arts 1993; Helsinki University of Technology, 1998.

Jens Schjerup Hansen was born in 1940 in Denmark. He received his M.A. degree in sociology in 1972 at the University of Copenhagen and his Ph.D. degree in 1995 at Nordplan in Stockholm. He is a senior researcher at the Danish Research Institute. His field of research is urban renewal, changes in our concept of nature and urban ecology. He has published numerous scientific articles and reports, including "Natursyn og planlægning" (The Concept of Nature and Planning) 1989 and "Koldinghus slotshave" (The Garden of Koldinghus) 1994.

Perla Serfaty-Garcon was born in 1944 in Marrakech, Morroco. She received her M.A. in Philosophy in 1967 and her Ph.D. in Psychology in 1972 from the University of Strasbourg, France. She received her Doctorat d'Etat in Sociology in 1985 from Sorbonne, University of Paris V René Descartes, Ecole practique des hautes études. During her twenty years as professor of psychology at the University of Strasbourg, she actively participated in the development of environmental psychology research and teaching in France and Europe and held visiting professor positions in the United States, Canada and Sweden. She is currently on leave from the University of Strasbourg and holds a position at the Bureau de la Coopération Internationale in the city of Montreal in Canada. She has published works on people's use and experience of urban spaces, sociability and interactions in public, urban preservation and heritage issues, as well as on the phenomenology of the home She has recently published a book on this subject entitled *Psychologie de la Maison. Une Archéologie de L'intimité.* Her forthcoming book will focus on sociability and urban spaces.

 Daniel Stokols was born in 1948 in Miami Florida. He received his B.A. degree at the University of Chicago in 1969, his M.A. degree in 1971, and his Ph.D. in 1973 in social psychology at the University of North Carolina, Chapel Hill. He is a professor of social ecology and Dean emeritus of the School of Social Ecology at the University of California, Irvine. His fields of research are the effects of physical and social conditions within work environments, the design and evaluation of community and worksite health promotion programs, the health and behavioral impacts of environmental stressors, the application of environmental design research to urban planning and facilities management, and the environmental psychology of the internet. He has published and edited numerous works, including *The Handbook of Environmental Psychology,* Volumes 1 and 2, 1987. He is co-director of the UCI Health Promotion Center and received the career award from the environmental research association in 1991.

Einar Strumse was born in 1957 in Oslo, Norway. He received his M.A. degree in 1991 and his Ph.D. in 1996 from the University of Bergen. He is an assistant professor of psychology at Lillehammer College, and coordinator of the Norwegian Research Council's programme on Environmental Quality of Life. He was a visiting research investigator at the School of Natural Resources & Environment, University of Michigan, Ann Arbor 1995-96, and a visiting research scientist at the Eastern Norway Research Institute, Lillehammer 1996-97. His field of research is environmental psychology, including the psychology of aesthetics, and psycho-social predictors of environmentally responsible behaviours.

David Uzzell was born in England in 1951. He read for a first degree in geography (B.A., Liverpool) but then moved into psychology with higher degrees in social psychology (MSc, London School of Economics and Political Science) and environmental psychology (Ph.D., Surrey). He is a professor in psychology in the Department of Psychology at the University of Surrey, and course director of the postgraduate programme in environmental psychology. His current research interests include the assessment of the visual impact of buildings, perceptions and attitudes to global environmental change, urban policy and environmental sustainability, and environmental education and heritage interpretation. He has recently been elected as President of IAPS, the International Association for People-Environment Studies.

Ann Westerman was born in Sweden in 1934. She graduated as an architect in 1964, and is a member of SAR (The Swedish Association of Architects). She received her doctoral degree in science in 1976 at the Royal University og Technology in Stockholm with the thesis "On Aesthetic Judgement of Building Exteriors". She practises architecture and exhibition projects at her architectural office in Stockholm. She has published several books and articles on experiencing architecture. Her scientific theory is that there are significant connections between a building volume's describable three-dimensional qualities and human beings' experiences of these, and that there are visually perceptive correlations between evaluation of building volumes and invisible attributes of the human body.

Appendix 1

Selected findings from the book *Aesthetics, Well-being and Health - abstracts on theoretical and empirical research within environmental aesthetics* (Cold (ed), Kolstad, Larssæther, 1998)

As mentioned, the book "Aesthetics, Well-being and Health —-" was the first step in investigating this field of knowledge. The book attempts to bring us closer to a common understanding of the subject. In the following we present a selection of our findings from the literature review, without references to the studies themselves, to give the reader an understanding of the subject. The list of reviewed literature is presented in Appendix 2 of this volume.

The roots to aesthetic preferences originate from surviving in nature
The roots to aesthetic preferences originate in our common sensory perception developed during thousands of years of survival in natural environments. This close contact with natural elements necessary for our survival has apparently created "a preferenda" influencing our aesthetic preferences. These are further shaped by cultural norms in close contact with the social and built environment and finally influenced by each person's knowledge structure and emotional experience.

Nature and natural elements have a positive impact on well-being and health
Realizing that we are part of nature with early man's environmental experiences deep in our minds and bodies, and even with modern man's apparent distance from "survival in and by nature", it appears to be difficult to disregard the significance of nature as "healer". Nature and natural elements and even simulations and symbolic images of nature appear to have a positive impact on people's well-being and health. Built environments with natural elements such as trees and greenery are generally preferred and better remembered than pure built environments. An increasing number of human-made materials, such as electricity poles, advertisements, displays and road constructions in the natural environment, cause a proportionally decreasing

evaluation of the overall quality.

Daylight is one of the natural factors which appears to be crucial for our well-being and health. Daylight in the interior, especially combined with a pleasant view of nature and aesthetically attractive environments which "lure" people to stay outdoors in the daylight, has a positive effect on our physiological health and psychological well-being.

Bearing the need for scientific evidence in mind, however, it is necessary to implement physiological and neurophysiological experiments, making conceptual links to psychological health and stress studies. This is a challenge for current research, even if we agree on the potential healing effects of nature and daylight.

Environmental coherence is essential for understanding the environment, and environmental complexity for the desire to explore and learn about the environment

Culture, evolution and individual knowledge and experience influence our aesthetic preferences on an unconscious and conscious level. Individually experienced environmental familiarity involving aesthetic perception, cultural meaning and emotional interest appears to have a deep impact on our individual day-to-day functioning and hence our well-being. However, it seems possible to also point out some general perceptual and cognitive factors which interact positively with certain environmental qualities. Understanding the environment and being able to "read" it and to feel secure is supported by environmental coherence. This is perceived when things are ordered and "fit together" somehow. At the same time there is a human affinity towards experiencing environments of a certain richness which cause arousal and positive stimulation and towards exploring such environments. Curiosity and an explorative desire are stimulated by environmental complexity and a certain "mystery" which promise exciting or new experiences "around the next corner". In the early days of man, an exploring nomadic behaviour was absolutely necessary in order to survive. Today this exploring behaviour has become part of our cultural desire to learn more about the surroundings and the outside world.

Pleasant, exciting and calm environments make us feel well
People do not prefer one style of architecture, but feel attracted to qualities such as a high degree of coherence, low contrast, medium complexity and high order. The balance between familiarity and novelty may be described as enough novelty to satisfy the curiosity drive, but sufficient familiarity to prevent overload. Certain qualities in the built environment appear to be generally preferred independently of people's knowledge structure, emotional "luggage", interests and the category of buildings and places. These qualities are found to be pleasantness, excitement and calmness. In other studies they are called coherence or harmony and balance, originality or authenticity, place adaptation or fittingness, and "cultivated simplicity" or good craftsmanship.

When focusing more on single buildings and features, experts and lay-people have different aesthetic preferences. Experts favour complexity, asymmetric design, new and interesting forms and attributes known from modernism and "new isms". The public prefer simplicity, symmetry and popular attributes known from traditional architecture. Their environmental and professional roles are different and consequently experts should know more about public preferences and what they are based on, and the public more about environmental aesthetics, in order to communicate and cooperate in planning and designing the environment. The challenge is to understand the background of aesthetic preferences and human needs and within the available resource framework transform these into artistic and functional wholes.

There is a need for "real-life" studies
Studies are often based on simulations concentrating on single environmental elements and people's aesthetic preferences. They do not help much in offering design criteria or a better understanding of the complex interaction of people and the environment. To build up comprehensive views on the subject, however, they appear to be necessary when placed side by side in a puzzle. Still there is a great need for real-life studies to take into account the complexity of the people-environment interaction.

Each situation and place has to be investigated as "new" or different, and thus no physical or architectural solution can automatically be repeated.

Environmental decision makers need to unveil their own and the users' environmental roles and assessments of places. The significance of these role structures and different assessments over time is also a strong reason for pursuing "real-life" research, and is a criticism of simulated "no-place" or laboratory research within environmental psychology because this type of research excludes many of the elements which influence environmental evaluations.

Many unanswered questions on the effects of environmental aesthetics
There are still many questions to ask and relatively few and novel answers to be found. Perhaps we should accept that it is not always possible to give clear and fresh answers, and that being aware of the unanswered questions may be more important than obtaining short-lived or deterministic answers. The danger is rather if we believe that we have found the one and only answer to a complex question.

Studying and discussing the influence of environmental aesthetics on our well-being and health appears to be very interesting and important for people and for experts within the aesthetic, social and psychological fields. The desire to explore this subject and learn more appears to be growing both generally and within these particular fields. This demands, however, an interdisciplinary approach and willingness to "bridge the gap" between them.

Appendix 2

List of reviewed literature from the book *Aesthetics, Well-being and Health - abstracts on theoretical and empirical research within environmental aesthetics* (Cold (ed), Kolstad, Larssæther,1998)

Papers, articles, monographs

Adams, E. (1991). Back to basics: Aesthetic experience. *Children's Environments Quarterly*, **8** (2), 19 - 29.

Allesch, C. G. (1993). The aesthetic as a psychological aspect of man-environment relations, or: Ernst E. Boesch as an aesthetician. *Schweizerische Zeitschrift für Pscychologie*, **52** (2), 122 - 129.

Baird, J. C. (1979). Aesthetic factors in adult and child evaluation of visual space. In J. C. Baird & A. D. Lutkus (eds). *Mind Child Architecture* (89-109). University Press of New England, USA.

Baird, J. C. & Lutkus, A. D. (1979). From spatial perception to architectural construction. In J. C. Baird & A. D. Lutkus. *Mind Child Architecture* (3 - 20). University Press of New England, USA.

Becker, F. D. & Poe, D. B. Jr. (1980). The effects of user-generated design modifications in a general hospital. *Journal of Non-verbal Behaviour*, **4** (4), 195 - 218.

Benjafield, J. (1985). A review of recent research on the Golden Section. *Empirical Studies of the Arts*, **3** (2), 117 - 134.

Boselie, F. (1991). Against prototypicality as a central concept in aesthetics. *Empirical Studies of the Arts*, **9** (1), 65 - 73.

Canter, D. (1991). Understanding, assessing, and acting in places: Is an integrative framework possible? In T. Gärling & T, Evans (eds). *Environmental Cognition and Action. An Integrative Multidisciplinary Approach.* (191 - 209). Oxford University Press, New York.

Coeterier, F. (1996). Permanent values in a changing world - The case of historic buildings. In M. Gray (ed). *Evolving Environmental Ideals* (120-128). Proceedings of the 14th conference of IAPS, Department of

Architecture and Town Planning, Högskoletryckeriet, Stockholm.

Cold, B. (1981). Kritikk av fire skoler (Norwegian). [Critical examination of four schools]. Byggekunst (1), Oslo.

Cold, B. (1990). What is good architecture? Discussion of modern and post-modern views. In P. Haluk, V. Imamoglu & N. Teymur (eds). Culture Space History. Symposia and Papers. Proceedings of the 11th conference of IAPS, Vol. 3, Faculty of Architecture Press, Ankara.

Cold, B., Asmervik, S. & Fathi, H. (1984). Glassgårder for folk og aktiviteter. Brukerundersøkelse av den glassoverdekte gata på Dragvoll (Norwegian). [Glass Buildings for People and Activities. A Study of the Glass-covered Street at Dragvoll]. SINTEF, Trondheim.

Colman, A. T., Best, W. M. & Austen, A. J. (1986). Familiarity and liking: Direct tests of the preference-feedback hypothesis. Psychological Reports, 58, 931 - 938.

Devlin, K. & Nasar, J. (1995). The Beauty and the Beast: Some preliminary comparisons of "high" versus "popular" residential architecture and public versus architect judgements of same. In L. Groat (ed) (Series ed D. Canter) Readings in Environmental Psychology. Giving Places Meaning (171 - 182). Academic Press Limited, London.

Evans, G. W. & Wood, K. W. (1980). Assessment of environmental aesthetics in scenic highway corridors. Environment and Behaviour, 12 (2), 255 - 273.

Fjeld, T. (1996). Samspill mellom planter og mennesker. Planter fra pryd til positiv påvirkning? (Norwegian). [Interplay between plants and people. Plants - from ornaments to positive influence?]. Lecture at NGF's winter course, 15 February, 1996.

Fredens, K. (1990). Kreativitet og sundhet (Danish). [Creativity and health]. Danske Fysioterapeuter (18), 4 -10.

Fredens, K. (1991). Den helbredende hjerne (Danish). [The healing brain]. Klinisk Sykepleje (1), 19 - 22.

Furby, L. et al. (1988). Public perception of electric power transmission lines. Journal of Environmental Psychology, 8, 19 - 43.

Gärling, T., Lindberg, E., Torell, B. & Evans, G. W. (1991). From environmental to ecological cognition. In T.Gärling, & G. Evans (eds). Environmental Cognition and Action. An Integrative Multidisciplinary Approach (335 -

344). Oxford University Press, New York.

Greenbie, B. B. (1982). Atavistic social symbolism in aesthetic response to the built environment. *Environmental Design Research Association* (13), 166 - 171.

Groat, L. (1995 a). Introduction: Place, aesthetic evaluation and home. In: L. Groat (ed). (Series ed D. Canter). *Readings in Environmental Psychology. Giving Places Meaning* (1- 26). Academic Press Limited, London.

Groat, L. (1995 b). Meaning in post-modern architecture: An examination using the multiple sorting task. In L. Groat (ed). (Series ed D. Canter) *Readings in Environmental Psychology. Giving Places Meaning* (141 - 160). Academic Press Limited, London.

Hartig, T., Mang, M. & Evans, W. (1991). Restorative effects of natural environments. *Environment and Behaviour*, 23 (1), 3 - 26.

Hartig, T., Böök, A., Garvill, J., Olsson, T. & Gärling, T. (1996). Environmental influences on psychological restoration. *Scandinavian Journal of Psychology*, 37, 378 - 393.

Heath, T. F. (1988). Behavioural and perceptual aspects of the aesthetics of urban environments. In J. L. Nasar. *Environmental Aesthetics. Theory, Research and Applications*. (6-10). Cambridge University Press.

Herzog, T. R. (1992). A cognitive analysis of preference for urban spaces. *Journal of Environmental Psychology*, 12, 237 - 298.

Hubbard, P. J. (1994). Diverging evaluations of the built environment: Planners versus the public. In S. J. Neary, M. S. Synnes & F. E. Brown (eds). *The Urban Experience. A People Environment Perspective* (125 - 133). Proceedings of the 13th conference of IAPS, E & FN Spon, London.

Janssens, J. & Küller, R. (1989). Vädertjänstens arbetsmiljö. Miljöpsykologisk studie av förhållandena vid Styrups flygplats (Swedish). [Working environment of the weather service. Environmental psychological study of the conditions at Styrup airport]. *Miljöpsykologiska Monografier* (7), Tekniska Högskolan i Lund, Sektionen för arkitektur.

Kaplan, S. (1992). Environmental preference in a knowledge-seeking, knowledge-using organism. In J. H. Barkow, L. Cosmides & J. Tooby (eds). *The Adapted Mind. Evolutionary Psychology and the Generation of Culture*. Oxford University Press.

Kaplan, S. (1995). The restorative benefits of nature: Towards an integrative framework. *Journal of Environmental Psychology*, 15, 169 - 182.

Kaplan, S. & Kaplan, R. (1989). The visual environment: Public participation in design and planning. *Journal of Social Issues*, 45 (1), 59 - 86.

Korpela, K. & Hartig, T. (1996). Restorative qualities of favourite places. *Journal of Environmental Psychology*, 16, 221-233.

Küller, M. (1986). Novemberfärger. Symposium om färg den 1. november 1984 (Swedish). [November colours. Symposium on colour, November 1984]. *Miljøpsykologiska Monografier* (6), Tekniska Högskolan i Lund, Sektionen för arkitektur.

Küller, R. (1988). Environmental activation of old persons suffering from senile dementia. In H. van Hoogdalen, N. L. Prak, T. J. M. van der Voordt & H. B. R. van Wegen (eds). *Looking Back to the Future. Symposia and Papers* (133 - 139). Proceedings from the 10th conference of IAPS, Vol. II, Delft University Press.

Küller, R. (1991). Environmental assessment from a neuro-psychological perspective. In T. Gärling & G. Evans (eds). *Environmental Cognition and Action. An Integrative Multi-disciplinary Approach.* (111 - 146). Oxford University Press, New York.

Küller, M. & Küller, R. (1990). Health and outdoor environment for the elderly. In P. Haluk, V. Imamoglu, N. Teymur (eds). *Culture Space History. Symposia and Papers* (236-245). Proceedings from the 11th conference of IAPS, Vol. III, Faculty of Architecture Press, Ankara.

Küller, R. & Küller, M. (1994). *City greenery, outdoor life and health of the elderly.* Byggforskningsrådet, R24:1994.

Küller, R. & Lindsten, C. (1992). Health and behaviour of children in class-rooms with and without windows. *Journal of Environmental Psychology*, 12, 305 - 317.

Laike, T. (1990). Relationen mellan hemmiljö och daghemsmiljö. 1. Metodstudier avseende miljövariabler (Swedish). [The relationship between home environment and day-care environment. I. Methodological studies regarding environmental variables]. *Miljöpsykologiska Monografier* (8), Tekniska Högskolan i Lund, Sektionen för arkitektur.

Laike, T. (1997). The impact of day-care environments on children's mood and behaviour. *Scandinavian Journal of Psychology*, **38** (3), 209 - 218.

Lang, J. (1988). Symbolic aesthetics in architecture: Towards a research agenda. In J. L. Nasar. *Environmental Aesthetics. Theory, Research and Application.* (11 - 26). Cambridge University Press.

Lawrence, R. J. (1992). Housing and Health: A complex relationship. *Archives of Complex Environmental Studies (ACES)*, 4(1-2), 49 - 58.

Lay, M. C. D & Reis, A. T. L. (1994). The impact of housing quality on the urban image. In J. Neary, M. S. Synnes, F. E. Brown (eds). *The Urban Experience. A People-Environment Perspective* (85-98). Proceedings of the 13th conference of IAPS, E & FN Spoon, London.

Levitt, L. (1989). Therapeutic value of wilderness. In H. R. Freilich (ed). *Wilderness Benchmark.* Proceedings of the National Wilderness Colloquium, 156 - 168.

Malinowski, J. C. & Thurber, C. A. (1996). Developmental skills in the place preferences of boys aged 8-16 years. *Journal of Environmental Psychology*, **16**, 45 - 54.

Marcus, C. C. (1997). Nature as healer. Therapeutic benefits in outdoor places. *Nordisk Arkitekturforskning* **10** (1), 9 - 20.

Merrill, A. A. & Baird, J. C. (1980). Perception and recall of aesthetic quality in a familiar environment. *Psychological Research*, **42**, 375 - 390.

Mikellides, B. (1988). Colour and psychological arousal. In H. van Hoogdalen, N. L. Prak, T. J. M. van der Voordt, H. B. R. van Wegen (eds). *Looking Back to the future. Symposia and Papers* (140-147). Proceedings from the 10th conference of IAPS, Vol II, Delft University Press.

Maaløe, E. (1972). *Æstetisk glæde og gentagelse af det fortsatt uforutsigelige* (Danish). [Aesthetic enjoyment and repetition of continued unpredictability]. Arktitekten, København.

Nasar, J. L. (1994). Urban design aesthetics. The evaluative qualities of building exteriors. *Environment and Behaviour*, **26** (3), 377 - 401.

Nasar, J. L. & Purcell, A. T. (1990). Beauty and the Beast extended: Knowledge, structure and evaluation of houses by Australian architects and non-architects. In P. Haluk, V. Imamoglu & N. Teymur (eds). *Culture Space History. Symposia and Papers.*(107-110). Proceedings from the 11th conference of IAPS, Vol III, Faculty of Architecture Press, Ankara.

Noschis, K. (1994). Rummets betydelse i vårdmiljön (Swedish). [The importance of space in care environments]. In *Kultur ger helse*. Nordisk konferens 1994, Esbo, Finland.

Oostendorp, A. & Berlyne, D.E. (1978). Dimensions in the perception of architecture. Identification and interpretation of dimensions of similarity. *Scandinavian Journal of Psychology*, 19, 73-82.

Orians, G. H. & Heerwagen, J. H. (1992). Evolved responses to landscapes. In J. H. Barkow, L. Cosmides & J. Tooby (eds). *The Adapted Mind. Evolutionary Psychology and the Generation of Culture* (555 - 579). Oxford University Press.

Parsons, R. (1991). The potential influences of environmental perception on human health. *Journal of Environmental Psychology*, 11, 1 - 23.

Porteous, D. (1982). Approaches to environmental aesthetics. *Journal of Environmental Psychology*, 2, 53 - 66.

Sivik, L. (1995). Om färgers betydelse (Swedish). [On the significance of colour]. In *Färgantologi bok 2. Upplevelse av färg og färgsatt miljö*. T5: 1995, Byggforskningsrådet.

Smith, C. D. (1984). The relationship between the pleasingness of landmarks and the judgement of distance in cognitive maps. *Journal of Environmental Psychology*, 4, 229 - 234.

Smith, S. G. (1994). The essential qualities of a home. *Journal of Environmental Psychology*, 14, 31 - 46.

Stamps, A. E. III. (1989). Are environmental aesthetics worth studying? *Journal of Architecture and Planning Research*, 6 (4), 344 - 356.

Stamps, A. E. III (1994). Validating contextual urban design principles. In S. J. Neary, M. S. Synnes, F. E. Brown (eds). *The Urban Experience. A People-Environment Perspective* (141 - 153). Proceedings of the 13th conference of IAPS, E & FN Spoon, London.

Stokols, D.(1988). Instrumental and spiritual views of people-environment relations: Current tensions and future challenges. In H. van Hoogdalen, N. L. Prak, T. J. M. van der Voordt & H. B. R. van Wegen (eds). *Looking Back to the Future. Symposia and Papers* (29 - 43). Proceedings from the 10th conference of IAPS, Vol II, Delft University Press.

Stokols, D. (1992). Establishing and maintaining healthy environments.

Towards a social ecology of health promotion. *American Psychologist,* 47 (1), 6 - 22.

Strumse, E. (1996 a). *The Psychology of Aesthetics: Explaining Visual Preferences for Agrarian Landscapes in Western Norway.* Doctoral dissertation, University of Bergen, Norway.

Strumse, E. (1996 b). *On the ontogenesis of environmental preferences.* Lecture given for the Dr. Philos. Degree, University of Bergen, Norway.

Strumse, E. (1996 c). *Environmental psychology: Taking the relationship between humans and their physical environment seriously. Implications for landscape planning and design.* Lecture given for the Dr. Philos Degree, University of Bergen, Norway.

Tennessen, C. M. & Cimprick, B. (1995). Views to nature: Effects on attention. *Journal of Environmental Psychology,* 15, 77 - 85.

Ulrich, R. (1983). Aesthetic and affective response to natural environment. In I. Altman, & J. F. Wohlwill (eds). *Behaviour and the Natural Environment* (Chapter 3). Plenum Press. New York and London.

Ulrich, R. (1985). *Aesthetic and Emotional Influences of Vegetation. A Review of the Scientific Literature.* Byggforskningsrådet, D22:1985.

Ulrich, R. (1991). Effects of interior design on wellness. Theory and recent scientific research. *Journal of Health Care and Interior Design,* 3. (Martinez Cal. USA.)

Ulrich, R., Simons, R. F., Losito, B. D., Fiorito, E., Miles, M. A. & Zelson, M. (1991). Stress recovery during exposure to natural and urban environments. *Journal of Environmental Psychology,* 11, 201 - 230.

Whitfield, T. W. A. (1995). Predicting preference for familiar, everyday objects: An experimental confrontation between two theories of aesthetic behaviour. In L. Groat (ed)(Series ed D. Canter). *Readings in Environmental Psychology. Giving Places Meaning* (183 - 199). Academic Press Limited, London.

Whitfield, A. & Wiltshire, J. (1995). Design training and aesthetic evaluation: An intergroup comparison. In L. Groat (ed) (Series ed D. Canter). *Readings in Environmental Psychology. Giving Places Meaning* (161 - 170). Academic Press Limited, London.